COMPLETING YOUR EdD

Praise for 'Completing your EdD'

Completing Your EdD: The Essential Guide to the Doctor of Education is designed to support anyone undertaking, or thinking about undertaking, a Professional Doctorate in Education (EdD). This book focusses on supporting EdD students at each stage of their study, from understanding the structure of EdDs to providing helpful information and guidance relating to the requirements of the thesis and preparing for the viva voce examination and beyond.

A particular strength of this book is that it starts from the perspective that the student is a complete beginner, making it accessible to those new to doctoral study. *Completing Your EdD: The Essential Guide to the Doctor of Education* addresses issues relating to several aspects of the EdD with which students frequently struggle including, for example, issues relating to understanding the essential components of the literature review, understanding what developing a theoretical framework really means and developing insights into the requirements of the final EdD thesis. This book covers important ground relating to the different chapters which traditionally make up an EdD thesis, as well as information about the supervisory support that can be expected. It also suggests ways in which students can share their research and develop a research profile following the successful completion of their EdD. Each chapter poses reflective questions to help the reader reflect critically on different aspects of their doctoral work. Case studies and real-life examples of EdD student experiences are also included, providing valuable insights into some of the situations doctoral students are likely to encounter and the factors that need to be considered at different stages of the doctorate.

The authors bring a wealth of experience in leading Professional Doctorate programmes and doctoral supervision and examining. This book provides essential reading to help students understand what an EdD entails. Through providing helpful guidance which addresses many of the issues and concerns frequently raised by EdD students, this book is also a valuable resource for EdD programme leaders and supervisors.

Carol Robinson, Professor of Children's Rights, Edge Hill University, UK.

We often use the metaphor of journeys in education, and doctoral study has been likened to a spiritual quest or voyage of discovery. For many, this will be a journey into the unknown, a journey without maps, and whilst there may be fellow travellers along the way, it is essentially a solo sojourn. Written by experienced supervisors of professional doctorate programmes in education (EdD), this edited collection is an essential guide for not only for those about to embark on a EdD but also those who have begun their studies.

This edited guide opens with a chapter designed to enable the reader to understand the distinctive nature of an EdD and how to select a programme to meet their individual needs. Subsequent chapters consider the essential components of a doctorate, such as writing the literature review; developing a theoretical framework; research design, methodological approaches and data collection methods; and data analysis. The guide also usefully includes chapters on research ethics, managing the supervisory relationship and how best to prepare for and perform at the viva. The final chapter, which focuses on what to do, and how you might feel post qualification, draws on the experiences of some of the authors. The chapter I return to most frequently is: 'Getting over the finish line' which provides constructive advice on bringing the various elements – chapters and sections – of the thesis together as a cohesive whole with the metaphorical 'golden thread'.

Each of the 10 chapters is written in an accessible style, with judicious use of call-out boxes and bulleted lists which break up the text; in some instances, posing reflective questions and exercises; and providing short case studies and suggested further reading. When research becomes 'curiouser and curiouser' and you become lost in a sea of texts, caught up in theoretical paradigm wars, dipping back into the guide will help you regain your focus and get you over the finish line.

Anthony Hudson, Doctoral Student, University of East London, UK.

COMPLETING YOUR EdD

The Essential Guide to the Doctor of Education

EDITED BY

IONA BURNELL

JODI ROFFEY-BARENTSEN

United Kingdom – North America – Japan – India
Malaysia – China

Emerald Publishing Limited
Howard House, Wagon Lane, Bingley BD16 1WA, UK

First edition 2020

Reprints and permissions service
Contact: permissions@emeraldinsight.com

British Library Cataloguing in Publication Data
A catalogue record for this book is available from the British
Library

ISBN: 978-1-78973-566-6 (Print)
ISBN: 978-1-78973-563-5 (Online)
ISBN: 978-1-78973-565-9 (Epub)

Printed and bound by CPI Group (UK) Ltd, Croydon, CR0 4YY

ISOQAR certified
Management System,
awarded to Emerald
for adherence to
Environmental
standard
ISO 14001:2004.

Certificate Number 1985
ISO 14001

INVESTOR IN PEOPLE

CONTENTS

AUTHOR BIOGRAPHIES

Dr Iona Burnell is a Senior Lecturer at the Cass School of Education and Communities at the University of East London. She currently teaches on the undergraduate Education Studies and the Doctor of Education programmes. Her teaching background is in Further Education where she taught Access to Higher Education (HE) courses. She completed her EdD at The University of Sheffield in 2013.

Dr Jim Crawley has worked for 40 years in and with the Further Education and Skills sector, in teacher education, adult and community learning, education studies, professional development and basic skills. He co-ordinated the Bath Spa University Post Compulsory Teacher Education programme, which gained two consecutive outstanding grades in OfSTED Initial Teacher Education inspections. He is now a Visiting Teaching and Learning Fellow.

Dr Jane Creaton is Associate Dean (Academic) for the Faculty of Humanities and Social Sciences and a Reader in Higher Education at the University of Portsmouth. She has been involved in the development, design and delivery of professional doctorates since 2007 and is a passionate advocate of the contribution that professional doctorates can make to transform the personal and professional lives of students.

Professor Gerry Czerniawski is Professor of Education at the Cass School of Education and Communities at the University of East London. He runs the doctoral programmes (PhD and Professional Doctorate in Education) at Cass and teaches on Initial Teacher Education courses. He is also a Council Member of the International Forum for Teacher Educator Development, the Chair of the *British*

Curriculum Forum, Lead Editor of the *BERA Blog* and a Trustee and Director of the British Educational Research Association.

Dr Kate Hoskins is a Reader in Education at Brunel University London. Her academic publications are concerned with issues of policy, identity and inequalities in further and higher education. She is the author of two books, *Women and Success: Professors in the UK Academy* (Trentham Books) and *Youth Identities, Education and Employment: Exploring Post-16 and Post-18 Opportunities, Access and Policy* (Palgrave).

Dr Richard Malthouse is a Senior Lecturer at the University of East London. He teaches research methods in education, undertakes seminars for the undergraduate Education Studies programme and is a Supervisor for doctoral students. He is a Fellow of the Higher Education Authority and of the Society for Education and Training. To date, he has published 33 books, many of which are dual-language publications.

Dr Leena Helavaara Robertson is Associate Professor in the Department of Education at Middlesex University, London. As a former primary/early years teacher, she has extensive experience of teaching multilingual children in schools and early years settings and working with families and community teachers. For many years, she led early years teacher education programmes in London; currently, she leads the professional doctorate programme in her department and supervises doctoral students.

Dr Jodi Roffey-Barentsen is Senior Lecturer at the School of Education at the University of Brighton. She is Programme Leader of undergraduate programmes in Early Childhood Education and contributes to postgraduate programmes including the MA and EdD, supervises EdD and PhD students and has experience in viva voce examinations. Furthermore, she co-leads the Children and Young People's Voice and Education Research and Enterprise Group.

Dr Sue Taylor is a Principal Fellow of the Higher Education Academy and an Associate Professor of Doctoral Education at University

College London. As Director of the EdD programme in the Centre for Doctoral Education, she has facilitated a number of changes to the EdD and was involved in restructuring the programme to enhance both student experience and progression. She has been instrumental in removing barriers to postgraduate research as part of the widening participation agenda. She designed and developed a pre-doctoral training programme that paved the way for mature professionals to access the EdD.

Professor Mike Watts is Professor of Education at Brunel University London, conducting 'naturalistic' people-orientated research principally in science education and in scholarship in higher education. He enjoys exploring new technologies for learning and writing about creative pedagogical approaches to learning and teaching. He is the Director of Internationalisation for the Department of Education at Brunel, teaches at all levels and currently supervises 14 PhD students.

Dr Paula Nadine Zwozdiak-Myers is a Senior Lecturer in Education and Programme Director for the Doctor of Education (EdD) at Brunel University London. Since undertaking this role in 2012, she successfully steered the validation of a new EdD programme (launched in 2017) which features a new approach to the taught component placing emphasis on a progressively staged curriculum that enables students to become more thoughtful about the complexities inherent within the research–improvement–practice nexus.

FOREWORD

Gina Wisker

*Professor of Contemporary Literature and
Higher Education at the University of Brighton and
Director of Brighton's Centre for Learning and Teaching.*

Many books and articles guide us with the doctorate. However, few offer insights on the doctorate based in professional practice. One of the strengths of this book on Education Doctorates, as professional doctorates, is its accessibility of structure and direct address. Another is its insider knowledge, which is turned in each chapter to clarify the shape, expectations and practice of the EdD, demystifying its structures and taking readers step by step through the expectations and the ways of working with the literature review, theories, ethics, research design, data analysis and writing for completion and the examination. It also tackles the practices of working effectively with your supervisor and directions after the doctorate, a contribution Sue Taylor notes, of the supervision relationship, that 'As mature professionals in demanding professional roles, you need particular support and guidance along your EdD journey'. The time pressures and demands, the relationship between that professional practice and the demands of researching it, often as insiders, to make effective research-based change, all of this lies behind the book as a whole. This is an accessible, well considered, well structured, essential insider guide.

INTRODUCTION

Iona Burnell and Jodi Roffey-Barentsen

Welcome to *Completing Your EdD: The Essential Guide to the Doctor of Education*, an accompanying guide that is somewhere between a handbook and a textbook. This book is designed specifically for anyone undertaking the Doctor of Education (EdD) programme, and can be utilised by students, lecturers, and anybody who is involved in facilitating the EdD.

We are very excited to present you with a comprehensive yet concise collection of chapters, each one related to an important aspect of the EdD. They have been expertly written by academics who are either working on, managing, or have been working on an EdD programme. Whether you have not yet started your EdD, are at the taught stage, or at the thesis writing stage, the collection of chapters within this book will be vital to your decision-making, your progress, and your success.

Education doctorates are a relatively new qualification in the doctoral series. Described as a professional or practitioner doctorate, it is distinctly different from the traditional PhD and is structured as part taught, part research. Another distinct factor of the EdD is the specialism – education. All professional doctorates have a specialism: Doctor of Engineering, Doctor of Social Science, and Doctor of Clinical Psychology. The EdD requires a text that has been specifically written for this specialism, and that is what we are presenting to you here.

Although there are many books that offer advice and guidance on PhDs and writing theses (some are recommended within this book as further reading), our book is a collection of 10 chapters; each chapter, as detailed below, covers a specific aspect of the EdD. Each chapter may aid you twice: once at the taught stage and again at the thesis writing/research stage. You may refer, for example, to the chapter on 'Research Design and Methodological Approaches' while undertaking a taught module in the first phase of the programme and again later while designing your research and writing your thesis.

The book chapters are laid out in what could be considered the chronological order in which your doctoral journey might take you – from making the decision to undertake the EdD, and meeting whoever may become your supervisor, to gaining ethical approval, writing the literature review and developing a theoretical framework, through to submission, and finally the viva. The last chapter in the series explores some options and suggestions for the post-qualification stage. Each chapter author was chosen for his or her expertise in that area of the EdD programme. Therefore, what you have here is a collection of professionals who are imparting their expertise and knowledge in order to enable you to success on your quest to fulfil your ambition to be a Doctor of Education.

The first chapter of this book is an in-depth look at what the EdD programme is, in relation to other professional doctorates, and the traditional PhD. Jane Creaton writes a fascinating account of the history of the EdD, and what makes it distinctly different from the PhD. This chapter identifies the key characteristics of the programme, including the potential advantages and disadvantages of the various programme structures, helping you to make an informed choice. Such choices may include the mode of delivery (weekends, evenings, etc.), content of the modules, the nature of the assessments, and supervision arrangements. Deciding to pursue a doctorate is a serious commitment, both financially and in terms of time and effort. It will form a large and important part of your life so making the right decision early on is very important.

The following chapter, Chapter 2, offers some very valuable advice about your relationship with your supervisor(s). Sue Taylor guides you through what, for some students, can be an awkward experience in unknown territory. Sue's advice includes identifying and approaching potential supervisor(s) (if your institution expects this of you), developing effective working relationship(s), and identifying possible measures if things do not go smoothly. She also draws on the benefit of her own experience by presenting in the case study, an example of best practice.

Chapter 3 raises some very important questions about ethics within educational research. Paula Zwozdiak-Myers discusses various theories of ethics and why this has become a crucial area for consideration for any research that involves human participants. This chapter encourages you to think through principles of ethics, scrutinise ethical guidelines, and very importantly, think reflexively. By the end of this chapter, you will have acquired a clear understanding of what ethical theories underpin research and what to consider when planning the design of your own research. Another important point that is raised here is – how to defend your ethical decision-making during your viva. This may seem like a long way off right now! But the importance of decision-making in the early stages cannot be stressed enough.

Chapter 4 is about writing the literature review. Leena Helavaara Robertson presents a thorough account of what constitutes a literature review. Leena demystifies what is sometimes a complex undertaking where many students feel lost and confused about what to include in their literature review. All of the important points are covered here including the purposes of a literature review, the selection process, developing criticality, and linking the literature to the research questions and your theoretical framework.

Chapter 5 is concerned with developing the theoretical framework within your thesis. Mike Watts explains why there is a need to articulate a theoretical framework for your research, and how this will inform the choices and consequential decisions you then need to make. Mike points out that defending your thesis at viva is, in fact, defending the numerous decisions you have made along the way. With that in mind, this chapter will guide you through the construction of your theoretical framework, ensuring that those choices and consequential decisions are the right ones for your research.

Chapter 6 begins with Kate Hoskins telling you that a key challenge for you as a doctoral researcher is deciding upon the research design that you will use to address your research questions and understanding how to justify your decisions about design.

This chapter clearly lays out the design process and what you will need to do in order to produce an effective methodology. From identifying the key features of quantitative and qualitative research, and making decisions about the various methods of collecting data, to defending your choice of methodology and methods, Kate provides you with valuable advice and guidance.

Chapter 7 is about analysing and interpreting your data. After gaining ethical approval, writing your literature review, decided on your theoretical framework, and designing your methods and methodology, how then to present the crucial and possibly final section: your findings from the data. Jim Crawley explains that analysing and interpreting data is at the heart of every piece of research and succeeding with this stage is crucial. Among other important advice within this chapter, Jim asserts that, in order to ensure validity, data analysis and interpretation must be adequate for the whole research project to be valid.

Chapter 8 is called 'Getting over the finish line' because, by now, you may well be thinking about making finishing touches in readiness for submission. As part of this chapter, Iona Burnell and Gerry Czerniawski offer some useful tips and insights to improving what could be the final stages of your draft thesis. The 'golden thread', for example, is the central argument that pulls through the thesis, creating cohesion, and connecting all of the parts together. Checking that the abstract is an appropriately distilled version of the thesis and that the introduction explains what you have done, how you have done it, and why, are important finishing touches. Iona and Gerry also include guidance on making last-minute checks to the methodology, presenting your findings, the criticality of your writing, and writing your conclusion. One of the aims of this chapter is for you to present a thesis that helps to reduce the amount of potential questions examiners ask in your viva.

Chapter 9 will help you to prepare for that crucial final stage: the examination process and the viva. Jodi Roffey-Barentsen and Richard Malthouse begin this chapter by explaining the examination process following submission of your thesis. They include very useful advice on preparing for your viva, including the importance of the mock, and guidance on how to anticipate questions from the examiner. Nobody can ever really know what the examiners will ask, but there are some questions that commonly occur in vivas, and this chapter will help you to prepare for those. Jodi and Richard also cover the possible outcomes of the examination process – what the outcomes are and what each one means, although these may vary slightly from institution to institution.

Chapter 10 is the final chapter in the book. Jodi Roffey-Barentsen presents a collection of interesting contributions from Jane Creaton, Kate Hoskins, Sue Taylor, Mike Watts, and Gina Wisker, in this chapter called 'Post qualification – now you're a doctor, what next?' The contributing authors offer guidance for publishing in journals, and they refer to general advice for Early Career Researchers. At the end of this chapter, you will be able to consider ways of sharing your research with the wider world, convert your thesis into (an) article(s) suitable for publication in a journal, and take steps to develop from an Early Career Researcher to a more experienced one.

In addition to the information provided in the chapters, each one also includes one or more case studies. The case studies are based on real-life scenarios from researchers' experiences. We would like to take this opportunity to thank those researchers who have contributed case studies to this book. We feel that the case studies bring the material to life and demonstrate that research in the social sciences, such as education, is often not straightforward or problem free. We don't want to deter you but rather encourage you; we hope that when you read the case studies you will appreciate that no researcher is immune to the difficulties that doing research poses, but that these difficulties can be dealt with and overcome.

Although doctoral research can be challenging and sometimes fraught with problems, it can also be an immensely rewarding experience. If you are reading this introduction because you are thinking of embarking, or about to embark on your EdD, we say 'go for it!'; you won't regret it. Doing an EdD is an amazing and incredibly fulfilling experience. We hope that you will find this book the ideal accompaniment to your journey, and we wish you every success.

1

THE STRUCTURE OF A PROFESSIONAL DOCTORATE IN EDUCATION; WHY CHOOSE IT?

Jane Creaton

INTRODUCTION

All doctoral-level qualifications in the United Kingdom

> *require the main focus of the candidate's work to demonstrate an original contribution to knowledge in their subject, field or profession, through original research or the original application of existing knowledge or understanding. (Quality Assurance Agency (QAA), 2015, p. 3)*

However, doctorates are delivered through a range of different models. The three main categories are subject specialist doctorates (PhD/DPhil), doctorates by publication and professional and/or practitioner doctorates. The latter category is distinguished by its application to professional practice and so tends to be structured differently from the other forms of doctorate. The aim of this chapter is to review and analyse the structure of professional doctorate in education (EdD) programmes. There are three key purposes: to enable you to understand the distinctive nature of a professional doctorate, to compare the professional doctorate with other options for doctoral-level study, and to assist you in choosing an EdD programme which best meets your requirements.

This chapter begins with a general overview of the structure of professional doctorate programmes, including level, credits, modules, delivery and assessment. It will then identify the key features of a professional doctorate and how these differ from other doctoral pathways. The final section will review some of the different ways that EdD programmes are structured and delivered and consider the advantages and disadvantages of the various approaches. The rationale is to enable you to choose a programme which is best suited to your aims and objectives, your style of working and your personal and professional circumstances.

At the end of this chapter, you should be able to:

- Identify the key characteristics of a professional doctorate.

- Understand the potential advantages and disadvantages of different EdD structures.

- Make an informed choice about which programme would best suit your needs.

WHAT IS A PROFESSIONAL DOCTORATE?

The UK Council for Graduate Education (UKCGE) defines a professional doctorate as:

> *A programme of advanced study and research which … is designed to meet the specific needs of a professional group external to the university, and which develops the capability of individuals to work within a professional context. (UKCGE, 2002, p. 62)*

The origins of professional doctorates can be traced back to the thirteenth century to the subject-based doctorates such as Doctor of Law and Doctor of Theology that were offered by European universities (UKCGE, 2002). The earliest modern professional doctorates in the United Kingdom were launched in 1992: an EdD at the University of Bristol and a Doctorate in Engineering (EngD) at the University of Warwick, the University of Manchester Institute of Science and Technology (UMIST)/University of Manchester and the University of Wales (Bourner, Bowden, & Laing, 2001). The UK frameworks for higher education (HE) qualifications do not differentiate between types of doctorate, requiring that all doctoral degrees are awarded for

> *the creation and interpretation of new knowledge, through original research or other advanced scholarship, of a quality to satisfy peer review, extend the forefront of the discipline, and merit publication. (Quality Assurance Agency for Higher Education, 2008, p. 23)*

There are, however, significant differences in how doctoral programmes are designed, structured and delivered (Ellis & Lee, 2005; Neumann, 2005; Pearson, 1999) which reflect the history and ethos of the different models. The link to professional practice and practitioner knowledge is fundamental, and Ellis and Lee (2005), for example, argue that 'application to practice is at the philosophical core of the professional doctorate' (p. 2). In contrast to the traditional PhD, which is generally conceptualised as an apprenticeship for aspiring academics, professional doctorates tend to be aimed at mid-career practitioners and hence are often described as being for 'researching professionals' rather than 'professional researchers' (Bourner et al., 2001, p. 71). Most programmes require participants to be employed or engaged in a professional capacity in the relevant sector, although there are some examples of professional doctorates (e.g. the Professional Doctorate in Forensic Psychology) which have been established as entry qualifications into a profession.

A report commissioned by the Higher Education Funding Council for England (HEFCE) into the provision of the professional doctorate in English HE institutions identified 72 EdD programmes offered by 54 different institutions (Mellors-Bourne, Robinson, & Metcalfe, 2016). The EdD is one of the most well-established professional doctorate programmes, being offered by nearly half of the 123 English HE institutions surveyed by the report's authors. The number of EdD programmes had nearly doubled from the previous survey of provision in 2009, which identified 38 programmes and education continued to be one of the dominant areas of professional doctorate provision (the others being business, health and social care and psychology). The growth of EdD programmes has also included an increase in specialisation, with the emergence of programmes focussing specifically on HE, educational psychology and education leadership.

In the early years of professional doctorate provision, there were some concerns about the parity of quality and standards between PhD and professional doctorates, linked to differences in the time requirements for completion, entry qualifications and the length of the final thesis (Ellis & Lee, 2005; Neumann, 2005; Pearson, 1999). These debates over the equivalence between the PhD and the professional doctorate can be seen as part of a wider scepticism within some elements of the academy about the status and value of professional knowledge. Although professional doctorate students are undoubtedly engaged in the creation of new knowledge, this is often informal, situated and contingent knowledge generated through professional practice (Eraut, 1994, 2000) rather than the more formal disciplinary-based knowledge associated with PhD study. These disciplinary boundaries, have however, come under considerable challenge from 'Mode 2 knowledge', which is produced outside the academy in the context of application and characterised by transdisciplinarity and heterogeneity (Gibbons et al., 1994).

As understanding of the different structures and approaches of professional doctorates has grown, a considerable body of academic literature has developed, focussing on the impacts of the professional doctorate on the personal and professional development of practitioners (Costley, 2013; Hawkes & Yerrabati, 2018; Lindsay, Kerawalla, & Floyd, 2017; Wildy, Peden, & Chan, 2015). This research identifies a number of positive impacts of the doctorate on candidates' career trajectories and professional identities. In relation to an EdD programme, Wellington and Sikes (2006) concluded that '… the doctorate is seen as being largely of benefit to the individual rather than the professional as a whole' (p. 733), but other research has also identified examples where research undertaken for doctoral projects has a direct impact on policy and practice within their own organisation (Costley, 2010, 2013). Interviews with professional doctorate candidates and alumni have also identified the development of 'more reflective practice and evidence-based professionalism valued by some employers' (Mellors-Bourne et al., 2016, p. vi).

> *Reflective question:*
>
> What personal, professional and other benefits do you hope
> you might get from the EdD?

THE STRUCTURE OF DOCTORAL PROGRAMMES

Another striking difference between doctorates lies in how programmes are structured. The traditional doctorate in humanities
and social sciences requires a three-year full-time period of research
supported by a supervision team. A more usual model for a professional doctorate programme is a two-year taught programme delivered part time on a cohort basis, followed by a research stage taking
between two and five years. The content of the taught element varies
across programmes but will typically include sessions on research
methodology and methods, publication and dissemination, professional reflection and practice and some subject-specific content. This
is delivered and assessed through a series of modules credited at masters or doctoral level. Assessments undertaken for the taught element
of the programme often involve an element of work-based learning,
professional reflection or action research. Although students write an
amount over the course of the programme that is broadly equivalent
to the total words required for a PhD thesis, the professional doctorate thesis is often shorter. The final research project undertaken for
the thesis is also undertaken in the context of the student's professional practice. This focus on the individual's professional practice
means that professional doctorates are also characterised by a greater degree of reflection and reflexivity than may be the case in a PhD.

It has been argued that the structure of professional doctorates is
becoming less distinctive because of the changing nature of doctoral
education (Bao, Kehm, & Ma, 2016; Kamler & Thomson, 2006;
Loxley & Kearns, 2018; Park, 2005). This includes the increasing
expectations that PhD students engage in formal research methods
and researcher development training, the growth of specialist Doctoral Colleges or Doctoral Schools to support the doctoral research community and the establishment of cohort-based approaches through
doctoral training partnerships and structured PhD programmes.

However, notwithstanding these developments, the experience of students on a professional doctorate programme is likely to differ quite significantly from a student on a PhD programme, at least in the taught phase of the programme. Furthermore, the experiences of professional doctorate students may also vary considerably by programme and by institution. Within the broad framework outlined above, there are significant variations in EdD programme structures, which can produce quite different learning experiences for participants at different institutions. Applicants for programmes should consider carefully the various elements before making a decision, and the purpose of this chapter is to provide more information about these structures, including size, length, volume and content, in order to guide you to make the best choice of programme for you.

HOW ARE PROFESSIONAL DOCTORATES IN EDUCATION STRUCTURED?

Although academic credit has not traditionally been assigned to PhDs, professional doctorates do sit within the relevant UK Frameworks of Higher Education Qualifications. The framework for England, Wales and Northern Ireland specifies 540 credits, at least 360 of which must be at level 8, and the Scottish framework specifies a minimum of 420 at level 12. Levels 8 and 12 are doctoral level and the QAA's Characteristics Statement for Doctoral Degrees complements and contextualises these frameworks by elaborating on the distinctive features of the doctoral degree. The majority of EdD programmes are offered part time, on the basis that practitioners will be juggling their studies with a full-time job. However, a growing number of programmes now offer a full-time pathway, to accommodate those who have more flexible working patterns. This is reflected in the minimum and maximum lengths of registration which can vary from three to four years full-time or from six to eight years part time, although some students may take longer to complete where they suspend their studies or have extenuating circumstances. It is worth asking course teams about the actual completion rates of people who have been through the course to get a realistic assessment of how much time and resource you will may need to budget for, even if your own circumstances will vary.

Choosing a professional doctorate: some questions to consider

- When would you like to finish? How long have you got?
- Do you have restrictions on travel (how far can you travel) or when (weekends/evenings)?
- Would you prefer to study face to face or online?
- How important is the cohort effect to you?
- Would it be helpful for you to have subject knowledge input in the taught element (do you have a master's in education?)
- Do you already know what you would like to do you thesis on?
- Have you already published in professional or academic journals?
- What are the professional backgrounds of people on most recent cohorts?

Even where a programme is being undertaken on a full-time basis, most programmes will require students to maintain an ongoing connection with professional practice. The nature and extent of this connection varies but must be sufficient to enable course participants to meet any module and course learning outcomes which require engagement with practice within the education sector. Some institutions also specify the length of experience within the sector and/or expectations about levels of seniority. Most programmes require a master's degree in education or a related discipline, but some will allow recognition of prior learning on the basis of equivalent knowledge, skills and experience. Others have some level of master's-level study incorporated into the programme. A final element to consider in relation to entry requirements is whether or not a research proposal is required as part of the application process. Some programmes do require a proposal to be submitted on application, partly to demonstrate suitability for study at this level and partly to ensure that there is the supervisory capacity and/or expertise. If you have a clear idea of what your research proposal will look like and what you want your project to be about, then you may want to choose a programme which asks for this to be submitted and proceeds on the assumption that you have a specific research project in mind. If, however, you are unsure about your proposed research project, are considering one or more alternatives and/or need more input in terms of research methodology or substantive content, then you should consider a programme which does not require a full research proposal in advance. These programmes may ask you to indicate what your area of interest is, so that they can ensure that they have the supervisory capacity, but the expectation is that your proposal will be developed over the taught phase of the project. It will be open to you to use the taught phase for exploring different ideas and approaches, but you will need to have a firm proposal by the end of the second year.

Reflective question:

Do you have a specific research proposal already in mind? What are some possible topics?

A note for HE staff: There are many people who work in universities either as academics or professional staff who are interested in doing a professional doctorate. In the case of academics, there are a number of staff who are recruited to teach in professional and/or vocational subjects on the basis of their practitioner experience. However, there is increasing pressure on most departments to recruit more staff with doctorates, and some universities have explicit targets to increase the percentage of academic staff with doctorates. For these staff, doing an EdD is an attractive option in that it enables them to combine their practitioner expertise with the HE context. For professional staff, there are a number of roles which merge academic and professional functions and where a doctorate adds value (librarians, learning developers, academic skills support, etc.) not only to the role but also to credibility and influence within the organisation. There are a number of advantages in doing the doctorate in-house – most universities offer discounts to staff, attending workshops is convenient, etc. However, there are also some disadvantages, particularly where the assessment is likely to be done with people that you are likely to be working with, and/or where you would like to be critical of your organisation.

THE TAUGHT ELEMENT

All EdD programmes begin with a taught element which usually consists of a number of assessed modules. These are usually credit rated so that you can accrue credit towards the 540 credits needed for the doctorate through a series of assessments. This is a significant difference from the PhD route, where the assessment is usually entirely through the thesis and viva at the very end of the period of study. The opportunity to build up credit as the programme progresses has a number of advantages. First, you will get regular feedback on your progress which will give you very specific and targeted feedback on whether you are at the appropriate level. Second, for busy practitioners, a series of interim deadlines for assessments may offer a more structured and productive way of working than where the degree rests on assessment at the end of the programme. Also, if you have to leave the programme before the end, the award of credit means that you can leave with a postgraduate award or transfer credit to another programme at a later date.

A common model for the delivery of the taught element is four or more modules delivered part-time over the first two years of the programme. The number of modules, the size of the teaching blocks and the assessment deadlines may be relevant if you have specific peaks and troughs in your workload or in your personal life that need to be accommodated. In general, longer modules provide more flexibility for students, although some prefer the motivation of regular deadlines. A related issue is the level of study. As mentioned earlier, the frameworks for HE qualifications specify that a minimum number of credits must be at doctoral level (level 8 in England, Wales and Northern Ireland and level 12 in Scotland). This allows programmes flexibility to offer some or all of the taught phase at level 7/level 12. Many programmes do this either because the modules are shared with a master's programme in education or to bridge the gap between postgraduate and doctoral study. If you have spent some time out of HE, you may find it helpful to choose a programme where at least one module is offered at master's level before you make the step up to doctoral level.

The final, and probably most important, consideration is the content of the programme modules in the taught phase. There are three main types of modules, and most programmes incorporate a mix of these. The first type of module is one which contains substantive or specialist subject content relating to education. This is often the case in programmes which offer a master's-level programme in the same subject area and students from both masters and doctoral programmes take the modules or where the EdD is targeted at a particular education sector or specialism, such as educational leadership. The availability of these types of modules is particularly appropriate if you have not previously studied education at undergraduate or postgraduate level and grounding in substantive aspects of educational theories, policies or practices would be useful to you.

The second type of module is the most common, and focus on aspects relating to research methods, methodology and related skills required by professional doctorate researchers. These modules are intended to prepare you for doctoral-level research and cover a large range of topics from research philosophies, specific research methods through to academic reading and writing skills. Many programmes deliver these in the specific context of practitioner research, focussing on particular types of practitioner-based methodologies, such as action research or practitioner-based enquiry, and on some of the specific ethical and methodological issues arising from researching your own workplace or area of professional practice. Although many of these modules may appear to be generic social science research modules, the delivery by educational researchers enables the content to be contextualised in the education discipline.

A final type of module relates to a specific stage of the doctoral process and can be seen as scaffolding the journey towards the final thesis. Thus, there may be a module which requires the development and assessment of the literature review, a small-scale pilot project, a scoping review of the organisation where the research will be undertaken or the final proposal that will be presented before transfer to the research phase. In some programmes, students start out with an initial research proposal, and each of the subsequent stages of the programme involves the development and refinement of the proposal. There are, of course, overlaps between these three different approaches, and most programmes are a hybrid, drawing together substantive content and research methodology and skills and/or the development of the research proposal. Table 1 shows examples of indicative module titles in each of the categories. Further information about individual modules can be accessed through institutional websites, although you may need to contact the course team for the full version.

It is also worth paying close attention to the nature and type of assessments offered on the programme. These will assess the learning outcomes of the modules, but there is a considerable range and diversity, from standard academic essays and presentations, through to more innovative forms of assessment such as blogging, journal articles, etc. You can expect that many of the assessments will have a reflective element, where you are either invited

Table 1: Examples of EdD Modules.

Subject Specialist Modules	Research Methods and Researcher Development Modules	Doctoral Process Modules
Perspectives on professionalism	Philosophy and practice of educational research	Identifying your research area
Leadership and organisational transformation	Advanced educational research methods	Writing the literature review
Professional education	Introduction to quantitative methods	Educational research proposal
Culture, interculturality and identity	Practitioner enquiry	Institution-focussed study
Curriculum, pedagogy and assessment	Developing thinking skills	Presenting and disseminating your research
Language and cross-cultural communication		

to reflect on your professional practice or reflect on the experience of doing the assessment itself and to consider its value in your learning and to your future research project. If you do not have much experience of reflective writing, then it would be useful to consult some of the established textbooks in this area. A feature which is common to all of the above approaches is the emphasis on professional practice and reflection. There are a number of ways in which this might be incorporated into the programme. One way is through a specific module in the programme. It may also be the case that it is incorporated into assessment tasks, often early in the programme, to enable reflection on the applicant's journey to date.

Other considerations relating to the taught phase include how the course is delivered. One of the distinctive features of professional doctorates is the cohort approach. For many students, this is one of the key advantages of doing a professional doctorate rather than a PhD. If you register on a PhD programme, then, depending on the size of the department, there will be other students who start at the same time as you, and you may meet these people at induction and/or at training and development sessions. However, these relationships are usually less productive and supportive than those which can develop through working with and building up relationships with other people on the same course. For many professional doctorate students, the opportunity to work in a cohort, to develop and share best practice and to work with others is one of the most satisfying and productive elements of the programme (Mellors-Bourne et al., 2016). There may be a reduced sense of isolation and loneliness and less reliance on a single supervisor or small supervision team for support and feedback. The cohort will consist of people from a range of backgrounds and professional experience who can enrich the learning experience and provide a community of learning. Some programmes make an active effort to build up a community through social media or a virtual learning environment and social events embedded in the programme. Others allow for these networks and relationships to emerge more organically through refreshment breaks in workshops, but all good professional doctorate programmes will be carefully planned so as to promote and develop opportunities for informal discussions, networking and the exchange of good practice. As professional doctorates cater primarily for people studying part-time whilst in full-time employment, most programmes are delivered through intensive teaching blocks or through workshops offered at weekends or in the evenings. Some professional doctorates are delivered partly or wholly online. A consideration here is the extent to which your desire to do a professional doctorate is motivated by your interest in being part of a cohort or community of practice. Whilst these relationships can, of course, be maintained online, you may prefer to meet you colleagues and build these relationships in person.

THE RESEARCH ELEMENT

In most programmes, the research phase can last between two and four years, and where there are valid extenuating circumstances or grounds for suspending study, it may be extended up to eight years. In most institutions, the research phase mirrors more closely the experience of PhD students, in that the primary relationship is with the supervisory team and there is little or no taught element. If you are attracted to a professional doctorate because of the structured approach, it is important to establish what activities are offered to the EdD cohort in this phase. Some programmes continue to offer cohort meetings and events, albeit on a reduced level, throughout the research phase, whereas in others, students are expected to maintain networks with the cohort themselves. It is important to prepare yourself for the transition as some students can find the disconnection from the structured programme unsettling. If you have relied heavily on the structured nature of the programme, there are a number of things that you can do in the research phase to try and address this. The first is to discuss with your supervisor your preferred way of working. If you find frequent interim deadlines helpful, then try and establish this at the outset and agree with your supervisor deadlines for drafts. Second, you may want to provide your own structure through creating deadlines, for example, through presenting papers at conferences on different aspects of your thesis or submitted a journal article based on your literature review, provided that these do not become displacement activities.

A second issue to consider as early as possible is the nature and involvement of your employer (if you have one) in the research phase of the project. The Characteristics Statement for Doctoral Degrees states that, for professional doctorates, '... successful completion of the degree normally leads to professional and/or organisational change that is often direct rather than achieved through the implementation of subsequent research findings' (QAA, 2015, p. 9). It does not follow that your research project will necessarily be in your workplace, or that you will need to demonstrate organisational change or impact, but it is important to establish at the outset what the university's expectations are. Some programmes will involve a workplace mentor, for example, or there may be an element of the assessment which is specifically work focussed. Other programmes have a much more flexible relationship with the place of work and there is no particular expectation in relation to the involvement of the employer. Nevertheless, the relationship with your employer remains an important one. At least half of professional doctorate candidates in recent research were fully self-funded (Mellors-Bourne et al., 2016), but some employers may provide study leave or more flexible working hours. If you are fortunate enough to be funded, you will need to establish what the strings attached might be, in terms of your employer being informed of your progress via a formal sponsorship agreement or an entitlement to read or comment on your thesis before publication. Even if you are not sponsored, you need to think about a number of practical and ethical issues relating to the project. If you are planning to research your own workplace, you will need to consider what access you have to the data and get your employer's permission to access it for research purposes.

A final consideration is what facilities and resources are available to you for the research element of the programme. These include working spaces. Although you are unlikely to be allocated a campus space, it is worth establishing what hot desking or library spaces might be available to you if you are able to spend a day on campus. Many universities have separate provision for postgraduate and/or doctoral students which you may entitled to access. Second, you should check to see what continuing professional development and researcher training programmes are available, particularly in relation to the type of methodology that you anticipate using.

This might include training in quantitative and qualitative data analysis programmes such as NVivo and SPSS, the use of reference management software, databases and so on. It should also include skills around completing the doctorate, for example, doing literature reviews, presentations, networking and managing the doctoral process. These skills and competences are often mapped against the Vitae Researcher Developer Framework which includes the knowledge, behaviours, abilities and attributes required by researchers. Although the taught element will give you a foundation in these skills, you may need to undertake this additional training in order to develop these at an advanced level for your thesis. Two final issues are whether your university offers funds to support your attendance at conferences and what support is available to promote researcher mental health and well-being. The latter is an increasingly important issue for all universities as the research indicates that there are particular issues around loneliness, transitions to doctoral study and managing unstructured time which are experienced by doctoral students which can result in decreased satisfaction and impact on successful completion.

Examples of types of training and development offered in the research phase:

Managing the supervisory relationship

Surviving and thriving in academia

Writing a successful abstract

Making the most of conferences

Being assertive: making yourself heard

The art of negotiation and influence

Surviving your viva

Writing and structuring an effective thesis

Communicating your research to a non-research audience

Social media: how to build and boost your research profile online

A key element of the professional doctorate programme is the relationship with your supervisor or supervisory team. The research on supervisory approaches and practices specifically relating to professional doctorates is fairly limited (Mawson & Abbott, 2017), but the report on the professional doctorate provision in England noted considerable inconsistencies in terms of the number of supervisors, the involvement of the employer and allocation of supervision hours (Mellors-Bourne et al., 2016). It is not usually possible to choose a supervisor, as they are allocated on the basis of a number of factors, including availability, expertise and the overall balance of the supervision team. It is increasingly common for supervision teams to consist of two or three people, although you will have a lead supervisor (a first supervisor or director of studies) who will be your primary contact. The team usually includes a subject expert, someone who has experience in your methodology or approach, someone who has contacts in this area and/or someone who has successfully supervised students through to completion. Establishing a good working relationship with your supervisor and having clear expectations on both sides is essential, particularly if you are working at a distance from the university. There will be university guidelines indicating what you can expect from your supervisor in terms of numbers of meetings, feedback on your work and other support and guidance. In a professional doctorate, the course leader usually maintains a role in the overall management of the research phase so that you have a point of contact if you need it.

Some tips for the research phase:

- Read completed theses from previous students on the course – what are the expectations and options?
- Read the work of your supervisors – what can they offer?
- Take the opportunity to have a complete break from study between the taught and research phase if you can (in most programmes this is possible in August and or September of the second year) to recharge your batteries for the research phase.

- Get into good working routine as early as you can – identify the best times of the week to set aside time for working and protect these as ruthlessly as you can.

- Write early and write often – it is never too early to start with outlines, reports, summaries.

- Use a research management software.

- Learn how to become a pro user of the word processing software of choice – getting headings, outlines, margins at the beginning can save time and stress later on.

The largest and most significant assessment in the doctorate is the thesis or project. Although there has been considerable discussion in the academic literature about whether a thesis is the most appropriate way of assessing a professional doctorate (Bourner & Simpson, 2005; San Miguel & Nelson, 2007), it still tends to be the most common form of assessment in EdD programmes. In most cases, the thesis is shorter (40–50,000 words) than that would be required for a PhD, reflecting the additional words that are produced for assessment in the taught element. In many institutions, there is no distinctive requirement for the professional doctorate thesis in the regulations, but others specify, for example, that the project must demonstrate an impact on professional practice. Some of the more practice-based professional doctorates may assess on the basis of portfolios which include a more explicit work-focussed or professional practice element.

A final element for consideration is the viva. This remains a universal mechanism for assessment, with institutions using usually two examiners (one external) to undertake an oral examination of the thesis. There are some variations in format. Some institutions, for example, incorporate a public presentation into the final assessment, requiring the candidate to present key findings to the examiners, colleagues and invited members of the public before undertaking the viva voce. Other institutions allow or require a candidate to be examined by a practitioner from the relevant subject area. If your department runs these open presentations in education or other subjects, it is highly recommended that you attend to get a feel of the requirements and what works in delivering your message to non-specialists.

Maxwell (2003) suggests that programmes which continue to privilege academic knowledge and outputs through the conventional assessment by thesis and viva are characteristic of 'first-generation' professional doctorates, which are hesitant to challenge the institutional status quo. However, as professional doctorates become more established, he suggests that 'second-generation' doctorates offer a more radical potential to reshape the academic and professional partnerships. In second-generation professional doctorates the 'realities of the workplace, the knowledge and the improvement of the profession and the rigour of the university are being brought together in new relationships' (Maxwell, 2003, p. 290). This might be reflected in alternative assessment strategies more suited to the assessment of different types of knowledge generation, including, for example, a portfolio of different outputs.

CASE STUDY – MY OWN EXPERIENCE

This case study draws on my own experience of undertaking doctoral study over a 20-year period, first and unsuccessfully, as a full-time PhD student and, second and successfully, as a part-time professional doctorate student. It was my experience that the nature and structure of the professional doctorate programme was perfectly suited to my personal and professional circumstances and provided the framework that I needed in order to complete my doctoral research project.

I began a PhD in law after completing an undergraduate degree in law and postgraduate degree in criminology. The PhD was fully funded as part of a postgraduate teaching assistantship which required me to teach several undergraduate criminal law seminar groups each week. My research topic (the legal and evidential implications of DNA profiling) has been suggested by a lecturer at the university where I had done my undergraduate degree, and although it was a subject that I found interesting, the proposal that had not been prompted by a particular passion or enthusiasm for this area of law. I had come from a university which specialised in socio-legal studies, that is the study of law in the wide social and political context, but the institution in which I was studying tended more to the 'black letter law' approach which prioritised the formal analysis of legal rules. My supervisors were experts in doctrinal analysis but did not have any experience of undertaking empirical research. In my three years as PhD student and postgraduate teaching assistant, I spent much of the time preparing teaching sessions and working on research projects with staff who were undertaking socio-legal research. I converted to part-time registration when I left the institution for a job as a research officer and then as a lecturer. Six years after I started the PhD, I got a job outside academia which gave me the opportunity to finally give up on the project.

However, five years later, I found myself back in academia and in a more senior position in which it was unusual not to have a doctorate. A colleague had recently completed an EdD and recommended exploring these programmes as an alternative to the PhD and so I began researching the options. I knew that a structured taught element was ideal for me as I responded well to deadlines and to structured learning opportunities. I was also unsure what my research topic would be, so I wanted a programme which had the flexibility to develop a proposal as the course progressed. I knew that the topic for my thesis would be HE related so I checked to see that there was a pool of expertise and indeed there was an established research group. The programme that I selected ran weekend workshops on Friday afternoons and Saturday and which was within a reasonable travelling distance. I paid less attention to some of the issues flagged up in this chapter, such as working space, library resources, etc. because I worked in a university and had ready access to these facilities. The structure of the programme was two modules in the first year and a year-long module in year 2, which provided a good warm up for the longer, unstructured research phase.

The informal learning opportunities that arose from the workshops were extremely important in developing my ideas and perspectives and provided the basis for a smaller working group established by six members of the cohort. This group was sustained through hundreds of messages that we exchanged through a social networking site over several years that provided the practical and emotional support to get the research completed and the thesis written. The group presented a joint conference paper which explored the pedagogical implications of our own experience for development of communities of learning in other contexts (Chandler-Grevatt et al., 2008). My supervisor was also an ideal match in terms of methodological orientation and productive working practices. By choosing a topic which directly aligned with my personal interests (in academic writing), professional interests (in assessment and feedback) and disciplinary interests (in criminology), I was able to complete the thesis in three years.

SUMMARY OF THIS CHAPTER

There are two key decisions to be made when deciding to opt for an EdD – the first is whether to do a professional doctorate rather than one of the other routes (a PhD/DPhil or a PhD by publication). The second decision is which EdD to choose, because, as has been shown above, there are significant differences in structure across different programmes.

In relation to the first decision, a professional doctorate is likely to suit you if some or all or the following factors apply:

- You enjoy learning with other people.
- You are able to make time in your schedule to attend face-to-face sessions or workshops.
- You prefer a structured approach to study with interim deadlines and smaller chunks of learning.
- You are motivated by gaining credit and passing assessments.
- You do not yet have a fully developed research proposal.

- You would welcome some structured input either on content or research methods/skills.

- You have not done an undergraduate or postgraduate degree in education and/or a related social science discipline.

- You have been out of formal HE for some time.

In relation to the second decision, there are a number of factors to take into account when making your decision, including:

- The structure of the programme – how many modules will you study, at what level and over what period of time?

- The content of the modules – are they subject based or research skills or both?

- When is the programme delivered (evenings, weekends, block delivery, online) and what support is available between these sessions?

- What is the nature of the assessments?

- How long the research phase is and what resources and support will be available to you during that time?

- What are the supervision arrangements? Are there staff available who have expertise in your likely area of research?

- What training opportunities and resources are available to you during the programme?

- What has been the experience of other students on the programme?

An EdD requires a considerable commitment of time and resources over a substantial period of time, and taking the time to find a programme which is likely to best match your needs and expectations is a very worthwhile investment.

FURTHER READING

British Library EThOS – e-thesis online service. Retrieved from https://ethos.bl.uk/

This resource is a UK-wide resource which aims to 'maximise the visibility and availability of the UK's doctoral research theses'. Although institutions now make theses available through online repositories, this service provides full-text access to over 260,000 theses from over 120 institutions. The advanced search function allows you to search for EdD theses only and is a great resource for familiarising yourself with the range and diversity of EdD topics and methodologies.

Drake, P., & Heath, L. (2010). *Practitioner research at doctoral level: Developing coherent methodologies.* Abingdon: Routledge.

This book is aimed at professionals undertaking doctoral study and researching practice. It covers all aspects of the doctoral process from the relationship between doctoral research and professional life, power and professional settings, insider research methodologies, ethical considerations, doctoral pedagogy and supervision, researcher identity and integrating academic and professional knowledge. Both authors did professional doctorates in education themselves and also draw on their insights from empirical research and experience as course leaders.

Mellors-Bourne, R., Robinson, C., & Metcalfe, J. (2016). *Provision of professional doctorates in English HE institutions: Report for HEFCE by the Careers Research and Advisory Centre* (CRAC). Retrieved from https://dera.ioe.ac.uk//25165/

This report examines professional doctorate provision in England, with the aim of understanding the different ways in which programmes are delivered, the skills and attributes developed and the impact of the programmes on graduates, employers and HE institutions. Drawing on a literature review, survey and interviews with staff, students and alumni, the report provides a very useful current professional doctorate landscape and a good insight into the different dimensions of studying for a professional doctorate.

Scott, D., Brown, A., Lunt, I., & Thorne, L. (2004). *Professional doctorates: integrating professional and academic knowledge.* Maidenhead: Open University Press.

This book is based on a research project which looked in detail at three professional doctorates (the EdD, the DBA and the DEng) to produce a comprehensive picture of the nature and purpose of professional doctorate study. Although it provides an in-depth look at recruitment, content, structure, teaching and assessment on professional doctorate programmes, it is most valuable for its detailed and scholarly exploration of the difference between academic professional knowledge.

REFERENCES

Bao, Y., Kehm, B. M., & Ma, Y. (2016). From product to process. The reform of doctoral education in Europe and China from product to process. *Studies in Higher Education*, 43(3), 524–541. https://doi.org/10.1080/03075079.2016.1182481

Bourner, T., Bowden, R., & Laing, S. (2001). Professional doctorates in England. *Studies in Higher Education*, 26(1), 65–83. Retrieved from http://www.informaworld.com/10.1080/03075070124819

Bourner, T., & Simpson, P. (2005). Practitioner-centred research and the Ph.D. *Action Learning: Research and Practice*, 2(2), 133–151. https://doi.org/10.1080/14767330500206789

Chandler-Grevatt, A., Clayton, S., Creaton, J., Crossland, J., Lefevre, M., & Robertson, S. (2008). Unpicking the threads: Facebook, peer learning and the professional doctorate. In *Society for Research in Higher Education Postgraduate and Newer Researchers Conference*. Liverpool, England.

Costley, C. (2010). Doctoral learning that leads to organisational and individual change. *Work Based Learning E-Journal*, 1(1), 177–201. Retrieved from http://wblearning-ejournal.com/archive/10-10-10/1014rtb.pdf

Costley, C. (2013). Evaluation of the current status and knowledge contributions of professional doctorates. *Quality in Higher Education*, 19(1), 7–27. https://doi.org/10.1080/13538322.2013.772465

Ellis, L. B., & Lee, D. N. (2005). The changing landscape of doctoral education: Introducing the professional doctorate for nurses. *Nurse Education Today*, 25(3), 222–229.

Eraut, M. (1994). *Developing professional knowledge and competence.* New York, NY: Routledge.

Eraut, M. (2000). Non-formal learning and tacit knowledge in professional work. *British Journal of Educational Psychology*, 70(1), 113–136. https://doi.org/10.1348/000709900158001

Hawkes, D., & Yerrabati, S. (2018). A systematic review of research on professional doctorates. *London Review of Education*, 16(1), 10–27. https://doi.org/10.18546/LRE.16.1.03

Kamler, B., & Thomson, P. (2006). *Helping doctoral students write: Pedagogies for supervision*. London: RoutledgeFalmer.

Lindsay, H., Kerawalla, L., & Floyd, A. (2017). Supporting researching professionals: EdD students' perceptions of their development needs. *Studies in Higher Education*, 43(12), 2321–2335. https://doi.org/10.1080/03075079.2017.1326025

Loxley, A., & Kearns, M. (2018). Finding a purpose for the doctorate? A view from the supervisors. *Studies in Higher Education*, 43(5), 826–840. https://doi.org/10.1080/03075079.2018.1438096

Mawson, K., & Abbott, I. (2017). Supervising the professional doctoral student: Less process and progress, more peripheral participation and personal identity. *Management in Education*, 31(4), 187–193. https://doi.org/10.1177/0892020617738182

Maxwell, T. (2003). From first to second generation professional doctorate. *Studies in Higher Education*, 28(3), 279–291. https://doi.org/10.1080/03075070309292

Mellors-Bourne, R., Robinson, C., & Metcalfe, J. (2016). Provision of professional doctorates in English HE institutions. Retrieved from www.crac.org.ukwww.vitae.ac.uk

Neumann, R. (2005). Doctoral differences: Professional doctorates and PhDs compared. *Journal of Higher Education Policy and Management*, 27(2), 173–188. Retrieved from http://www.informaworld.com/10.1080/13600800500120027

Park, C. (2005). New variant PhD: The changing nature of the doctorate in the UK. *Journal of Higher Education Policy and Management*, 27(2), 189–207. https://doi.org/10.1080/13600800500120068

Pearson, M. (1999). The changing environment for doctoral education in Australia: Implications for quality management, improvement and innovation. *Higher Education Research & Development*, 18(3), 269–287.

Quality Assurance Agency. (2015). Characteristics statement: Doctoral degree. Retrieved from www.qaa.ac.uk/publications/information-and-guidance/publication?PubID=2843

Quality Assurance Agency for Higher Education. (2008). *The framework for higher education qualifications in England, Wales and Northern Ireland*. Gloucester: The Quality Assurance Agency for Higher Education.

San Miguel, C., & Nelson, C. D. (2007). Key writing challenges of practice-based doctorates. *Journal of English for Academic Purposes*, 6(1), 71–86. https://doi.org/10.1016/j.jeap.2006.11.007

UK Council for Graduate Education. (2002). *Report on professional doctorates*. Dudley: UKCGE.

Wellington, J., & Sikes, P. (2006). 'A doctorate in a tight compartment': Why do students choose a professional doctorate and what impact does it have on their personal and professional lives? *Studies in Higher Education*, 31(6), 723–734. https://doi.org/10.1080/03075070601004358

Wildy, H., Peden, S., & Chan, K. (2015). The rise of professional doctorates: Case studies of the Doctorate in Education in China, Iceland and Australia. *Studies in Higher Education*, 40(5), 761–774. https://doi.org/10.1080/03075079.2013.842968

2

YOUR RELATIONSHIP WITH YOUR SUPERVISOR

Sue Taylor

INTRODUCTION

The Doctor of Education (EdD) programme is a challenging journey (Wellington & Sikes, 2006). As mature professionals in demanding professional roles, you need particular support and guidance along your EdD journey. This support and guidance will be available in many guises: cohort/peer support, tutor support, support from colleagues and from friends and family. Some of these relationships already exist, whereas others will need to be germinated and nurtured. One such relationship is with your supervisor(s) – you may have more than one supervisor, and this may bring particular considerations as to how to get the most from your supervisory journey. Some of the key questions answered in this chapter are as follows: how to get the most out of supervision, how to use supervision effectively and what to do if the relationship isn't going so well. At pertinent points, there will be some questions to facilitate reflections on working effectively with your EdD supervisors. First, some background and context.

WHAT WILL I LEARN FROM THIS CHAPTER?

Irrespective of the place in your EdD journey, it is important to reflect on your relationship with your supervisor(s) and help them be your guide. Every student's relationship with their supervisor(s) is different and individual to them. However, preparing effectively for meetings, putting dates in the diary and making the most of precious supervision time are important factors for every student to consider. In writing this chapter, I consulted with a range of EdD students at various stages in their professional doctoral journey to ascertain what they thought would be useful inclusions – I hope I have captured what both they and you would like to know through supporting case studies.

OBJECTIVES OF THIS CHAPTER

At the end of this chapter, you should be able to:

- Identify and approach potential supervisor(s) (if your institution expects this of you).
- Develop effective working relationship(s) with your supervisor(s).
- Communicate effectively with supervisor(s).
- Identify possible measures if things do not go smoothly.

BACKGROUND/CONTEXT FOR THIS CHAPTER

I completed my own EdD in 2006. Since then, I have been involved in leading and teaching across all elements of an EdD programme and am now EdD Director. I have supervised many EdD candidates to completion as well as having examined EdD theses. In short, I am passionate about the EdD and its relevance to professionals in deepening understanding of practice and policy. As module leader for a transitional phase of the EdD, bridging the structure and building blocks of the taught courses, and the independent research (thesis) phase, I dedicate time to workshops specifically on 'working with your supervisors'. I also offer EdD-specific supervisor professional development, timely given the introduction of the Good Supervisory Practice Framework (GSPF; Taylor, 2018a) and the Research Supervision Recognition Programme (RSRP; UKCGE, 2019).

It is within this context that I'd like to support you with your own EdD journey, specifically in developing effective student–supervisor relationships. When studying for my own EdD, very little was written specifically for EdD students. Fortunately, this is now not the case although Mellors-Bourne, Robinson, and Metcalfe (2016) found little in terms of supervision of professional doctorates and also reported supervision practices to be diverse. Those studying for professional doctorates and in particular for an EdD have very specific needs due to their usually demanding professional roles and the fact that they undertake insider research (Burnard, Dragovic, Ottewell, & Lim, 2018).

IDENTIFYING AND APPROACHING SUPERVISORS

Some UK universities (Brunel, UCL Institute of Education (IOE)) require prospective EdD students to identify and make contact with potential supervisors. Brunel, for instance, explains that the relationship with your supervisory team will be 'at the core of your research studies …' (brunel.ac.uk, 2019). Like IOE, they suggest making contact with your proposed supervisor(s) to share your research ideas/proposal in advance of the application. In other institutions (University of Manchester and University of Brighton), supervisors are allocated by the EdD Director with the allocation being based on your field of study. In the case of University of Strathclyde, supervisors are brought in at the thesis stage only. But what might you be looking for in your supervisor(s)?

Many universities match EdD students to supervisors in respect of topic or broad research area, and of course, this is extremely important. But should this be the only consideration when identifying and approaching a prospective supervisory team? Most EdDs are studied between four and eight years, albeit a proportion of this time, that is, the last four years, might be where the majority of time is spent with your supervisor(s). Nevertheless, a sustained duration is required, and so careful consideration should be given to who might be the best person/people to support you in your research endeavours.

Identifying Supervisors: Skills, Methodology, Knowledge and Experience

As EdD students, you are probably researching an aspect of practice and/or policy within your professional capacity. Indeed, this is more than likely a requirement of the EdD at the institution of your choice (Pratt, Tedder, Boyask, & Kelly, 2015). As such, there may be specific methodological considerations with such insider research (Corbin Dwyer & Buckle, 2009; Hellawell, 2006) and so choice of supervisor(s) might involve those who have expertise within the profession (Taylor, 2018b) and/or with methodologies suitable for insider research. Equally, selecting supervisor(s) with an understanding of the specific ethical issues and considerations of insider research might also be pertinent. At the point of considering applying to undertake a professional doctorate, you need to research potential supervisors. You will probably have already read journal articles by a range of 'authorities' in your chosen research field and reviewing reference lists might be a good place to start in your search for potential supervisors. You might wish to consider what research they are currently undertaking, what research they have previously done as well as their standing in the field. It is highly unlikely that your research focus will align exactly with your potential supervisors, so be prepared to be flexible to an extent. You might also want to consider their preferred methodologies and how well these align with your proposed research. Equally, it might well be worth considering their experience of supervising doctoral students, particularly EdD students, so they can be empathetic to the demands and focus of the EdD programme. How might you find all this out? Using a general search engine will help if you type in keywords. However, if you are confining yourself to a particular institution, then using the institution's own search engine in the same way would be a useful way forward. Getting to know as much as possible about potential supervisors before approaching them (Lee, 2017) is the start of developing a good working relationship.

Case study 2.1 reflects how important a Year 1 EdD student felt about the importance of identifying a potential supervisor.

Case Study 2.1 – Research in Identifying a Supervisor

I was proactive in thinking through my choice of supervisor. I undertook what I felt was the necessary research to accompany the usual quest for research alignment, such as seeking referrals and testimonies (and who the most appropriate sources of such referrals might be).

Approaching Supervisors

At many institutions, there are regulations governing how many research students' supervisors can supervise at any given time, as well as time allocations for supervision (Mellors-Bourne et al., 2016). Equally, there may be regulations governing whether supervisors can be principal or subsidiary supervisor. Given the likelihood of such regulations, there could be capacity issues and therefore competitiveness of securing the supervisor(s) of your choice could be high. Therefore, once you have identified possible supervisor(s), you will need to approach them. You need to entice them into wanting to build a long-term relationship with you. What is so interesting about your proposed research and how well does it align with their current thinking? How well formulated are your ideas? How could the potential supervisor support you in making a contribution to professional knowledge (Scott, Brown, Lunt, & Thorne, 2004; Scott, 2014)? It might be useful to put some key points down into an email that will act as an enticement. Try to avoid writing an overly long email at this stage as you want to whet a potential supervisor's appetite without them having to read a lengthy email where key points may be lost (or not read sufficiently carefully – academics are busy people). If you add an attachment with more detail, this is more likely to have the desired effect since if your email is sufficiently tantalising, the prospective supervisor(s) are likely to open the attachment and read on. In sending an initial request, try and demonstrate how you think your research interest aligns with your potential supervisors' areas of research. It might be worthwhile explaining something of your previous relevant research, say at master's level, outlining the critical contributions to your success at that level. It may take numerous emails to several academics before receiving any response let alone a positive one. You may also need to follow up on emails if you've had no response, asking if they've had time to read and consider your initial request, and if there's anything further they wish to know at this stage in making a decision about whether to continue the dialogue. This initial approach is the second stage in developing a relationship with your prospective supervisor(s).

Questions for reflection 2.1

- What will influence your choice of supervisor(s)?

- Which institutions allow/expect you to approach your preferred supervisor(s)?

- What are the protocols at your preferred institution in approaching potential supervisors?

Developing Effective Working Relationships with Your Supervisors

Both you and your supervisors will want the same outcome: for you to be successful in your EdD journey. This section considers how to establish effective working relationships from the start.

The First Meeting

Some EdD programmes do not call for supervision from the outset (even if supervisors are in place). Many EdD programmes have taught elements and are structured so the research phase commences in Years 2 or 3. Nevertheless, it might be useful to start and build relationships with your supervisor(s) from the commencement of your EdD journey. The only potential difficulty might be in supervisors agreeing to meet if there is no (or very little) time allocation for supervision in the early stages. Mellors-Bourne et al. (2016) report discrepancies in time allocation for supervisors. So how can you entice your supervisor(s) in taking an interest in you and your EdD from the early stages? Get to know them. For instance, take an interest in their current as well as previous research as well as in their current and previous research students – what contributed to their respective successes? Also, help your supervisor(s) get to know you and keep them abreast of the direction your research ideas are taking as a result of any taught modules (the direction is likely to develop and evolve). If you keep supervisors updated with your current thinking and progress, it will make for a smoother transition once you commence the research phase as they will be more familiar with your evolving research.

The first meeting with your supervisor(s) might be a good time to set a few parameters and agree roles, responsibilities and expectations within the remit of the supervisory role at your institution.

Setting Expectations

Setting expectations is an essential element in developing a successful working relationship. It is not necessarily a case of having a formal contract, but it may be useful to broach the subject as to what supervisors expect of you. As an EdD Director, a question I always ask of EdD applicants, is what they expect of a supervisor, but equally what they will bring to the relationship and what they see as their roles and responsibilities. Supervisory meetings usually work best when there is a shared understanding of each other's roles, and establishing clear expectations from the outset is a good way to avoid a mismatch of goals later on.

Supervisors' understanding of their roles is likely to include supporting you in refining your research questions and designing the research project, conducting and managing the research project, writing the thesis and preparing and making arrangements for the viva. In addition, they may point you in the direction of research activities both within and outside of your home institution including dissemination of your research (at whatever stage you're at) both orally at conferences and as journal publications. How this support is given is the negotiable aspect of the relationship.

As an EdD student, you probably need guidance and advice around several different areas. Writing might be one (it could have been some time since you last wrote for an academic audience) and so feedback will be important to you (dealt with later in this chapter). Equally, your supervisors might need some guidance from you as to the expectations of the EdD versus a PhD (Drake & Heath, 2011). The rigour and quality of an EdD is no different from a PhD, but the contribution to type of knowledge (Scott et al., 2004) might be different. The length of the thesis might be different from the expectations for a PhD thesis, since EdD students will have submitted a large amount of coursework prior to their research phase. Most universities will provide support and training for supervisors (UKCGE, 2019), but it is worth being proactive in this respect, that is, you will normally have an entitlement in terms of allocation of time depending on what year and at what stage of your EdD you're at. It's worth ensuring that both you and your supervisors are in agreement what this time allocation is and how the entitlement might change (increase) throughout the duration of your EdD journey. If you have two supervisors, it will also be necessary to establish their respective roles and how the time will be allocated between them.

Frequency of Meetings

As EdD students working in demanding professional roles, regular meetings with supervisors might pose a challenge due to work commitments. There may be a range of ways of maintaining regular contact with your supervisors and equally in ensuring that you and your supervisors are kept abreast of progress. Setting of parameters and expectations and negotiating ways of working that are mutually acceptable to all parties will be important. The frequency and mode of meetings may change depending on where in your EdD journey you are and the amount and type of support required at a given time. The use of digital technologies could support you greatly here by arranging to Skype or using telephone conferencing. These digital technology modes for meetings will be particularly applicable to those of you from overseas (or undertaking a solely online EdD programme). It will be of paramount importance, given your hectic professional roles that you maximise on opportunities to 'meet' with supervisors. This 'maximisation' can be achieved in a number and variety of ways. For instance, by ensuring that you submit work in advance of the meeting; that you set an agenda for the meeting; that if Skyping or meeting via conference call and you are doing this from work premises, that you ensure you are 'unobtainable' to work colleagues during this time. It is so easy to be called away with professional demands. What will be important is for you and your supervisors to be strategic in deciding whether meetings are needed, and if so, when and when correspondence via email will be more appropriate. There will be a time allocation for supervisors per year of registration, and it will be worth thinking through how that time will be utilised. The time would normally include responding to queries via emails, reading drafts of chapters and support with interpretations and analysis of findings as well as meetings and identifying and nominating examiners and organising upgrades (where applicable) and the viva voce. Case study 2.2 illustrates some of the ways my EdD students have tried to manage their time with their supervisors effectively.

Case Study 2.2 – Setting Parameters

I obtained a very clear outline of my entitlement: number of tutorials and time within those, how often and also emails and boundaries within those. It is easy to ping off an email, but I carefully consider what might be perceived as asking too much. On the flip side, I make sure I get what I need so that I am not left unsure as to what to do. To ensure time is managed well, I comply with previously negotiated agreements set within the parameters identified at the very beginning of the relationship with my supervisors. I am also proactive in reminding my supervisors of these negotiated agreements. I recognise and acknowledge that the relationship is twofold, in which both supervisors and I have responsibilities. I agreed a structure for cadence of meetings with my supervisors and general ways of keeping in touch. My supervisors were not as familiar with the EdD as with PhD supervision and so I shared information about the EdD, including deadlines, with my supervisors. These approaches to working with my supervisors helped clarify everyone's responsibilities from the start.

Planning for Supervision Meetings

Once parameters have been set as well as roles and expectations, you will be able to prepare better for meetings with supervisors. It might be wise to set an agenda and you should be proactive in this as you should have a clear idea of what you want to gain from each meeting, irrespective of the mode that meeting takes. Where applicable, you should have agreed what your responsibility is at the end of the previous meeting and whether you should read and/or write something in advance of the next meeting ready to discuss and critique an article maybe. Stick to agreed deadlines as your supervisors will no doubt, having agreed deadlines and dates of the next meeting in advance, set time aside to act on anything sent. Many of my EdD students, particularly those for whom English is a second language, record the conversation. Even if you don't do this or your supervisors are not happy with an audio recording, you should get into the habit of writing notes and keeping a record of what you think was agreed and of your reflections of the meeting and then sharing these with your supervisors. This will ensure a shared understanding of what has been agreed and an opportunity to gain clarity: engaging in meaningful discussion and listening isn't always conducive to maintaining clear notes during the meeting itself. One of my EdD students uses checklists to support pre- and post-supervision meetings (Case study 2.3).

Case Study 2.3 – Preparing for Supervisory Meetings

To support progress and a well-managed and structured supervisory meeting, I write a self-evaluation progress checklist to think through before each supervision and a suggested reflections and actions checklist to be completed after each supervision. I keep notes of what has been said during supervision meetings, so that they can be referred back to and send those to my supervisors to check that they are representative. I am proactive in setting supervision sessions and believe that taking responsibility for arranging meetings and engaging has to be led by me for the most part. Together with my supervisors, I continually review timescales for successful completion, building in time for revision, iterations, etc.

These preparations are equally important if you are an overseas EdD student. Taking responsibility to constantly monitor your own EdD journey and the flow of your relationship with supervisors will be essential to your success.

> *Questions for reflection 2.2*
>
> - What are your expectations of your supervisor(s) at the outset of your EdD journey?
> - What expectations do your supervisors have of you at the start of your EdD journey?
> - How will you ensure a shared understanding of the roles and responsibilities of each of you?

Partnerships – Changing Dynamics: Expert Versus Novice

As an education specialist, you are an expert in your professional role. You will bring your experience and expertise as a professional to the EdD journey. Nevertheless, you will rely on your supervisors and probably view them as experts in the research field as well as in understanding the research process, possibly viewing yourself somewhat as an 'apprentice' (Taylor, 2018b). Given the levels of expertise and experience on both sides, you will form a partnership. However, in a successful supervisory relationship, this partnership will be dynamic and organic and the expert – novice continuum will shift (Fullerton & Ghérissi, 2015). As you become confident that you have well-defined research questions and that these are operationalisable (Cohen, Manion, & Morrison, 2018) with your research design and methods, you will have a good way forward, guided by your supervisors. However, once you start collecting/generating data the expert – novice continuum is likely to become less well defined. Your supervisors may well steer you in possible approaches to analysis and interpretation. Your supervisors will not necessarily know about all approaches, but they are likely to be able to point you in the right direction for additional further research training both within and outside your own institutions. They will support you in becoming generative learners. But by the time you start analysing and interpreting *your* data, you are becoming the expert as these will be your findings. Of course, interpretations are always open to challenge and a good supervisor will question your thinking and your interpretations as they will start to 'mimic' what they believe your examiners will challenge you on. This will be a constructive approach to ensuring you will eventually be able to defend your thesis. Your supervisors will support you in giving you the confidence that your research is valuable and that it will have impact through a contribution to professional knowledge, policy and practice (Lee, 2009).

The reciprocal relationship may encompass co-authoring of journal articles. Supervisors will usually support you in publishing your EdD research from its very early stages through to completion. In recognition of this support, acknowledgement of the supervisors' involvement is usual.

A requirement to hold a doctorate as a university-based tutor means that increasingly, you may be undertaking an EdD in your place of work and this may become a source of tension in that your supervisor may well be a close professional colleague (Taylor, 2018b). The reciprocal relationship becomes even more important in such instances and the relationship could be viewed along the whole of the expert–novice continuum, that is, expert–expert; expert–novice and novice–expert. Nevertheless, supervisors as colleagues may have its advantages in understanding your professional role and supporting you in making organisational impact (Lundgren-Resenterra & Kahn, 2019).

Questions for reflection 2.3

- Do I view my supervisor as an authority figure or as a partner?
- Where am I currently on the expert–novice continuum?
- Do I want my supervisor to pose questions in order to support me finding my own solutions?

Headspace?

Above, I've alluded to the particular challenges that a professional doctorate such as the EdD poses. Any doctoral research is challenging, but the fact that you are experienced professionals in complex professional roles with high levels of responsibility adds to the challenge. Hawkes and Taylor (2014) used evidence of EdD completions from 1996 to 2013 at IOE. Particular groups were most at risk of not successfully completing their EdD due to being unable to leave the 'day job' behind. For instance,

> head teachers frequently face the most challenges balancing their professional life with their study and personal life, by virtual of the nature of the role ... [and] are consistently the slowest, although ... the higher education academic is equally slow to complete the EdD. (Hawkes & Taylor, 2014, p. 6)

The relationship between doctoral research and professional life is discussed at length by Drake and Heath (2011). It is essential that you work closely with your supervisors, so they understand your professional commitments. Equally, you should respect the time given by your supervisors and be prepared to create the necessary headspace for engaging in cerebral discussions. This necessity is captured well in Case study 2.4.

Case study 2.4 – Cognitive Mindset

With many on this course being very busy professionals it can be tempting to fit in a meeting in an already packed schedule. As EdD students, we should consider whether we are in the headspace to make the most of that interaction, to present our thinking and be ready to respond to critiques.

Questions for reflection 2.4

- Have I negotiated time from my employer to devote to my EdD studies?

- Do I respond to work emails just prior to or immediately following supervisory meetings?

- If the answer to Question 2 is affirmative, what impact might this be having on the way I view my relationship with my supervisor and my ability to act on their advice and guidance?

Feedback

As EdD students working in a professional role within education, writing is likely to play a large part in your daily lives. However, as you will be aware from studying at master's level, writing for purpose and writing for audience, in particular an academic audience, will be different from the writing in your professional capacity. It is a question of genre and even within your EdD programme, there are likely to be different requirements depending on the phase you're at and the structure your EdD programme follows. Therefore, submitting written work for comment from your supervisors will be crucial to developing the necessary critical reading and writing skills expected of doctoral students. You should work closely with your supervisors on developing these skills and should negotiate the type of feedback you require. Be proactive in this regard and learn to be self-evaluative, acknowledging what you think you have done well, what might require further development and what specifically you would like feedback on. Some universities adopt a dialogic and ipsative approach (Hughes, 2017; Hughes, Smith, & Creese, 2014) to support this process.

Setting predetermined dates to submit samples of work for feedback will support maintaining the momentum and help keep you on track for timely completions. Of course, you will need to be realistic when setting these negotiable deadlines with your supervisors, taking into account personal and professional commitments. Once set, ensure you stick to the deadlines and then be mindful about the amount of time your supervisors may require to comment and provide feedback and set a meeting to align with these dates (Case study 2.5). Remember you will not be your supervisors' only research candidate, and they too will be pragmatic in identifying and agreeing when they will be able to read your work and provide constructive comment. Once you have submitted work for comment, you do not need to wait for feedback, there will be a lot of other productive things you can be doing such as more reading or writing for another chapter, etc. On receiving writing for comment, I usually send an email acknowledging receipt and give an indication as to when I might be able to give feedback. Equally, I will often indicate, in consultation with my EdD student, what they might be getting on with in that time.

The nature and purpose of feedback is likely to change over time. Initially, there might be a focus on big messages and on academic writing. Eventually, your supervisors will try and think about the 'final' intended audience for your thesis – the examiners. At this stage, they may be super critical even down to semantics (sentence construction can lead to multiple interpretations and you need to avoid ambiguity in your writing). Your supervisors will also no doubt be calling for succinctness in the extreme and will want you to say what you need to but in far fewer words. This is an important skill worth working on from the outset as there are usually strict rules on word counts for EdD theses. It will not be a question of what you should omit (the problem is usually being way over the word count) but how to be more concise and retain meaning in fewer words. Case study 2.5 explains how one EdD student is proactive in seeking feedback from their supervisor. You'll note how he has built dialogic feedback into his expectations.

Case Study 2.5

I send my supervisors things to read in advance of meetings. I negotiate mutually agreed deadlines. Mine is happy with about four days in advance but some I am sure would appreciate seven. As an EdD student, I am intentional and generative when seeking feedback. I identify where I seek guidance, where I feel improvements are needed, and share the issues I am facing as I write. Similarly, I am open to, and engage with feedback in the spirit of academic endeavour and continuous improvement.

Constructive feedback on your work will mean making changes, some will be minor, but some feedback might result in making some huge conceptual and possibly even paradigm shifts. Being open to this critical appraisal is important whilst maintaining your own voice, hence dialogic and ipsative processes being supportive of your development as a writer. Your supervisors will take into consideration the audience for your writing whilst supporting the value, impact and contribution to professional knowledge (Fenge, 2009) that you will need to demonstrate to your examiners.

In receiving feedback, you may need to interpret what your supervisors are suggesting. Feedback will need to be transformative and generative in that it should challenge your thinking and develop your ideas and writing and your ability to interpret your research findings. Occasionally, as experienced professionals, you might interpret challenge from supervisors as personal or negative, sometimes finding it difficult to focus on the positive comments. If you have developed the trust, honesty and expectations as set out above, you will feel comfortable in talking to your supervisors to gain more clarity about what is going well and where amendments need to be made and importantly, why.

Questions for reflection 2.5

- Who do I submit work for feedback to?
- What form will the feedback take?
- Am I proactive in requesting feedback?
- Do I explain what would be helpful to have feedback on?

Contradictions?

The expectation of some institutions is to have more than one supervisor. This is usually to 'protect' and enhance your experience. Having more than one supervisor will offer the opportunity to gain multiple perspectives. These multiple perspectives are sometimes perceived as contradictions, and some EdD students feel they are being given conflicting advice. It is helpful to acknowledge multiple perspectives and that those of your supervisors may differ from your own. Equally, so might your examiners. Our ontologies and epistemologies (how we view knowledge and how knowledge is constructed; Mason, 2018) shape our research. Therefore, using multiple lenses to view your research is crucial to success in your viva, and your supervisors will guide and steer you along your journey. Therefore, these multiple perspectives should be viewed positively. Case study 2.6 is an example of how I work with co-supervisors. We are clear to our EdD students that we are modelling how they might deal with challenges and how this modelling of discussing different perspectives might support them in eventually defending their thesis.

Case Study 2.6

When co-working with a second supervisor, we often 'model' how to provide rationales for our differing standpoints. These are not necessarily opposing views but rather the other side of the same coin. We do this to demonstrate three things: first, to show that a perspective has to be argued for with 'evidence'; second that there are different ways of viewing knowledge (ontology); and third, that there is not necessarily a right/wrong perspective, but rather it is a question of providing rationales.

Having more than one supervisor will also provide 'protection' and continuity in the absence of one of your supervisors at any given time, for example, sabbaticals, annual leave, conferences and leaving the institution. Having more than one supervisor involved in your research from a very early stage means that more than one person is familiar with your work and has learned to be on your 'wavelength' and can therefore continue with supervisory support in the event of planned and unplanned supervisory absences. This may help prevent delays throughout your EdD journey.

Institutions offering the EdD will regard the policy of more than one supervisor differently. Some will expect both supervisors to be involved equally and throughout the whole of your EdD journey whilst others will expect the supervisory team to divide their time allocation between them. It is important that from the very beginning, you each have a shared understanding of how co-supervision will be organised and that the approach to supervision is amenable to all of you. If, for instance, one supervisor is expert in the research field, whilst the other has expertise in a particular methodological approach, this makes the division of supervision quite straightforward. However, it may well be that both supervisors are equally well placed to advise on all aspects of the research process and the research field. The way you work with more than one supervisor becomes part of the early nego-tiations in terms of expectations and setting parameters as discussed above. For instance, it might well be that it is unnecessary for both supervisors to be present at every meeting, although it would be wise to always include both supervisors in any email communications, in sharing notes from supervisory meetings with both supervisors and for both supervisors to be aware of deadlines negotiated.

Some of you may have an experienced supervisor and one less experienced (whilst it is usual for all supervisors to undergo training and there are sources of information for good supervision of research students, learning how to supervise comes with the practice of supervision). In these instances, it is usual for the more experienced supervisor to take the lead and for both supervisors to be present at all meetings and to be included in all communications.

Questions for reflection 2.6

- Do I have a clear understanding of each of my supervisor's roles and responsibilities?
- Do I know what time allocation I have from each of my supervisors?
- Which supervisor will take the lead?
- Do I communicate with both supervisors at all times?
- What mode and frequency of communication is preferred by all?

Communicating Effectively with Supervisors

If supervision as outlined thus far has gone/is going well, you will be communicating effectively with your supervisors and the relationship could be regarded as successful. However, things do not always go well, and the next section focusses on possible ways forward to resolve any difficulties (perceived or actual) within the supervisory relationship.

When Things Start to go Wrong

There are particular challenges for EdD students, as both you and your supervisors will need to navigate 'the power hierarchy'. The EdD student–supervisor relationship is complex, because it is a relationship between academics and established professionals, nuanced in the EdD as a professional doctorate.

As successful professionals, you might never, or very rarely, have experienced 'failure'. Therefore, on undertaking the challenges of a professional doctorate such as the EdD where you are juggling the demands of a highly responsible professional role alongside the demands of a challenging academic research programme, you might find yourself in a situation where you experience self-doubt. Most EdD programmes provide opportunities for introspection and critical reflection (Cunningham, 2018). Nevertheless, when things do not appear to be going as well as anticipated, these skills are sometimes forgotten. Argyris (1991) explains that successful professionals sometimes cast blame outward rather than critically examining their own behaviour. If your EdD journey doesn't appear to be going to plan, the first step might be to critically reflect and be honest in thinking about all of the above sections. From my own experience (both as an EdD alumni and as an EdD supervisor) and from the shared experiences of my EdD students, things might go wrong as a result of:

- A lack of communication on either the EdD student's part, the supervisor's part or both.

- A lack of understanding or misunderstanding of what has been advised.

- Perceived or actual differences in advice given from each of the two supervisors leading to lack of clarity.

- Supervisors leaving the institution – even with a new supervisor in place and with continuity provided by the existing supervisor, there needs to be some discussion as to ways of working within a different team.

- Tensions in research methodology, that is, approach to take.

- Lack of 'trust' from one or both sides, for instance, the changes in the relationship as the EdD student becomes expert.

- Not devoting the necessary 'headspace' for your EdD studies.

Institutions usually have a range of processes in place to support you if your supervisory relationship might not be working quite according to plan. Some processes are specific to each institution. However, there are some general guidelines you might like to consider.

Support Mechanisms

Gaining awareness of where to seek help, who to seek help from
and the forms of help available will be crucial from the earliest
stages of your EdD journey. It may be necessary to seek help and
advice from outside the supervisory team, and it may well be that
at the time that you are seeking this type of support and guidance,
you might not be in a 'good place'. This will make navigation of
the types of support available to you more difficult, so knowing
the forms of support in advance will be a good investment of time.
This knowledge will also facilitate you being able to escalate any
difficulties whilst remaining in 'control' of your journey.

Regulatory Support

First and foremost, you should make yourself aware of the regulations for your EdD programme and know where these can be
found. These regulations might also include procedures to follow if
you have difficulty in meeting deadlines or in the event of supervision not working out as you had hoped. Many universities will have
general sections for postgraduate research students that will provide information for both students and supervisors. They may also
have specific regulations, codes of practice and regulatory frameworks that govern EdD candidates.[1] UCL, for instance, has regulations and codes of practice for postgraduate research students and
specifically for EdD candidates.[2] These regulations are accessible to
both candidates and to supervisors with information outlined as:
'Regulations and Codes of Practice' including appropriate forms
of supervision, *Academic Manual* (which has specific sections for
EdD students), 'General Information' including a *Doctoral School
Handbook*, 'Essential Procedures and Policies' and 'Useful Contact
Lists'. You should similarly be able to locate postgraduate research
regulations and regulatory frameworks and codes of practice for
your home institutions.

These regulatory frameworks will be comprehensive and will
outline processes and procedures to follow in the event of your
EdD supervision going awry. They will normally outline a 'hierarchy of support', that is, it is usually better to raise any concerns at
a 'local' level in the first instance before escalating. Nevertheless,
there may be an occasion when higher level mediation is necessary.

Mediational Support

Above, I talked of the importance of honesty and trust in the supervisory relationship. If things start to go wrong, then the first course of action would be to have a frank discussion with both supervisors before any difficulties (perceived or actual) spiral. This is a two-way process and you should anticipate that supervisors would also feel able to have these frank discussions if they are concerned about your progress.

In the event that difficulties cannot be resolved between you and your supervisors, the type of regulatory frameworks outlined above are likely to provide you with contact information and the 'hierarchy of support'. For instance, in addition to your supervisors, you may have an assigned personal tutor and it might be appropriate to discuss any difficulties with them. You may well have departmental and faculty graduate tutors who can offer assistance, as well as the EdD Programme Director. To facilitate fairness and equity, any persons involved in mediation will turn to the regulatory frameworks in providing advice, guidance and counselling.

In addition to mediation services offered by academic staff, you are likely to have access to support from the Student Union.

Being aware of how to locate the regulatory frameworks and sources of support and guidance will ensure you have routes to a mutually acceptable resolution.

Well-being Support

Although not explicitly about supervision, given the challenges of the EdD programme, you might also make yourself aware of any Student Support and Well-Being Services. Seeking help and guidance from such support might mitigate against the need for requiring regulatory support services.

Questions for reflection 2.7

- What are the regulations for my EdD programme?
- Where are these regulations located?
- If I am experiencing difficulties who do I talk to in the first instance?
- What is the 'hierarchy of support' available to me?

SUMMARY OF THIS CHAPTER

In writing this summary, I decided to use an extended case study
(Case study 2.7). This is because this particular case encapsulates
how successful and enjoyable the supervisory relationship can be.
It incorporates an example of best practice when working with
two complementary supervisors who do not usually work closely
together as they come from different disciplines within social sciences and education. Nevertheless, together with the proactive student, they navigated and negotiated good working relationships
that have thus far resulted in the EdD student making excellent and
timely progress throughout his EdD journey.

Case Study 2.7

My own experience of the supervisory relationship has been fantastic. I have two excellent supervisors and I've been guided and
supported by them both so splendidly since I started. We've worked
really well together. In light of that that, suggestions I can offer
don't come from a negative perspective. So, why have things have
gone so well?

From the start I engaged with my supervisors (not a requirement
at this institution). I always made sure that if I wanted feedback,
I gave them enough time to digest it and consider a response. I was
careful to remember that I am not the only supervisee they have on
their list and that they have their own teaching and writing commitments. Sometimes, I got in contact too much, but they've always
been great. It's important that EdD students are not sending things
to supervisors imagining that they are sitting around waiting for us
to get in touch so that they have something to do (as a mentor and
supervisor of aspiring sign language interpreters I have to remind
them that I have more than one task in my life – supporting them –
and if they want me to give feedback on something, sending it to
me and saying they need feedback tomorrow won't work).

It's important that EdD students are realistic – our journey is
our own and our supervisors can't make it for us. They can guide
us and suggest paths to take, but they can't make the journey for
us, they have made theirs already.

They challenge me, but I feel supported within that. They push me, but I sense that they have faith in me and feel that I am capable of some great work. That encouragement and support has been invaluable to me. I left school with no qualifications and didn't do 'O' levels or 'A' levels. Through my undergraduate degree and my two master's degrees (and some other postgraduate qualifications in teaching), I have battled with the idea that I am a fraud and I'm going to get caught out. I still have that with the doctorate. So, their belief in me, and their genuine interest in my research and professional role, empowers me.

We meet regularly but have clear, planned objectives for the times in-between. I keep them updated with what it is that I am doing and where I am at.

Feedback has always been very thorough. It is detailed and specific rather than vague or unhelpful. EdD students need to plan for feedback – if we don't allow time to act on the feedback, there's no point.

As I have developed these past three years as a student on the EdD course, I have become more confident and know when to absolutely agree with my supervisors and when to suggest that I think differently about things and we have a great dynamic in that regard.

Letting supervisors know your intentions and plans and thought processes before you embark on certain activities is really important. I've always endeavoured to do that because it would be a waste of time to go down one road only for them to offer a suggestion that really makes sense and have to rethink it all. So, I'm always open, always engaging and in a nutshell – using them as much as I can (whilst being mindful I'm not the only person they are dealing with).

I honestly struck gold with my two supervisors. I don't think everyone has that experience, but I have.

As this EdD student states, the supervisory experience can vary (Mellors-Bourne et al., 2016) even within the same institution. However, as Case study 2.7 demonstrates, being proactive and keeping lines of communication open is crucial in having a successful supervisory experience and therefore an enjoyable EdD journey. I wish you every success with yours.

FURTHER READING

Hawkes, D., Syerrabati, S., & Taylor, S. (2018). The EdD at 20: Lessons learned from professional doctorates. *London Review of Education*, *16*(1), 1–3. Retrieved from http://www.ingentaconnect. com/content/ioep/clre/2018/00000016/00000001

This special issue of the *London Review of Education* is edited by two EdD programme leaders. It incorporates articles from EdD students as well as from EdD alumni and EdD supervisors involved in doctoral research. The focus is the EdD programme from multiple perspectives and has a foreword by Ingrid Lunt who has written extensively about professional versus academic knowledge.

Lee, N.-J. (2009). *Achieving your professional doctorate*. Maidenhead: Open University Press.

This book is useful as a general 'toolkit' in thinking about undertaking a professional doctorate. It considers what is a professional doctorate and who would consider studying for one and why. It takes a global view of the EdD and considers the role of the supervisor on the EdD.

Scott, D., Brown, A., Lunt, I., & Thorne, L. (2004). *Professional doctorates: Integrating professional and academic knowledge*. Maidenhead: Open University Press.

This book provides EdD students with an understanding of how their EdD thesis could make an original contribution to knowledge and makes a distinction between professional and academic knowledge, acknowledging the importance of professional knowledge and the supervisor's role in supporting this acquisition of and contribution to professional knowledge.

Taylor, S. (2018a). *Good supervisory practice framework*. Dudley: UKCGE.

This new framework outlines possible best practice for doctoral supervision. However, it is aimed at all doctoral supervision.

NOTES

1. University of Bristol, http://www.bristol.ac.uk/academic-quality/pg/cop-research-degrees.html; University of Newcastle, http://www.bristol.ac.uk/academic-quality/pg/cop-research-degrees.html; and University

of Stirling, https://www.stir.ac.uk/about/professional-services/student-academic-and-corporate-services/academic-registry/regulations/postgraduate-research-regulations/.

2. https://www.grad.ucl.ac.uk/essinfo/

REFERENCES

Argyris, C. (1991). Teaching smart people to learn. *Harvard Business Review*, May–June.

Brunel University. (2019). *Research Degrees*. Rerieved from https://www.brunel.ac.uk/research/research-degrees

Burnard, P., Dragovic, T., Ottewell, K., & Lim, W. M. (2018). Voicing the professional doctorate and the researching professional's identity: Theorizing the EdD's uniqueness. *London Review of Education*, *16*(1), 40–55. https://doi.org/10.18546/LRE.16.1.05

Cohen, L., Manion, L., & Morrison, K. (2018). *Research methods in education* (8th ed.). Abingdon: Routledge.

Corbin Dwyer, S., & Buckle, J. L. (2009). The space between: On being an insider–outsider in qualitative research. *International Journal of Qualitative Methods*, *8*(1), 54–63.

Cunningham, B. (2018). Pensive professionalism: The role of "required reflection" on a professional doctorate. *London Review of Education*, *16*(1), 63–73. https://doi.org/10.18546/LRE.16.1.07

Drake, P., & Heath, L. (2011). *Practitioner research at doctoral level: Developing coherent methodologies*. Abingdon: Routledge.

Fenge, L. A. (2009). Professional doctorates: A better route for researching professionals? *Social Work Education*, *28*(2), 165–176.

Fullerton, T., & Ghérissi, A. (2015). Midwifery professional relationships: Collaboration across the novice-to-expert continuum. *International Journal of Childbirth*, *5*(1), 3–11. Retrieved from https://search.proquest.com/docview/1663355931?accountid=14511

Hawkes, D., & Taylor, S. (2014). So who wants to do an EdD anyway? Evidence from the Institute of Education EdD completions 1996–2013.

Work Based Learning e-Journal International, *4*(1), 1–10. Retrieved from http://wblearning-ejournal.com/currentissue.php

Hellawell, D. (2006). Inside-out: Analysis of the insider–outsider concept as a heuristic device to develop reflexivity in students doing qualitative research. *Teaching in Higher Education*, *11*(4), 483–494. http://dx.doi.org/10.1080/13562510600874292

Hughes, G., Smith, H., & Creese, B. (2014). Not seeing the wood for the trees: Developing a feedback analysis tool to explore feed forward in modularised programmes. *Assessment and Evaluation in Higher Education*, *40*(8), 1079–1094.

Hughes, G. J. (2017). Exploring the relationship between ipsative assessment and institutional learning gain. In G. Hughes (Ed.), *Ipsative assessment and learning gain: Exploring international case studies* (pp. 33–56). Basingstoke: Palgrave Macmillan.

Lee, A. (2017). Establishing a good relationship from the beginning. Tool adapted from Brown, G. and Atkins, M. (1988). *Effective teaching in higher education* (pp. 146–147). London: Methuen.

Lee, N.-J. (2009). *Achieving your professional doctorate*. Maidenhead: Open University Press.

Lundgren-Resenterra, M., & Kahn, P. (2019). The organisational impact of taking a professional doctorate: Forming critical leaders. *British Educational Research Journal*, *45*(2), 407–424. https://doi.org/10.1002/berj.3503

Mason, J. (2018). *Qualitative researching* (3rd ed.). London: Sage.

Mellors-Bourne, R., Robinson, C., & Metcalfe, J. (2016). *Provision of professional doctorates in English HE institutions: Report for HEFCE by the Careers Research & Advisory Centre, supported by the University of Brighton*. Higher Education Funding Council for England.

Pratt, N., Tedder, M., Boyask, R., & Kelly, P. (2015). Pedagogic relations and professional change: A sociocultural analysis of students' learning in a professional doctorate. *Studies in Higher Education*, *40*(1), 43–59. http://dx.doi.org/10.1080/03075079.2013.818640

Scott, D. (2014). Academic and professional knowledge in the professional doctorate. *International Perspectives on Higher Education Research*, *13*, 17–30.

Scott, D., Brown, A., Lunt, I., & Thorne, L. (2004). *Professional doctorates: Integrating professional and academic knowledge.* Maidenhead: Open University Press.

Taylor, S. (2018a). *Good supervisory practice framework.* Dudley: UKCGE.

Taylor, S. (2018b). The UCL EdD: An apprenticeship for the future educational professional? *London Review of Education, 16*(1), 104–120. https://doi:10.18546/LRE.16.1.10

UKCGE. (2019). *Research recognition programme.* Dudley: UKCGE.

Wellington, J., & Sikes, P. (2006). 'A doctorate in a tight compartment': Why do students choose a professional doctorate and what impact does it have on their personal and professional lives? *Studies in Higher Education, 31*(6), 723–734. http://dx.doi.org/10.1080/03075070601004358

3

ETHICS IN EDUCATIONAL RESEARCH

Paula Zwozdiak-Myers

INTRODUCTION

Grounded in 'moral philosophy' or the 'philosophy of morality' ethics, as it relates to educational research, is principally concerned with deliberating between right and wrong – good and bad. The questions: What ought I to do? How might I find out or know about what I ought to do? Once I find out, why should I do it? form the substantive content of this branch of philosophy along with debates about what constitutes a moral judgement, how it may be distinguished from other types of value judgement, what kind of truth claims can be made within the moral domain and why responding to such questions matters.

This chapter introduces ethical theories from four philosophical orientations, aligned to ethical principles and procedures within historical and current guidelines. These should enable you to think through ethical dimensions of educational research with a reflexive stance from a well-informed platform. The authentic case study exemplifies how one doctoral researcher navigated and responded to ethical issues associated with online research.

At the end of this chapter, you will be able to:

- Situate consequentialism, deontology, virtue ethics and an ethic of care within educational research.

- Appropriate key ethical principles and guidelines for conducting your research.

- Recognise ethical issues pertinent to online research.

ETHICAL THEORIES

Consequentialism (Utilitarianism)

Consequential (utilitarian) theories (see also Macleod, 2016 on John Stuart Mill) maintain that an action or decision can be viewed as morally defensible or desirable if it produces the greatest possible balance of good over bad (right over wrong). This means we need to understand what constitutes good and bad and be able to evaluate the balance between good and bad in relation to any action or decision we may choose to take. The principle of *maximum benefit* involves thinking through what the foreseeable positive and negative consequences may be for each possible action or decision, and selecting that which maximises benefits and minimises risks and/ or harm (Sinnott-Armstrong, 2003, however, questions whether it is entirely possible to evaluate all the possible consequences of each and every action and for all individuals). This inevitably raises the question of benefits and risks to whom and whether or not the possible consequences for all key stakeholders (e.g. research participants, researchers, institutions, educational community and wider society) hold the same weighting. Utilitarianism (one form of consequentialism) focusses on the 'utility' of consequences aligned to possible actions (and those affected by them) and suggests 'an individual ought to do that act that promotes the greatest good, happiness, or satisfaction to most people' (Kimmel, 1988, p. 45). From this perspective, which treats individuals instrumentally *as a means to some chosen end* (if this maximises benefits and produces the best possible consequences) rather than as ends in themselves, no one individual is privileged nor considered more important than other individuals, which also includes the decision maker.

Picture this scene:

One school judged five years ago by Ofsted as 'requires improvement' has recently been judged 'outstanding'. Although morale is seemingly positive, this follows a period of turbulence with high staff turnover. Ben has been fast tracked into middle leadership and for his doctoral research aims to examine what factors led to this improvement. The headteacher granted permission for this research to go ahead yet with the caveat to review findings before they were made public. Ben's documentary analysis reveals General Certificate of Secondary Education (GCSE) results have seen an increase year on year, so too has data concerning exclusions. Teachers who experienced this transition were not wholly in accord with new policies and practices. Reflecting on students when interviewed one teacher remarks:

> *two of those excluded were diagnosed with social, emotional, behavioural disorders and from disadvantaged backgrounds ... now they have been further stigmatised ... I worry about their future prospects and life chances.*

Reflective questions:

What is the purpose (utility) of Ben's research?

What are the positive and negative consequences of actions he could take?

What weightings should he attach to different stakeholders when gathering evidence and reporting findings?

Deontology

Deontological theories dismiss the notion that determining what is morally good or ethically right can solely be realised by assessing the weight of any given action in terms of positive and negative consequences. In deontology, certain acts are regarded as inherently good or bad, inherently right or wrong and, therefore, from an ethical perspective are obligatory, notwithstanding any of the possible consequences, for example, always telling the truth, not betraying a trust nor a confidence. An influential proponent of this approach, Immanuel Kant (1758/1993) advanced the thesis that moral obligations do not stem from consequences but rather from categorical ethical principles. In coming to recognise what constitutes the 'right' thing to do his categorical imperative is that, as rational agents, we should only act in ways we would wish and will all other people to act (his appeal in also trying to identify universal rules). Israel (2015, p. 12) distinguishes this tenet from the deontological Golden Rule: 'do unto others as you would have them do unto you'. Kant's (1758/1993) categorical imperative embraces the notion that we should always treat people with human dignity, respect and as of equal worth, as *ends in themselves* and never solely as a means to some given end:

> *Act in such a way that you treat all humanity, whether in your own person or in the person of any other, always at the same time as an end and never solely as a means to an end. (p. 36)*

Ross (1930) widened the lens of these principles of deontology and ethical conduct to incorporate prima facie duties around such concepts as beneficence (doing good), fidelity (honesty), justice (fairness and equity), non-maleficence (not causing harm) and self-improvement. When these principles are in conflict with one another, as is so often the case in educational research, Ross advocates that we should choose between the principles by performing the most important duty. In so doing, we must draw upon our intuition and moral judgement to discern what it is that we really should and ought to do.

Reflective questions:

From a deontological perspective, there are several conflicting principles which Ben might be challenged by. Consider the following:

For the reputation of the school, what is the most important duty?

For the protection of participant teachers, what is the most important duty?

For students at risk of exclusion, what is the most important duty?

For the integrity of his doctoral research, what is the most important duty?

How have you arrived at these moral judgements?

Virtue Ethics

Virtue ethics is an agent-centred (as opposed to consequence, act or rule centred) theory concerned with the moral character of ethical decision makers. From an Aristotelian (1984) perspective, the concepts *aretê* (excellence, virtue), *phronêsis* (practical, moral wisdom) and *eudaimonia* (human flourishing, happiness) give primacy to virtuous character. Within this tradition, a virtue can be understood as a deep and enduring disposition that motivates ethical researchers to pursue the 'good' and 'right' course of action, especially when faced with uncertainty, challenges and difficulties. In general, we act from our own character and our dispositions to see, value and behave in certain ways, which is why

> being an ethical researcher requires an authentic engagement with our own beliefs and the values of our disciplines. Ethics is a bit like jazz, in that it is about more than simply following the notes on the page, it demands an ability to improvise and to think for ourselves. (Macfarlane, 2010, p. A30)

Moral virtues and intellectual virtues are particularly important character traits for educational researchers to harness. Moral virtues incorporate such dispositions as courage, concern for justice, caring for others' welfare, honesty and perseverance. Intellectual virtues capture those dispositions concerned with integrity, trust and truthfulness in the pursuit of knowledge. Sockett (2012, p. 57) argues that the 'linchpin of trust' resides in our:

> *openness of mind to fresh new avenues of enquiry and criticism; concern for accuracy; interest in clarity of communication; and, impartiality in face of rival interpretations and selections of evidence.*

The complex interrelationship between moral and intellectual virtues (and their respective deliberations) when the deeply entrenched virtue 'truthfulness' disposes the researcher to act in the best interests of the research has been elaborated by Pring (2015, p. 185) as:

> courage *to proceed when the research is tough or unpopular;* honesty *when the consequences of telling the truth are uncomfortable;* concern for the wellbeing *of those who are being researched and who, if treated insensitively, might suffer harm;* modesty *about the merits of the research and its conclusions;* humility *in the face of justified criticism and the readiness to take such criticisms seriously.*

He further exclaims: 'the virtuous researcher would be horrified at any attempt to "cook the books" or to stifle criticism or to destroy data or to act partially' (Pring, 2015, p. 185).

Picture this scene:

Children missing education is of significant concern for one Borough in London. As the Education Welfare Officer, Stella decides to investigate factors that may underpin this issue for her doctoral research. Whilst conducting home visits and interviewing some of these children and their families, recurrent themes surfaced – extreme levels of poverty, children as young carers and intergenerational families from diverse communities living in overcrowded accommodation. There are clearly multiple complex issues to address within her professional role and as a researcher. When Stella approaches local schools, she questions the extent to which individual family circumstances should be fully disclosed in the interests of all key stakeholders yet is also mindful that crucial support may not be forthcoming if she withholds certain information. She is also exercised about how to protect the privacy of these families and their 'stories' when writing up and disseminating her findings.

> *Reflective questions:*
>
> What moral and intellectual virtues might Stella need to harness to perform her professional and researcher roles effectively?
>
> Are there situations where these virtues are diametrically opposed?
>
> If yes, how might you advise Stella to proceed? Explain why you privilege this decision over an alternative course of action?

ETHICS OF CARE

The 'interpretive turn' (Rabinow & Sullivan, 1987) of the twentieth century paved the way for an epistemological shift in educational research from positivism towards hermeneutics, and with this, new and revitalised perspectives of moral theory and ethics. The interpretive lens recognises attitudes, beliefs, customs and identities are 'dialogically' created within social relationships and the use of language – negotiated and constructed through the interactions between researchers and those they study. This methodology calls upon researchers to 'seek out and listen carefully to "voices" embedded in their social contexts to gain a true understanding of what people are saying and why they do what they do' (Howe & Moses, 1999, p. 32). These *value-laden descriptions* and *ends* are part and parcel of interpretive approaches to educational research and, as MacIntyre (1982, p. 175) writes:

> *not only do social scientists explore a human universe centrally constituted by a variety of obedience to and breaches of, conformities to and rebellions against, a host of rules, taboos, ideals and beliefs about goods, virtues and vices ... their own explorations of that universe are no different in this respect from any other form of human activity.*

As key proponents of care theory, Gilligan (1982) and Noddings (1984) challenged the premise that moral actions can solely be (nor are) grounded in abstract rational principles, especially since ethical questions can also appeal to the emotional domain. Their ethics of care theory signals the primacy of compassion, cooperation, empathy, consensus and trust when establishing and sustaining positive relationships and social networks. Gilligan (1982) questioned the predominantly male-dominated traditional ethical theories which place an emphasis on autonomy, rights and duties/obligations and identified two alternative ways in which we can think ethically. The first based upon an ethics of justice and rights and the second an ethics of care. Findings from her landmark research into the psychological development of girls and young women challenged the developmental theories of psychological theorists such as Lawrence Kohlberg, who not only had excluded female voices from his research but generalised findings to include both males and females. Similar studies that involved bias and unjust labelling include those of Willis (1977) into working-class male youth and Ogbu and Matute-Bianchi's (1986) work concerning people of colour.

Noddings (2002a, p. 2) distinguishes between an ethics of care and virtue ethics, noting that 'it is relation centered rather than agent centered, and ... more concerned with the caring relation than with caring as a virtue'. In her view, caring provides the foundation on which virtues are built. In advancing her vision of the ethical *self* or ethical *ideal*, Noddings (2002b, p. 223) writes:

> We put great emphasis on moral interdependence – our shared responsibility for the moral strength or weakness of each member of our society. In 'educating the (caring) response', caring parents and teachers provide the conditions in which it is possible and attractive for children to respond as carers to others. We show them how to care. Children educated in this way gradually build an ethical ideal, a dependable caring self. A society composed of people capable of caring – people who habitually draw on a well-established ideal – will move toward social policies consonant with an ethic of care.

In relation to educational research, Noddings (1986) advanced two theses concerning the application of an ethics of care. First, the relationship between researchers and participants should exemplify caring, especially mutual respect and trust. The second widens the lens of the first and is concerned with the whole research enterprise: the selection of research questions and overall conduct of the research should be based on their potential to contribute towards caring school communities. She persuasively cautions against conducting research purely on the basis of intellectual curiosity or in ways that may be harmful or destructive to an individual student, groups of students or school communities. The overall purpose of educational research should, in Nodding's (1986, p. 506) view, be '*for* teaching' and not simply '*on* teaching'.

When questioning what the empirical evidence points towards in educational practice, Noddings (2003, p. xv) found:

> *individuals only rarely consult moral principles when making decisions that result in the prevention of harm. More often, people respond directly as carers (out of sympathy) or as faithful members of a community that espouses helping and not harming.*

Reflecting on their own research, Schultz, Schroeder and Brody (1997, p. 473) recognise:

> *At the very least, Noddings urges us to weigh the effects that our research decisions have on the development of the other as a caring person and of a community of caring.*

They further suggest

> *ethical dilemmas arising from complex human relationships cannot be resolved by invoking rules and protocols ... researchers need to struggle continuously with the larger questions and how to share their stories in meaningful and ethical ways. (Schultz et al., 1997, p. 483)*

Critical and relational approaches to educational research including communitarian, covenantal, environmental, feminist and indigenous frameworks (e.g. Bannon, 2013; Brabeck & Brabeck, 2009; Brydon-Miller & Hilsen, 2016) view researchers as thoughtful, active agents whose relationships and commitment to participants in the research process are understood to deepen the research endeavour and contribute to more ethical research practices. In the quest for just, equitable and relational outcomes to ethical questions, researchers consider how power relations, basic human rights, respect, sensitivities and reciprocity can guide their actions and relationships with research participants within very particular and specific social contexts.

Reflective questions:

How do you exemplify an ethics of care for your research participants within your design, before and during the process of gathering data, in your analysis and reporting?

How might you continue to be sensitive to their future selves, whilst at the same time, faithful to the moment?

ETHICAL PRINCIPLES

Historical watershed cases of research misconduct, especially those concerning harmful and deceptive research practices (such as Milgram's, 1974 obedience to authority studies in the 1960s and Humphreys', 1970 covert observation during the Tearoom Trade studies of the 1970s) led to the emergence and formulation of ethical guidelines and regulations not only in biomedical and behavioural research but also in social science and educational research. The Belmont Report (NCPHSBBR, 1979, B. 1) which still has widespread national and international currency set out three principles to guide our understanding about key ethical issues associated with research involving human participants – respect for persons, beneficence and justice.

Respect for Persons

This principle places considerable emphasis on autonomy and has two strands: individuals should be acknowledged as autonomous agents and individuals with diminished autonomy should be protected. The Report (NCPHSBBR, 1979, B. 1) states:

> *An autonomous person is an individual capable of deliberation about personal goals, and of acting under the direction of such deliberation. To respect autonomy is to give weight to autonomous persons' considered opinions and choices, while refraining from obstructing their actions, unless they are clearly detrimental to others. To show lack of respect for an autonomous agent is to repudiate that person's considered judgments, to deny an individual the freedom to act on those considered judgments, or to withhold information necessary to make a considered judgment, when there are no compelling reasons to do so.*

As autonomous agents, individuals should be given the opportunity to decide whether to participate in research on a voluntary basis and be provided with sufficient information about the research project and their role within it. Individuals with diminished autonomy, such as children, those with an illness or disability where their freedom to choose may be limited must be protected, based on an assessment of potential benefit and risk of harm. The Report advises, as an individuals' capacity of autonomous decision-making may alter during their lifespan 'the judgment that any individual lacks autonomy should be periodically re-evaluated and will vary in different situations' (NCPHSBBR, 1979, B. 1). Kant's deontological perspective of individuals as rational, autonomous agents as well as not using individuals simply as a means to some end are reflected in this principle.

Beneficence

This principle focusses on actively doing good to maximise possible benefits and well-being of individuals, avoiding the potential of imposing such conditions as emotional, psychological, physical or emotional distress and harm. This means 'investigators and members of their institutions are obliged to give forethought to the maximisation of benefits and the reduction of risk that might occur from the research investigation' (NCPHSBBR, 1979, B. 2). Although benefits may relate to an individual, a group, community and the wider public, the Report gives particular attention to the risk assessment of research involving children, especially where benefits may significantly improve the life chances of children in the future, yet have little or no immediate effect on the lives of those directly involved in the research. The Report acknowledges that 'as with all hard cases, the different claims covered by the principle of beneficence may come into conflict and force difficult choices' (NCPHSBBR, 1979, B. 2). The prima facie duties of beneficence and non-maleficence (avoiding harm) in Ross' (1930) deontology have particular salience with this principle.

Justice

This principle is concerned with the distribution of benefits and burdens amongst people within research and places particular emphasis on the selection of participants. Drawing from case studies that signalled ethical misconduct and exploitation of vulnerable people, the Report persuasively argues that systematically selecting some groups of people for research is unjust when simply premised on 'their easy availability, their compromised position, or their manipulability, rather than reasons directly related to the problem being studied' (NCPHSBBR, 1979, B. 3). The Report advanced the notion that justice may be broadly understood in terms of 'equals being treated equally' yet also questioned how equality might be construed in light of multiple differences including age, competence, gender and status. Distributive justice was presented as an alternative formula for calculating the possible distribution of benefits and burdens: 'to each person an equal share' ... 'to each person according to merit' ... or ... 'to each person according to individual need' (NCPHSBBR, 1979, B. 3). The inclusion and exclusion criteria for selecting research participants will be dependent upon which formula is the most appropriate (rather than most convenient) for each research enterprise.

Picture this scene:

Alastair works in a prestigious higher education institution which has recently been exposed to negative scrutiny from the media in relation to the alarming number of Tier 4 students falling off the radar by not actively engaging with their studies. For his doctoral research, he is particularly interested in finding out more about international students' motivations and aspirations for wanting to study in the United Kingdom and has identified an overseas cohort of students as potential research participants. They have explicitly expressed an interest for their voices to be heard, identity to be revealed and made public. Alastair's proposal to the university Research Ethics Committee (REC) has been challenged on several grounds, for example, not ensuring participant anonymity and confidentiality, possible institutional damage as well as compromising future international relations.

Reflective question:

How might Alastair negotiate and settle these perplexities in terms of respect for persons, beneficence and justice?

The Belmont Report translated the three principles into applications (and requirements) when conducting ethical research which include

Respect for persons: informed consent, with sufficient and comprehensible information so individuals can choose to participate, voluntarily.
Beneficence: assessment of risks and benefits;
Justice: in the selection of research participants, fair procedures to provide fair outcomes.

These principles and their applications informed the development and augmentation of ethical guidelines and regulations for researchers within a range of disciplines and underpin ways in which many RECs evaluate research proposals. Those presented in Table 1 exemplify research ethics principles associated with social science and educational research.

These sources aim to set out good practice and illuminate key principles and expectations of researchers, research organisations and RECs. The British Educational Research Association's (BERA) *Ethical Guidelines for Educational Research* (2018) reflect (explicitly or implicitly) the AcSS principles and are consistent with ethical principles of respect developed in previous iterations of BERA guidelines since the first publication in 1992.

ETHICAL GUIDELINES FOR EDUCATIONAL RESEARCH (BERA, 2018)

The Association's main aspirations for these guidelines are to remind us that:

> [...] *all educational research should be conducted with an* ethic of respect *for: the person; knowledge; democratic values; the quality of educational research; and academic freedom. Trust is a further essential element within the relationship between researcher and researched, as is the expectation that researchers will accept responsibility for their actions ...*
>
> *Applying* an *ethic of respect may reveal tensions or challenges ... there will usually be a need to balance research*

Table 1:   Research Ethics Principles.

Five Ethics Principles for Social Science Research (AcSS, 2015, p. 1)	Framework for Research Ethics (FRE): Six Key Principles (ESRC, 2015, p. 4)
Social science is fundamental to a democratic society and should be inclusive of different interests, values, funders, methods and perspectives	Research should be designed, reviewed and undertaken to ensure integrity, quality and transparency
All social science should respect the privacy, autonomy, diversity, values and dignity of individuals, groups and communities	Research staff and participants must normally be informed fully about the purpose, methods and intended possible uses of the research, what their participation in the research entails and what risks, if any, are involved
All social science should be conducted with integrity throughout, employing the most appropriate methods for the research purpose	The confidentiality of information supplied by research participants and the anonymity of respondents must be respected
All social scientists should act with regard to their social responsibilities in conducting and disseminating their research	Research participants must take part voluntarily, free from coercion
All social science should aim to maximise benefit and minimise harm	Harm to research participants must be avoided in all instances
	The independence of research must be clear, and any conflicts of interest or partiality must be explicit

> *aspirations, societal concerns, institutional expectations and individual rights. It is recommended that researchers undertake a risk-benefit analysis, beginning at the earliest stage of research planning, to reflect on how different stakeholder groups and the application of this ethic of respect can be considered in the research design. (BERA, 2018, p. 5)*

These guidelines are set out in five sections and some key messages embedded within each are presented here for illustrative purposes.

Responsibilities to Participants

This section addresses multiple ethical issues concerning how to protect research participants including consent, transparency, right to withdraw, incentives, harm arising from participation in research, privacy and data storage and disclosure, and places great emphasis on respecting the rights and dignity of diverse research populations. The ethic of respect means

> *individuals should be treated fairly, sensitively, and with dignity and freedom from prejudice, in recognition of both their rights and of differences arising from age, gender, sexuality, ethnicity, class, nationality, cultural identity, partnership status, faith, disability, political belief or other significant characteristic. (BERA, 2018, 1 p. 6)*

Researchers are called upon to be mindful of ways in which structural inequalities, gatekeepers' consent and power relations arising from dual roles within some approaches to research may influence children and young people and their relationships. In light of the United Nations Convention on the Rights of the Child (UNCRC) (UNICEF, 2010),

> *the best interests of the child are the primary consideration, and children who are capable of forming their own views should be granted the right to express those views freely in all matters affecting them, commensurate with their age and maturity. (23 p. 15)*

Researchers are advised to think about such issues as avoiding non-disclosure and confidentiality as well as their duty of care in advance of data collection so as to recognise and minimise potential risks, distress and discomfort that may arise. Certain approaches to research such as visual and participatory methods raise very specific questions concerning the reveal of participant identities as juxtaposed with anonymity. How personal data are to be stored and used must comply with General Data Protection Regulation (GDPR, 2018) which in essence stipulates 'citizens are entitled to know how and why their personal data is being stored, to what uses is it being put and to whom it may be made available' (48 pp. 23–24). The GDPR (2018) also clarifies citizens have the right to access 'personal data that is stored, and which relates to them' (48 pp. 23–24).

Responsibilities to Sponsors, Clients and Stakeholders in Research

This section considers the rights and duties of researchers particularly in relation to collaborative and/or sponsored research. Written contracts and agreements especially for publicly funded research should normally be agreed from the outset and take into account research methods to be employed as well as ways in which research participants and sponsors are to be acknowledged when publishing and disseminating research outcomes. Researchers should be well informed about different approaches to research and

> within the context and boundaries of their chosen methods, theories and philosophies of research, communicate the extent to which their data collection and analysis techniques, and the inferences to be drawn from their findings, are robust and can be seen to meet the criteria and markers of quality and integrity applied within different research approaches. (BERA, 2018, 60 p. 28)

Responsibilities to the Community of Educational Researchers

Researchers are called upon within this section to protect the reputation and integrity of educational research by ensuring they conduct research to the highest standards. In so doing, they 'contribute to the community spirit of critical analysis and constructive criticism that generates improvement in practice and enhancement of knowledge' (BERA, 2018, 62 p. 29). Particular attention is given to complaints procedures when concerns of malpractice are evident, expectations concerning the appropriate attribution of authors of digital content and the requirement to report negative results of evaluations and interventions rather than conceal them.

Responsibilities for Publication and Dissemination

This section clearly sets out the expectations associated with communicating research findings and the significance of research in a clear and cogent manner, using appropriate language for the intended audience(s). This is aligned to making research results public for the benefit of educational professionals, policymakers and wider audiences. Of particular importance is educational researchers

> *must not bring research into disrepute by in any way falsifying, distorting, suppressing, selectively reporting or sensationalising their research evidence or findings, either in publications based on that material, or as part of efforts to disseminate or promote that work. (BERA, 2018, 77 p. 33)*

The scope and format in which research can be published are also considered.

Responsibilities for Researchers' Well-being and Development

This section is new to this edition and considers ways in which the physical and psychological well-being of researchers can be safeguarded, especially when conducting qualitative research and fieldwork on sensitive issues in situations that may incur risk. For example, 'specialist training should be made available to researchers entering conflict or post-conflict settings internationally, or areas with high risk of disease' (BERA, 2018, 84 p. 36). Consideration is also given to supporting researchers' personal and professional career development.

Hammersley and Traianou's (2012a) *Ethics and Educational Research* (commissioned by BERA) is an online resource which complements these guidelines and discusses perplexities associated with – conflict amongst the principles; varying interpretations of the principles, multiple dealings; the research goal; and situated judgements. They also question the notion of consent being – fully informed and free? Their bibliographic appendices signpost literature available within this field, which includes ethics and survey research; ethics and action research; research on children, internet research; and ethics in visual research.

The BERA website (www.bera.ac.uk) has several case studies to highlight ways in which the guidelines can be translated in ethical research practice.

> *Reflective question:*
>
> How do the ethical guidelines for educational research (BERA, 2018) inform and map onto the ethical dimensions of your research proposal and doctoral research?

AUTHENTIC CASE STUDY OF ONLINE RESEARCH

Introduction

Within the context of social media data and online research, questions concerning ethical issues are currently evolving and examples of best practice are still a dynamic area of discussion and debate. As Boyd and Crawford (2012, p. 672) argue:

> *it is problematic for researchers to justify their actions as ethical simply because the data are accessible ... the process of evaluating the research ethics cannot be ignored simply because the data are seemingly public.*

The British Psychological Society (2017, p. 7) advise:

> *when there is a level of ambiguity concerning whether data are 'in the public domain' or not, researchers should consider the extent to which undisclosed observations may have potentially damaging effects for participants, before making decisions on whether to use such data and whether gaining valid consent is necessary.*

Townsend and Wallace (2016) note researchers are more ethically bound to seek informed consent in some scenarios than others and present an example of using data accessed via social media which the user expects to be private.

Background Context

Niamh* has worked for a local authority in England for 15 years and within her role as Early Years Special Educational Needs (SEN) Advisory Teacher has experienced significant tensions, particularly

---

* Benedict-Owen, 2019.

since the economic downturn of 2008 and change in governance from 2010, between legislative statutes along with their concomitant complex and much reduced funding streams and subsequent limited availability and quality of provision of Early Years education at the point of delivery. For her research, she aims to identify and consider key issues that influence the capacity of Private, Voluntary and Independent (PVI) group-based practitioners (key providers of early years education) to support the SEN of children within their care and develop an effective online early years intervention model for use by practitioners within the early years phase of education.

From her literature review, Niamh identified the following problem areas affecting SEN support at the point of delivery in PVI group-based settings:

- Low sense of professional efficacy and esteem amongst practitioners.

- Prohibitive costs of training.

- Difficulty in accessing specific training in a timely fashion.

- Additional costs to maintain adult–child ratios during release time for staff training.

- High levels of staff turnover leading to a loss of SEN expertise.

Niamh experimented with the creation and development of a number of social media/network platforms over a period of time including NING and Facebook, to recruit and interactively engage with PVI group-based practitioners. Ethical concerns Niamh addressed to undertake her online research are discussed below using one Facebook platform for illustrative purposes. She gained ethical approval from her university REC before she proceeded.

Ethical Considerations

Niamh found the Social Media Ethical Framework advanced by Townsend and Wallace (2016, p. 8) particularly insightful as it invites researchers to consider the following questions concerning legal, privacy and risk, reuse and publication issues:

- Does your research involve social media data?

- Have you consulted the terms and conditions of the specific platform?

- Have you consulted the relevant disciplinary, funding, legal or institutional guidelines?
- Can the social media user reasonably expect to be observed by strangers?
- Are the research participants vulnerable (i.e. children or vulnerable adults)?
- Is the subject matter sensitive?
- Will the social media user be anonymised in published outputs?
- Can you publish or share the data set?

To be of value, Niamh decided her online intervention model should be mobile/smartphone compatible as well as easily accessible, easily navigated and offer such functionality as the capacity to share images/videos, provide hyperlinks to other sites, capacity for practitioners to be able to engage with each other, ask questions and share expertise.

Her membership base was set up and designed to allow practitioners access to a wide geographic spread of professional views and to support the ongoing development of a dynamic and interactive virtual community of practice (CoP) (Lave & Wenger, 1991). To secure group membership, Niamh as administrator had set up a function which enabled her to screen potential Facebook users before allowing them to join. Potential members would be denied access if it was apparent their motive for wanting to join the group was to promote their own products and services.

Niamh ensured the purpose of her research was published on the social networking interface used for the purpose of research and that 'participants providing valid consent are given sufficient details about the study, and the nature of their participation, as well as possible associated risks' (British Psychological Society, 2017, p. 10). Her Facebook Group publicity post reads:

> I am a PhD student [...] a part of my research involves studying how Early Years Practitioners access SEND information and knowledge in order to support the children in their setting.
>
> I am a member of a number of amazing EYFS groups where practitioners are very generous in supporting each other and offering guidance to help ensure the best possible outcomes for the children in their care.

I decided to set up a closed group as a space where practitioners can expressly share and discuss concerns around SEND – where everyone is supportive and non-critical of each other – willing to share their experiences and advice with other practitioners.

As always, the confidentiality/anonymity of any child that you might be seeking advice/strategies for is paramount – so please make sure when discussing any concerns that a specific child cannot be identified.

Niamh used online posts and additional research information to make explicitly clear that any data generated could be used for research purposes and stated in her own Facebook space that:

This page is part of a PhD research project and provides SEND information for practitioners in The Early Years Foundation Stage.

She also made participants aware via a hypertext link to members that they could withdraw from the research at any point without any obligation placed upon them as to why they chose to withdraw:

Thank you to everyone who has contributed to the Early Years Intervention model. As you know this intervention is a key component of the research for my PhD. Please could you let me know by 31.08.2018 if you do not want any of the contributions you have made to form part of the published thesis.

The British Psychological Society (2017) argues that questions concerning whether online postings are 'public or private' can to some extent be determined by the online setting itself as well as whether there is a 'reasonable expectation of privacy on behalf of the social media user'. Niamh ensured data drawn from her Facebook platform was located within her own profile/page/group, all clearly identified as being set up for the purpose of her research. She also posted the following message concerning individuals posting on Facebook wishing to express their right to anonymity within the research findings:

> *I will be publishing some of these posts in my doctoral*
> *thesis – some of which may contain your name. As you will*
> *appreciate, I have thousands of members on Facebook. As*
> *I am sure you will also appreciate contacting everyone indi-*
> *vidually is impossible. In the circumstances, unless I hear*
> *from you by the end of October 2018, I will assume that*
> *you are happy with this.*

Recognising that it was not possible to confirm with absolute certainty all contributors would have seen nor paid attention to these 'opt-out' postings, Niamh decided all data sourced from Facebook and used within her research would be codified following transcription and any identifiable attributes such as names and personal images would be obscured. In this way, 'protecting the identity of unwitting participants' (Townsend & Wallace, 2016, p. 7) would be assured.

The Association of Internet Researchers (2012) considers a researcher's ethical responsibility to research participants is exponentially linked to levels of risk and/or vulnerability of participants. Niamh argues throughout her thesis that none of the data sought or obtained featured participant content of a sensitive personal nature nor was there any question participants would be placed in a position of risk or caused any harm. This was borne out by the way in which she selectively captured and presented data specifically related to the focus and purpose behind her research.

The data generated primarily took the form of text-based comments and conversation strings encapsulated within a 'post' format. The content generally consisted of posted comments and shared communications between colleagues, other individuals accessing the site and/or Niamh as the researcher. A particular strength with this type of qualitative data acquisition was it made possible the capture of 'practitioner voice'. Typically, communications followed a narrative conversational pattern which could be captured through screenshots of the exchanges. This type of data representation allowed 'recording' the data set within its precise and original contextual form.

A significant amount of data was embedded within narratives of practitioners in the context of their professional working environment. For analysis and reporting purposes, these narratives have widely remained in their purest form and represented through pictorial data capture inserted thematically within the body of her main text. This device ensures the research 'story' can be viewed through the lens of practitioner/group-based setting and depicts the emotions and experiences of practitioners, as expressed by them. In reporting findings, Niamh ensured a critical analysis of the evidence base and balanced view to capture all nuanced 'voices' prevalent within her research.

The notion of *positionality* has resonance with this research since Niamh views herself as an 'outsider' within her capacity to gather/interpret data as a researcher and LA representative as an Early Years SEN Advisory Teacher: the demands and requirements of her professional role included implementing LA decisions some of which were unpopular amongst the PVI group-based sector. As a specialist colleague and educator working within the PVI group-based sector, she also views herself as an 'insider' since this enabled multiple opportunities for her to hear and see first-hand examples of operational challenges in relation to SEN delivery across a number of PVI group-based settings across a wide geographic spread. On the one hand, acknowledging this 'insider' positionality may have led to a degree of empathy towards PVI group-based practitioners with whom she had worked was important, yet on the other hand, it was imperative that this did not lead to any factual distortion and/or bias that would be detrimental to the objectivity, direction or findings of her research. Niamh exercised caution not to influence the direction of interactions between users of the intervention model by not offering personal perspectives/opinions to the comments posted as these interactions formed an integral part of the qualitative data.

When considering copyright issues and sharing content and information, it is important to be mindful that online sites and platforms may have very different parameters. The terms and conditions of Facebook in 2017 stated:

> *You own all of the content and information you post on Facebook, and you can control how it is shared through your privacy and application settings. In addition:*

> *For content that is covered by intellectual property rights, like photos and videos (IP content), you specifically give us the following permission, subject to your privacy and*

application settings: you grant us a non-exclusive, trans-
ferable, sub-licensable, royalty-free, worldwide license to
use any IP content that you post on or in connection with
Facebook (IP License). This IP License ends when you
delete your IP content or your account unless your content
has been shared with others, and they have not deleted it.

Niamh's interpretation of this statement was in essence, whilst the originator of a Facebook post owns the copyright, Facebook's terms and conditions are such that as a matter of principle, when an individual post is on Facebook, both Facebook and anyone to whom the post has been distributed have the right to use it provided it is held on Facebook servers.

The debate over 'public' or 'private' social media data is particularly important with this type of research: even though contributors of 'posts' may be aware they are in the public domain, this does not necessarily endorse permission for research use nor does it ensure contributors would express the same views if aware that these may form part of research.

SUMMARY OF THIS CHAPTER

Moral reasoning can be a complex phenomenon, and ethics in educational research cannot simply be codified or reduced to a set of principles especially since there is 'considerable room for reasonable disagreement about research ethics' (Hammersley & Traianou, 2012a, p. 12). The purpose of this chapter has been to open your eyes and encourage you to think reflexively about how the ethical theories, principles and guidelines presented (by no means exhaustive) may be inherent within the ethical dimensions of your doctoral research and offer some guidance about possible ways in which you might address them.

As Howe and Moses (1999, p. 56) argue, educational research 'is always *advocacy* research' since it 'unavoidably advances some moral-political perspective'. Research involving vulnerable children and young people, for example, is likely to have some impact on their educational opportunities and schooling experiences. In addition to harnessing a strong moral compass, to be truly ethical, you must also be prepared to defend what your research is *for*.

Key questions for you to consider:

- What ethical theories underpin your research?
- What ethical issues 'ought you' to consider within the design and implementation of your research?
- How might you defend your ethical decision-making in your viva?

FURTHER READING

Brooks, R., te Riele, K., & Maguire, M. (2014). *Ethics and education research*. London: Sage.

This book provides a comprehensive and balanced view of ethics in educational research and draws on case studies to exemplify ethical questions and dilemmas that need to be addressed in relation to theories, principles and guidelines; regulatory contexts; research design; informed consent and reciprocity; identity, power and positionality; data analysis; and dissemination.

Hammersley, M., & Traianou, A. (2012b). *Ethics in qualitative research: Controversies and contexts*. London: Sage.

This invaluable book raises ethical issues in qualitative enquiry, which generally involves flexible and emergent research designs and collecting relatively unstructured data in natural settings. The authors illuminate the difficult and controversial nature of ethics, examine the philosophical assumptions involving the social contexts in which key ethical principles arise and consider implications for research practice.

Israel, M. (2015). *Research ethics and integrity for social scientists: Beyond regulatory compliance* (2nd ed.). London: Sage.

This book considers traditional and recent developments and debates concerning researching ethically and complying with ethical requirements. It incorporates a range of national ethics regimes that are destabilising the social sciences and discusses issues relating to indigenous, interdisciplinary, international and internet research.

REFERENCES

Academy of Social Sciences (AcSS). (2015). Five ethics principles for social science research, London. Retrieved from https://www.acss.org.

uk/wp-content/uploads/2016/06/5-Ethics-Principles-for-Social-Science-Research-Flyer.pdf. Accessed on October 21, 2019.

Aristotle. (1984a). Nicomachean Ethics. In J. Barnes (Ed.), *The Complete Works of Aristotle* (Vol. 2, pp. 1729–1867). Princeton, NJ: Princeton University Press.

Aristotle. (1984b). Politics. In J. Barnes (Ed.), *The Complete Works of Aristotle* (Vol. 2, pp. 1986–2129). Princeton, NJ: Princeton University Press.

Aristotle. (1984). Nicomachean ethics, and politics. In J. Barnes (Ed.), *The complete works of Aristotle* (2 Vols.). Princeton, NJ: Princeton University Press.

Association of Internet Researchers. (2012). Ethical decision-making and internet research. Retrieved from http://aoir.org/reports/ethics2.pdf. Accessed on October 20, 2019.

Bannon, B. (2013). From intrinsic value to compassion: A place-based ethic. *Environmental Ethics*, *35*(3), 259–278.

Benedict-Owen, S. (2019). *Factors influencing provision of Special Educational Needs support at the point of delivery within the Private, Voluntary and Independent group-based Early Years Education and Childcare sector*. Unpublished PhD Thesis. Brunel University, London.

Boyd, D., & Crawford, K. (2012). Critical questions for big data. *Information Communication and Society*, *15*(5), 662–679.

Brabeck, M., & Brabeck, K. (2009). Feminist perspectives on research ethics. In D. Mertens & P. Ginsberg (Eds.), *The handbook of social research ethics* (pp. 39–53). London: Sage.

British Educational Research Association (BERA). (2018). *Ethical guidelines for educational research* (4th ed.). London: BERA. Retrieved from https://www.bera.ac.uk/researchers-resources/publications/ethical-guidelines-for-educational-research-2018. Accessed on October 24, 2019.

British Psychological Society. (2017). *Ethics guidelines for internet-mediated research*. Leicester: British Psychological Society. Retrieved from www.bps.org.uk/publications/policy-and-guidelines/research-guidelines-policy-documents/research-guidelines-poli. Accessed on October 20, 2019.

Brydon-Miller, M., & Hilsen, A. (2016). Where rivers meet: Exploring the confluence of ecofeminism covenantal ethics and action research. In M. Phillips & N. Rumens (Eds.), *Contemporary perspectives on ecofeminism* (pp. 95–108). New York, NY: Routledge.

Economic and Social Research Council (ESRC). (2015). ESRC framework for research ethics. Retrieved from www.esrc.ukri.org/files/funding/guidance-for-applicants/esrc-framework-for-research-ethics-2015/. Accessed on October 12, 2019.

General Data Protection Regulation (GDPR). (2018). Retrieved from www.gov.uk/government/publications/guide-to-the-data-protection-regulation. Accessed on September 10, 2019.

Gilligan, C. (1982). *In a different voice: Psychological theory and women's development*. Cambridge, MA: Harvard University Press.

Hammersley, M., & Traianou, A. (2012a). Ethics and educational research, BERA online resource. Retrieved from www.bera.ac.uk. Accessed on July 10, 2019.

Howe, K., & Moses, M. (1999). Ethics in educational research. *Review of Research in Education*, 24, 21–60.

Humphreys, L. (1970). *Tearoom trade: A study of homosexual encounters in public places*. London: Duckworth.

Kant, I. (1758/1993). In J. Ellington (Trans.), *Grounding for the metaphysics of morals* (3rd ed.). Indianapolis, IN: Hackett.

Kimmel, A. (1988). *Ethics and values in applied social research*. London: Sage.

Lave, J., & Wenger, E. (1991). *Situated learning: Legitimate peripheral participation*. Cambridge: Cambridge University Press.

Macfarlane, B. (2010). Researching with integrity. *Chronicle of Higher Education*, 56(3), A30.

MacIntyre, A. (1982). Risk, harm and benefit assessments in instruments of moral evaluation. In T. Beauchamp, R. Faden, R. Wallace, & L. Walters (Eds.), *Ethical issues in social science research* (pp. 175–192). Baltimore, MD: John Hopkins University Press.

Macleod, C. (2016). John Stuart Mill (1806–73). Retrieved from https://plato.stanford.edu/entries/mill/. Accessed on November 10, 2019.

Milgram, S. (1974). *Obedience to authority*. New York, NY: Harper and Row.

National Commission for the Protection of Human Subjects of Biomedical and Behavioral Research (NCPHSBBR). (1979). Belmont report: Ethical principles and guidelines for the protection of human subjects of research. Report, Department of Health, Education and Welfare, Office of the Secretary, Protection of Human Subjects, Michigan. Retrieved from http://www.hhs.gov/ohrp/humansubjects/guidance/belmont.html. Accessed on September 12, 2019.

Noddings, N. (1984). *Caring: A feminine approach to ethics and moral education*. Berkeley, CA: University of California Press.

Noddings, N. (1986). Fidelity in teaching, teacher education and research on teaching. *Harvard Educational Review, 56*, 496–510.

Noddings, N. (2002a). *Educating moral people: A caring alternative to character education*. New York, NY: Teachers College Press.

Noddings, N. (2002b). *Starting at home: Caring and social policy*. Berkeley, CA: University of California Press.

Noddings, N. (2003). *Caring: A feminine approach to ethics and moral education* (2nd ed.). Berkeley, CA: University of California Press.

Ogbu, J., & Matute-Bianchi, M. (1986). *Beyond language: Social and cultural factors in schooling language minority students*. Sacramento: Bilingual Educational Office, California State Department of Education.

Pring, R. (2015). *Philosophy of educational research* (3rd ed.). London: Bloomsbury.

Rabinow, P., & Sullivan, W. (1987). The interpretive turn: Emergence of an approach. In P. Rabinow & W. Sullivan (Eds.), *Interpretive social science* (pp. 1–21). Los Angeles, CA: University of California Press.

Ross, W. (1930). *The right and the good*. Oxford: Oxford University Press.

Schultz, R., Schroeder, D., & Brody, C. (1997). Collaborative narrative inquiry: Fidelity and the ethics of caring in teacher research. *Qualitative Studies in Education, 10*, 473–485.

Sinnott-Armstrong, W. (2003). Consequentialism. Retrieved from https://plato.stanford.edu/entries/consequentialism/. Accessed on November 10, 2019.

Sockett, H. (2012). *Knowledge and virtues in teaching and learning.* London: Routledge.

Townsend, L., & Wallace, C. (2016). *Social media research: A guide to ethics.* University of Aberdeen. Retrieved from https://www.gla.ac.uk/media/media_487729_en.pdf. Accessed on October 21, 2019.

UNICEF. (2010). *The United Nations Convention on the Rights of the Child.* London: UNICEF. Retrieved from www.unicef.org.uk/wp-content/uploads/2010/05/UNCRC_united_nations_convention_on_the_rights_of_the_child.pdf. Accessed on September 12, 2019.

Willis, P. (1977). *Learning to labour: How working-class kids get working class jobs.* New York, NY: Columbia University Press.

4

WRITING THE LITERATURE REVIEW

Leena Helavaara Robertson

INTRODUCTION

Curiouser and Curiouser

There is a moment in time during the process of writing your doctoral study, when your supervisory team will suggest something like 'you might as well now start compiling your literature review'. In response perhaps you may think, 'great, yes, I can write about texts and my reading'. And then, almost as an afterthought, your supervisors may say, 'Yes, you need to start developing your own theoretical framework'. And that may well be the precise moment when you, like Alice in Wonderland (Carroll, 1865/2015), start going down the Rabbit-Hole and things will never be the same again.

If you have never read Alice – this wonderful, classic British children's book – or you have forgotten what happens in it, it may help to know that the story is about a little girl called Alice who falls accidently down a hole in the ground. As she falls, she shrinks in size and arrives at a Rabbit-Hole which consists of never-ending, criss-crossing underground tunnels. It is here that strange creatures appear, like White Rabbit, Mad Hatter or the grin of a Cheshire Cat. Or they run and often argue with Alice and each other and seem utterly convinced that they are right even when Alice can see that they talk nonsense. One of the ways Alice can cope in the Rabbit-Hole is to ask clear-headed questions. 'Through the Looking Glass and What Alice Found There' (Carroll, 1871/2015) is the sequel to the first book about Alice, and this time Alice enters a different world through a mirror, and suddenly everything is reversed as in reflection. This leads to other new, illogical, mad encounters. 'What does this mean', is a question that Alice keeps asking herself and others. She also asks about the meanings of words and who has the authority to attach new meanings to old words. She survives and remains strong because she is good at maintaining her energy and agency; she recognises the power of a good question and keeps on using that power.

Doctoral students, who become tangled in readings of texts, or in unstable meanings and contradictory points of view, or get caught in theoretical paradigm wars, may feel frustrated. There tends to be a stage in the process when research matters do indeed become 'curiouser and curiouser' as Alice once said. Seeking answers to big theoretical questions may well be an arduous, bothersome or near impossible part of the process, but finding your own kinds of answers is also deeply satisfying. In short, finding answers tends to have a transformative effect. You will move on theoretically and never look back.

This chapter will aim to help you to find your way out of the mountain of literature and various metaphorical Rabbit-Holes. By posing questions, this chapter will support you in remaining in control. The ultimate aim is to help you to write and to see writing as a complex social practice and human endeavour.

Where there is a gap between institutional demands, such as raising the number of research degree completions, and fewer resources to ensure that this happens, the universities' pedagogical response, in the last two decades or so, has been to frame writing as a 'skill' (Lillis, 2001). This is pertinent to British context, where I work, but the problem is global. I am Finnish and often visit Finnish universities where my colleagues discuss similar worries. Promoting writing as a 'core transferable skill', that can be delivered in few online sessions, is difficult for all. It is particularly difficult for 'international' students who are very welcome to the British Higher Education Institutions (HEIs) because of the higher fees they pay, but who may not feel at home in HEI systems. Doctoral students, from around the world, and home-grown ones who have arrived at HEIs via non-traditional academic routes, and those who may come from social groups that have been historically substantially excluded from HEIs, may feel that academic writing practices are shrouded in mystery. The sessions focussing the development of 'writing skills' are clearly not enough, and students often feel that they have to struggle on their own. Or that they are expected to learn academic writing by breathing the air of the institution.

This chapter views writing as a complex undertaking and aims to demystify the process. Writing takes time to develop, and there are no quick solutions, but it is not impossible to learn what makes a successful literature review either. It should and can emerge after the various writing processes. Its success, always to be discussed with supervision teams, will be inherently connected with the ways *you* have constructed *your* review, and made it relevant, critical and interesting:

- *Relevant*: You will have reviewed appropriate and relevant literature *and* you will have presented your argument why this selection of texts is relevant for your study. You learn to make the case for your chosen texts in supervisory meetings and in discussions with others significant in your doctoral research process and defend verbally your choice. No one can ever read all potentially relevant texts, so you need to rehearse an argument and defend the significance of your material and then make this argument transparent in your writing.

- *Critical*: You will have synthesised – or brought together in a conceptual way – different texts and made a claim of these texts facilitating the examination of your ideas. No one text can do it all, and it is in the processes of writing that synthesis happens, and your theoretical framework emerges. By remaining critical, you will have also identified a gap in literature that your study aims to address, and later, after the processes of analysing data, in the final chapters of your study will make the claim for contributing something new and original to theory.

- *Interesting*: Finally, you will have completed the review with rigour and made it interesting. The style of writing is yours but thinking about the ways you can hold readers' attention is an easy way of steering them to your central ideas. Aim to structure the chapter and provide clear signposts for readers. Refer to earlier sections with page numbers where necessary and tell the reader when something will be returned to in the later sections, and refer to your appendices, again with page numbers, where additional information can be found. Help the reader to follow your line of argument.

The rest of this chapter is structured in the following nine sections:

- Literature review and its purposes.
- Selection processes.
- Naming of the separate parts.
- Developing criticality.
- Theoretical framework.
- Contribution to knowledge.
- Checklist for submission.
- Case study.
- References.

At the end of this chapter, you should be able to:

- Critically reflect on academic writing as a complex social practice.
- Demystify the processes of reviewing literature and theoretical frameworks.
- Know and understand what makes a successful literature and how to make yours relevant, critical and interesting.
- Plan appropriate subsections and provide signposting.
- Evaluate and analyse texts and develop criticality.
- Remain in control of the many processes of writing a literature review.

LITERATURE REVIEW AND ITS PURPOSES

One of the main purposes of writing about literature is that you are expected to 'place' your own emerging ideas in the existing academic literature. More of this so-called 'placing' later. The first consideration, however, relates to your research aims and your own specific research questions. What you review, and how and the whole purpose of the literature review is entwined with and connected to the ways you have decided to frame your research aims and questions. The words and terms you have used tend to suggest certain bodies of literature and perhaps even schools of thought.

The following questions evoke and call for different kinds of literature to be reviewed, and though there is an overlap, there are also clear differences:

Question	Some Possible Questions About Literature
How do mentoring and co-coaching develop successful professionals?	• What is mentoring and what is co-coaching? How do different writers explain them and their difference and relevance? And whose ideas will be adopted and why?
	• How have others explained 'successful professionals' – what would count as 'success' in literature?
	• How to explain the connection between mentoring and co-coaching and 'success'?
	• Why this focus on current buzz-words of mentoring and co-coaching?
Why do mentoring and co-coaching play a part in the development of successful professionals?	• What is mentoring and what is co-coaching?
	• How have different writers explored what kinds of overall approaches and strategies lead to being a successful professional? How does mentoring and co-coaching relate to these other approaches and strategies?
	• Whose testimonies are to be trusted?
	• What alternatives have been suggested for the development of successful professionals?

(Continued)

(Continued)	
What is the legacy of mentoring and co-coaching strategies in this workplace/community of practice?	• What is mentoring and what is co-coaching? How have these terms been used in professional context over the period of time? What has changed? • What are professionals' long-term views of mentoring and co-coaching strategies?

It is common for the research question to evolve as a direct consequence of reading and writing – at the very least the question becomes
more focussed. Generally, it also becomes clearer and more interesting, because it has become more original and better justified. Most
students actively seek to rephrase the main question after becoming
more familiar with key texts. So, whilst the actual research questions
are not set in stone at the initial phase of your research process, the
connection between the question and literature has to remain solid
and transparent, and such that you can defend it well later on when
you enter the final oral examination, viva voce. My own supervisor
used to start tutorials often with the same question: 'How would you
frame your research question today?' Now I do the same with my
own students.

The old conundrum what comes first, chicken or egg – or in
this instance posing the question or reading around the topic – is
worthy of some thought because it is very difficult to pose a valid
and original question without knowing what kinds of questions
others have asked before. However, it is also difficult to know what
to read without some kind of a question. The best advice is to do
the two in tandem. Reading and considering the actual words and
concepts in your research question are your two guiding lights.

According to Bakhtin (1981),

> *The word in language is half someone else's ... it exists in
> other people's mouths, in other people's contexts, serving
> other people's intentions: it is from there that one must
> take the word, and make it one's own. (pp. 293–294)*

Here Bakhtin was not discussing writing for theoretical purposes,
but ordinary everyday uses of language. Yet, the same applies to
writing for theoretical purposes. The main purpose of a literature

review is to make your theoretical base transparent – the reader needs to know where you are coming from with your ideas and your words, and whether you can be trusted to discuss other writers' work. Ultimately, you need to show that you know enough to be able to synthesise conceptual ideas.

A literature review is never just a list of studies, or an extended or annotated bibliography, although it can start off that way. It is a critical look at existing research that is significant to the work that you are planning to carry out. A literature review always offers an argument about a body of research. One part the argument is a carefully developed rationale for selecting the texts reviewed, and the other parts show an ability to critically analyse texts.

Most literature reviews will explore the following:

- Establish key terms and theoretical constructs and explore how they tend to be used in your chosen context in general. You will need to discuss your own take on these terms and how you will use them. Aim to own your terminology like Alice did! Here is Alice talking to Humpty Dumpty, 'When I use a word', Humpty Dumpty said, in rather a scornful tone, 'it means just what I choose it to mean – neither more nor less'. 'The question is', said Alice, 'whether you can make words mean so many different things'.

- Provide some historical notes about terminology and the use of concepts and any relevant background information. You will probably stand on the shoulders of some giants who in their time constructed parts of your theoretical foundation. Acknowledge them and state explicitly what aspect of their thinking remains a part of your foundation, and what needs updating or refreshing, and why this updating is relevant. This kind of excavation adds an interesting dimension to your review and identifies something of your theoretical position. A wider historical overview of the context may similarly be helpful.

- Set out what other researchers and theoreticians have written about your topic, and how they have answered similar questions to yours. Identify where they are coming from. Initially, this may simply involve thinking about their discipline and the favoured traditions of that discipline. Then move towards their subject and topics, or their context, and aim to work out what theoretical ideas they have favoured or emphasised. In essence identify their contribution to knowledge. Learn to evaluate the quality and the relevance of literature; this becomes possible and relatively easy when you know the pieces you are reviewing. Read them well. Show that you are familiar with them; perhaps use a direct quotation that supports your thinking.

- Set out the differences between various researchers, writers and theoreticians and identify what their main current debates or perspectives are. Consider well-established local ideas and practice as well as new cutting-edge ideas; move between local, national and international writers and audiences.

- Explain carefully what the writers reviewed have not yet answered; set out text against text and discuss what is missing. Here you aim to carve out space for your study, for your own original contribution to knowledge, as well as for further research.

- For some research studies, national or international policies or laws need to be reviewed; is yours one of them? Would it help to reveal and examine the changes in practice, policy or legal matters?

- Media may play a powerful part in creating dominant discourses that may influence your participants' thinking around your central ideas. Critical discourse analysis (Fairclough, 1989, 1995) may give you tools to unpack media-driven assumptions and fallacies but there are many other well-established ways to do this, too. In my own work, post-colonialist writers, especially Said (1979, 1994), have been helpful. Others may be fired up by Foucault's (1972/1969) and Bourdieu's work (see, e.g., Bourdieu & Passeron, 1977). Your supervisors and your research significant others (such as co-doctoral students) can suggest others more relevant for your topics.

- Demonstrate your own scholarly stance and showcase your familiarity of texts, perspectives and paradigms. Establish yourself as an expert of your topic.

SELECTION PROCESSES

The selection of texts is often one of the first big problems and a dilemma. There are simply far too many texts to read, and subsequently far too many to write about. The task seems colossal. Unsurmountable.

So, what would Alice do? Perhaps Alice would have listened to the advice of others when it was good advice, 'Begin at the beginning', the King said, very gravely, 'and go on till you come to the end: then stop'.

The start of the process is greatly helped by search engines, such as Google Scholar, and every university library has both online information for developing keyword searches and individual people who will show you how to begin to look for relevant texts. Just do it, Alice would probably say! Do not procrastinate too long.

Or you may want to find writers whose ideas resemble mostly your own, or the ones that inspire you – who take your breath away. Take time to study carefully the bibliographies they have developed for their journal articles or books. The early roadmap is probably contained in their list of references: follow it. You may still have many concerns about getting lost, and these may well linger on throughout the writing process, but at least you have made a start and are now moving ahead.

The problem, of course, is that eventually it becomes problematic to know when the end has been reached. In fact, there is no such thing as an end. (In this case the King was wrong.) Each day something new is published, somewhere, and yet, you must learn to stop. Your task is to write a literature review not an encyclopaedia.

You will probably always harbour some insecurities as to whether you have found the right kinds of texts and whether you have read enough. Part of the process is to learn to cope with this feeling of helplessness and to develop a rationale for the selection. You need to rehearse your argument that you have read around sufficiently and taken on board key ideas from writers who are trustworthy to you. Not from everyone. The decision to stop reading is a stage in itself – self-imposed and arbitrary – and in real life your reading and your search for deeper understanding continues. It continues after you have been awarded the title doctor, too; in fact, many see the doctoral study as a beginning. My own supervisor used to tell me again and again, 'this study is only a start'. And she was right.

In writing your literature review – and perhaps by now we should acknowledge the process as crafting – you provide layered evidence that your research question is appropriate and an important one to be asking from your context. Interestingly, it is the process of *writing* that deepens your thinking and not just reading. Wisker (2015, p. 67) makes a point stating that 'reading, thinking, applying, interpreting and writing in an iterative fashion' is the key in facilitating the deepening conceptual quality and confidence. Wisker's focus is on the *iterative* processes, on the layered repetition of reading, thinking and writing and including reading and rereading your drafts with an aim of improving them. My own take on this is the emphasis on writing; writing allows you to better shape your ideas and to crystalise your thoughts. Over time, this becomes curiously satisfying. You move from simple description to a critical analysis, from describing what has been written about your ideas before to an up-to-date critical evaluation.

This then begins to provide evidence of you 'placing' your ideas in academic literature. The processes of crafting, reading and rereading drafts and developing your writing take time. You return to the literature review at different stages of the study – it is an iterative process and you will become more confident in adding more texts and deleting ones that seem less relevant at the end of the process.

NAMING OF THE SEPARATE PARTS

Structuring the literature review chapter for the reader, or for an ambiguous audience that is often referred to as academia, is another challenge. What kinds of elements does your literature review need to consist of?

Planning different sections, and naming them, will help you to remain in control. Most students find it satisfying to report on literature through the use of themes – themes being a good way to showcase your own emerging theoretical framework – and they aim to avoid addressing one author after another. By selecting themes, you can address more than one author at a time and focus on major controversies or debates between different authors.

Or you may want to organise the chapter chronologically or at least partly chronologically. Focussing on time, decade after decade, may support you in showing the emergence of trends and new ideas.

It is worth stating and learning to accept that the process of working out the constituent parts of the chapter to support the reader is not complete until at the end of the whole research process. In fact, the sooner you accept that like all other chapters in your study, literature review is more than 'just' one chapter in your study, the sooner you begin to become comfortable with its multi-level nature. It has its tentacles, or struts that that are based on earlier parts of the study, and others that in turn continue and reach into later parts of the study. For example, in your literature review you will continue with and elaborate and strengthen the overall theoretical argument that was probably briefly acknowledged in the introductory chapter. It defines key terms, as already discussed, so that your ideas can feed into methodology and become a workable part of a method (surveys, interviews, stakeholder questionnaires and so on). After analysing your data sets, you need to revisit the literature review and possibly add some new sections. The findings will perhaps reveal an area, a theme or a problem that was not discussed. Or perhaps the participants' frame of reference, their perspectives and worldviews, was not accounted for earlier on. All chapters support one another and are inherently connected.

DEVELOPING CRITICALITY

Writing about reading seems a straightforward idea, but as soon as you start putting down your own words, the task may morph into a messiness that causes you to shrink back to the size of young novice. (Back to the Rabbit-Hole again!) In your professional role, you may have had years of experience and tacit knowledge, but you may feel that it has suddenly lost its relevance. The words on your screen seem basic and trivial, and you may well hear your supervisors' voices in your head 'don't write an annotated bibliography in the style of "she said, they said, he said"; write an analysis'. But as Kamler and Thomson (2008) put it, 'the difficulty of writing as an authority when one does not feel authoritative' (p. 508) is genuine and occasionally destabilising. At the same time, this is probably the time when you have begun the process of constructing a new identity – that of a researcher working on theory – but simply feel unsure about moving between different old and new identities.

Lamott (1994) shares an astonishingly beautiful example of feeling utterly paralysed when facing a task of writing:

> *Thirty years ago, my older brother, who was ten years old at the time, was trying to get a report on birds written that he'd had three months to write, which was due the next day. We were out at our family cabin in Bolinas, and he was at the kitchen table, close to tears, surrounded by binder paper and pencils, and unopened books on birds, immobilized by the hugeness of the task ahead. Then my father sat down beside him, put his arm around my brother's shoulder, and said, 'Bird by bird, buddy. Just take it bird by bird'. (p. 19)*

As an experienced writer, I can still easily empathise with this child, and the good advice of his father: bird by bird. The ability to write critically cannot develop unless we have some drafts. We all have to start somewhere. Word by word. Sentence by sentence. Once we have some drafts in front of us, the task of rereading and rewriting begins, and it becomes feasible to improve the level of discussion and analysis.

The idea that academic literature is about reliable content and about communicating factual information which is somehow separate from social relationship – meaning that it is objective (not subjective) and neutral – has been successfully challenged by many and over many decades. There are no words, and thereby texts, that carry autonomous meanings. Meaning is always created in the act of reading. Academic writing, like all writing, is a social act. Each author brings his or her own subjectivities (such as age, gender, social class, background, language, life histories and so on) to the writing processes, and their actual words echo the 'speech communities' (Hymes, 1977) in which they live. Their 'habits of meaning' (Halliday, 1978) with reference to interpreting texts reveal each reader's values and life experiences. 'The habits of meaning' can also be understood as a metaphor for 'reading' real lives or making sense of social practices and human experience.

All academic writing is, therefore, ideologically informed, and since different speech communities do not have equal status in the production of academic texts, many writers have shown how particular identities (typically male, white, middle-class, European) are privileged within societies, and thereby their perspectives are also valorised within academic discourses (Cameron, 1992; hooks, 1987; Mirza, 2018). Lillis (2001, p. 80) asks pertinently 'To what extent are existing dominant conventions intrinsic to intellectual inquiry' and moves on to explicitly challenge textual biases.

In the early stages, it is possible to develop criticality by reviewing texts by simply asking pertinent questions, such as who is the author and what kinds of subjectivities he/she may bring into the text? Avoid ethno-centricity and question the power of dead, white, male writers' work. Decolonise theoretical paradigms and search for alternatives. If no reliable alternatives can be found, identify it as a weakness in theoretical works in general. Not only do theoretical perspectives include taking account of different subjective perspectives but also as Troyna and Carrington (1989) crystallised it, you have to decide 'whose side are you on'. Whose life story and whose narrative have shaped this writing? Whose experiences have been neglected and why? Who is silenced? Who remains a winner when evaluating the impact of the text? Who is the loser?

For Ely et al. (1997) who strove to remain focussed on social justice, the answers became clearer when they explicitly considered the participants of the study,

> *We ask over and over during the multiple drafts leading to the final writing: What language will I use to communicate the experience? What forms will best do justice to the people who were my participants. (p. 37)*

From these initial questions, criticality can be further developed by looking at texts with different lenses. Post-colonialism, Marxism, post-structuralism, post-modernism, feminism and so on, and the more recently developed theoretical positions and paradigms such as new-materialism and post-humanism, can each offer a lens that reveal very clearly some of the shortcomings of the writing being reviewed. These shortcomings are not necessarily observable in the texts per se; rather you make the claim of the text not going far enough, or deep enough, within your own adopted theoretical position.

Correspondingly, your own writing reveals parallel shortcomings. According to Fairclough (1989, p. 23):

> *Linguistic phenomena are social in the sense that whenever*
> *people speak or listen or write or read, they do so in ways*
> *which are determined socially and have social effects. Even*
> *when people are most conscious of their own individuality*
> *and think themselves cut off from social influences – they still*
> *use language in ways which are subject to social convention.*

Because it is impossible to eliminate all social influences (with reference to the quotation above), the task of the student writer is to know himself/herself well and to reflect on his/her own position-alities and possible deep-seated preoccupations. At the same time, it is important to make own positions and drives transparent and to write reflexively.

The Thesis Whisperer, that is the self-description of Inger Mewbur, is also skilled at giving additional advice and, for example, setting your free of perfectionism. You can follow her and check her work on this website, see https://thesiswhisperer.com/. Another excellent resource is Pat Thomson's website Patter, see https://patthomson.net/.

THEORETICAL FRAMEWORKS

The actual forms of writing, rhetorical and literary devices, layouts, and not just individual words, can all configure meaning in writing. For each of us writers, there is a stage when we must stop to ask whether our writing style is suited for the task. For instance, here I am asking whether it is acceptable to use fictional characters such as Alice and Humpty Dumpty when writing about theoretical frameworks? The answers tend to be unique, and highly personal, and relate to both of our own ideas of making meaning and of our long-term professional and research aims.

For me, it was important to breathe some life into this topic, and therefore, I needed a character like Alice. I like the quirkiness of her – and her gender. I also think that using Rabbit-Holes as a metaphor for making sense of literature, begins the process of demystifying terms such as 'theory'. If theoretical frameworks are often thought to have been constructed in the ivory towers of academia – with peace, solitude, beauty and shining white ivory being some of the most durable and strongest images of this metaphor – I prefer the way Rabbit-Hole brings the focus back to earth and to the messiness of mud and dirt. They seem a bit more accessible by all. Ivory towers suggest exclusiveness and elitism. For me Rabbit-Holes are, therefore, convenient spaces for levelling hierarchies and thereby hopefully constructing more ethical theoretical frameworks.

Dear reader, please note that I am not making a claim that using Alice is correct. I am offering my thoughts as an example of demonstrating how choices can be made transparent. Afterwards, readers will always make their own judgements.

In the writing processes of your literature review, you need to be thinking with theory and not just writing about theory. All theories are a set of ideas that explain a phenomenon or phenomena, and your task is that of application, using it, rather than description. Your aim is to think initially what is it that you want the chosen theory to do for you? What does it explain about your research question and your central ideas? What does it add? Does it help you to challenge taken-for-granted assumptions? What does it not do?

Start by thinking with theory to problematise ideas relevant to your research question and then apply these problematised ideas to your context. Make the connections between theory and context explicit. It is likely that no one theory can explain all of the above, so you will need different theoretical frames, and once you combine these frames together, your unique theoretical framework begins to emerge.

As Thomson advices students on her website (https://patthomson.net/), literature should be reviewed as a resource: it helps you to think. And she reminds us about the exciting aspect of reviewing other's' texts,

> The literatures don't do the thinking for you. The thinking is up to you. But you don't do it alone. You're in the company of loads of other scholars who've thought about the same topic and left resources for you to use. (Thomson, 2019, n.p.; https://patthomson.net/2019/08/26/orientations-to-reading-think-of-the-literatures-as-a-resource/)

CONTRIBUTION TO KNOWLEDGE

When getting to the end of the process and beginning to outline your own original contribution to knowledge, you return to your literature review again. You start by reflecting on what exactly does your study contribute in closing a gap in previous research studies and theoretical ideas? Examine your literature review very carefully and evaluate it. How did you discuss the key theoretical concepts earlier? Do you now need to make the discussion more sophisticated, add more detail or change the nuance?

Once you have reviewed your literature review and yet again improved your writing, you need to name the contribution that the study makes explicitly and discuss it. The following questions may help you:

- Did you replicate an important study in a new context or in a different era? Did your study explore an aspect of a theory in a new context, with different twenty-first-century challenges? What was different, and have you used terms in the literature review that supports you to discuss the difference?

- How are new policies enacted? What is the relationship between the policy and the processes of policy enactment? Did your theoretical framework explain this, and what can you add to this?

- Did your study improve aspects of methodology? How did you discuss this before? Reviewing your theoretical framework now, did you miss some themes or concepts?

- Did your study add some new information about resolving debates or conflicts? Have you clearly referred to the writers whose work contributed to the earlier debates or conflicts?

Wisker (2015) emphasises 'threshold crossings' as a critical aspect of recognising the newness of the contribution to knowledge that your study makes:

> Conceptual threshold crossings are seen to take place in doctoral students' work when they make learning leaps or breakthroughs in their learning, start to fully own the process and realise their contribution to knowledge and to conceptual understanding. (p. 65)

It is comforting to recognise that these 'learning leaps' take place at all stages of the process. And that they are inherently part of a creative process which are often facilitated by growing in confidence. The processes of feeling that you belong to this new group of like-minded writers rest on understanding the group's internal and situated practices and its unspoken rules and traditions. This feeling may take some time to develop. It also rests on having the right to speak and having others willing to listen.

Many academic writers tend to like a good verbal debate. They might say that being challenged, and in return challenging others, helps them to facilitate a stronger justification for their work and ideas. Again, it crystallises their perspective. It is also important to recognise that theoretical ideas have been traditionally considered to belong to men. And for white, middle-class men for that. Not women. Sadly, for some academic writers, heated debates are also part of showing off and for constructing and maintaining a hierarchy between ideas and establishing personal superiority.

Once Alice commented that, 'Who in the world am I? Ah, that's the great puzzle'. So, it is for doctoral students, too. Many speak of feeling like an impostor, or that they do not feel comfortable in academia, or that the word writer or academic is not quite an integral part of their identity. My personal view is that academia needs creative people – whoever they are – who will change practices and make them less combative, more collective and more inclusive for all.

CHECKLIST

- Has your central theoretical argument been developed and logically pursued throughout the chapter and throughout the study?

- Are there disjointed sections that do not 'belong' anywhere? If so, are they really needed, or can they be deleted? If they do have their place in this study, add more specific connections and increase the internal cohesion of the whole chapter.

- Are there other sections that in the end need to be deleted – sections that were considered relevant at the start of the process but are no longer appropriate?

- Whose voice is dominant? Does your own 'voice' come through clearly enough or are you using other writers' words too much? Is the literature review clearly connected with your context, your research questions and ideas?

- Have you used primary sources? Whilst initially secondary sources may be useful for showing you how others have applied ideas that you are also interested in, in a doctoral study, you must consult primary sources.

- Have you used too many outdated references?

- Have you checked that all sources cited in the literature review have been listed in the references?

SUMMARY OF THIS CHAPTER

One of the main purposes of this chapter, and the reasons why I have constructed it in this way – and with Alice! – has been to develop your confidence in tackling this whole area of literature and theory and demystifying the processes of writing. In addition, this chapter has aimed to:

- Acknowledge and accept the complexity of the task and provide easy-to-understand guidance and advice on how to begin.

- Support you in understanding that you are making your own theoretical journey. No one else can do that for you.

- Challenge you to accept that the journey is never *just* about being awarded a doctorate though for now that is a good goal.

- Welcome you to academia and hope that you will share the long-term goals about various theoretical journeys that involve collaboration with human beings and seek social justice for them.

- Develop your acceptance for the need to remain ethical in your journey.

CASE STUDY: MY OWN EXPERIENCE

My own doctoral study, many moons ago, started by wanting to understand why books for English primary schoolteachers did not explore or explain multilingual children's school learning experiences. This was in the mid-1990s and as a primary schoolteacher my everyday reality called for better understanding of multilingualism. The majority of my reception class (five-year-olds) were learning to speak English at school because they spoke different languages at home. Yet, particularly the books that focussed on learning to read, seemed to assume that all children were already highly competent in using English. Why would these books make this odd assumption, I wondered? How come all these multilingual children's learning experiences were rarely counted for in theoretical texts that explored the processes of learning to read? Why were their experiences neglected and their voices silenced? Why had my teacher education course *not* prepared me to understand my multilingual pupils early experiences of learning to read?

There were some rare examples, but the majority of texts that I found emphasised the deficit view of this group of children. Their lack of English was perceived as a problem, a barrier to their learning and strangely the languages that they used at home were not recognised or discussed. It was as if these 'other' languages did not exist.

These early questions, and feelings of anger and disappointment, developed later into my central argument about forms silencing, and how theories tend to start from the dominant groups' experiences and neglect minoritised groups' experiences. I had found a gap theory. Much later, I learnt to locate these ideas in post-colonialism (Said, 1979, 1994) and Critical Race Theory (Gillborn, 2008).

I began to ponder on my pupils' literacy development and, by doing so, had already begun to deepen my conceptual understanding. My main research question was beginning to become settled around 'how do young multilingual children learn to read in their everyday contexts?' My supervisor Eve Gregory (1993, 1994) was, and remains, a wonderful role model who led me to sociocultural theories of learning, and I have never looked back. For me, the area of 'learning to read' soon developed into an aspect of literacy development; there were then already an expanding bank of theoretical ideas and books about 'literacy' as a social practice (Heath, 1983; Street, 1984). Soon I was moving towards the development of my theoretical framework, though perhaps I was not yet aware that this was actually happening. It felt as if I was simply exploring general topics.

In my doctoral study, I followed the progress of a small group of multilingual children who between the ages of five and seven years were learning to read in three languages. For two years, on and off, I observed this group of pupils during their English literacy lessons at a state school in England, and at their local community school where they learnt to read in Urdu (the national language of Pakistan), and at the local Mosque where they were learning to read in classical Arabic for spiritual and Qur'anic purposes. All of the participants of the study were of British-Pakistani background.

I became interested in 'literacy events' (Heath, 1983), that is the kinds of everyday activities that different groups of people engage in. This was a construct that enabled me to explain what these children were experiencing. I also needed other ideas, particularly those that explored bi/multilingualism in schools (Cummins, 1984, 1991; Edwards, 1983). Combining these theories together and being selective and clear as to what specific aspects I needed for explaining my own emerging ideas, I had successfully developed my main theoretical framework (Robertson, 2002, 2006).

REFERENCES

Bakhtin, M. M. (1981). In M. Holquist (Ed.) and C. Emerson & M. Holquist (Trans.), *The dialogic imagination: Four essays*. Austin, TX: University of Texas Press.

Bourdieu, P., & Passeron, J. C. (1977). *Reproduction of education, society and culture*. London: Sage.

Cameron, D. (1992). *Feminism and linguistic theory* (2nd ed.). Basingstoke: MacMillan Press Ltd.

Carroll, L. (1865/2015). *Alice's Adventures in Wonderland and Through the Looking Glass*. London: Penguin Classics.

Carroll, L. (1871/2015). *Alice's Adventures in Wonderland and Through the Looking Glass*. London: Penguin Classics.

Cummins, J. (1984). *Bilingualism and special education: Issues in assessment and pedagogy*. Clevedon: Multilingual Matters.

Cummins, J. (1991). Language shift and language learning in the transition from home to school. *Journal of Education*, *173*(2), 85–98.

Edwards, V. (1983). *Language in multicultural classrooms*. London: B. T. Batsford Ltd.

Ely, M. Vinz, R., Downing, M. and Anzul, M. (1997) *On Writing Qualitative Research, Living by Words*. London: Falmer Press.

Fairclough, N. (1989). *Language and power*. London: Routledge.

Fairclough, N. (1995). *Critical discourse analysis*. London: Longman.

Foucault, M. (1972/1969). In A. M. Sheridan Smith (Trans.), *The archaeology of knowledge*. London: Tavistock.

Gillborn, D. (2008). *Racism and education, coincidence or conspiracy?* London: Routledge.

Gregory, E. (1993). Sweet and sour: Learning to read in British and Chinese school. *English in Education*, *27*(3), 53–59.

Gregory, E. (1994). Cultural assumptions and early years pedagogy: The effect of home culture on minority children's perceptions of reading in school. *Language, Culture and Curriculum*, *7*(20), 111–124.

Halliday, M. A. K. (1978). *Language as a social semiotic*. London: Edward Arnold.

Heath, S. B. (1983). *Ways with words*. Cambridge: Cambridge University Press.

hooks, b. (1987). *Ain't I a woman? Black women and feminism*. London: Pluto Press.

Hymes, D. (1977). *Foundations in sociolinguistics*. London: Tavistock.

Kamler, B., & Thomson, P. (2008). The failure of dissertation advice books: Toward alternative pedagogies for doctoral writing. *Educational Researcher*, *37*, 507–514.

Lamott, A. (1994). *Bird by bird: Some instructions on writing and life*. New York, NY: Pantheon Books.

Lillis, T. M. (2001). *Student writing: Access, regulation, desire*. London: Routledge.

Mirza, H. (2018). *Dismantling race in higher education: Racism, whiteness and decolonising the academy*. London: Palgrave Macmillan.

Robertson, L. H. (2002, November). Parallel literacy classes and hidden strengths: Learning to read in English, Urdu and classical Arabic. *Reading, Literacy and Language (UKRA)*, *36*(3), 119–126.

Robertson, L. H. (2006). Learning to read 'properly' by moving between parallel literacy classes. *Language and Education*, *20*(2), 44–61.

Said, E. W. (1979). *Orientalism*. New York, NY: Vintage.

Said, E. W. (1994). *Culture and imperialism*. New York, NY: Vintage.

Street, B. (1984). *Literacy in theory and practice*. Cambridge: Cambridge University Press.

Thomson, P. (2019). *Patter*. Online https://patthomson.net/category/thesis/ [Accessed on 28 May 2020]

Troyna, B., & Carrington, B. (1989). Whose side are we on? Ethical dilemmas in research on 'race' and education. In R. Burgess (Ed.), *The ethics of educational research*. London: Falmer Press, pp. 205–223.

Wisker, G. (2015). Developing doctoral authors: Engaging with theoretical perspectives through the literature review. *Innovations in Education and Teaching International*, *52*(1), 64–74.

5

DEVELOPING A THEORETICAL FRAMEWORK

Mike Watts

INTRODUCTION TO THIS CHAPTER

Three questions to be answered here: What is theory? How to formulate a theoretical framework for your Doctor of Education (EdD) thesis? Why the need for such a framework anyway? I begin with an example drawn from my own work – research in science education – to illustrate how research questions in themselves contain the seeds for a theoretical perspective, and how these can bloom to a full framework for the study. Research questions, and therefore theoretical directions, derive essentially from personal orientations – essentially it is you who drives both the questions and the choice of 'theoretical window' through which to view these.

In that opening paragraph, I have used a number of metaphors (growing seeds, windows, drives, directions, orientations – even the term framework itself), and I structure this chapter by continuing this metaphoric impetus through a discussion of (1) theoretical 'layers' using causal layered analysis (CLA), (2) 'logic chains' that inform each of the central ingredients of the thesis, (3) 'decisions trains' that you take (and take you) along the route of your research study and (4) theoretical validation as one of the key 'filters' through which to view your work as it develops.

By the end of this chapter, you will be able to:

- See the need to articulate a theoretical framework for your research.

- Appreciate how theory-driven thinking forms the 'DNA' for your thesis, the core internal shape of your work from beginning to end.

- Begin formulating both theory and framework for your own research, perhaps using a 'layered approach' such as CLA.

- Articulate your initial theoretical assumptions and therefore the likely choices and consequential decisions you then need to make.

- Criticise other work in the field from the vantage of the theory or theories you are adopting and adapting.

- Explore the theoretical validity of your work.

- Identify the limits to your own work and the extent to which you can comment and generalise from your own research outcomes.

SETTING OUT

'I really *hate* science', said the teenage girl with a degree of venom.

Being a science educator, I felt a powerful need to understand just why she spoke that way, exactly what lay behind such a very clear statement of aversion. Was it something about being a teenage girl? Was it a consequence of the setting in which she found herself at the time of speaking? Was it her experiences of classroom science and of her school science teachers? Did she catch that loathing from family, peers or siblings? Was it a consequence of being a girl of Asian heritage living in a socio-economically disadvantage part of London? Or was it some intersection of all of these possible influences on her system of likes and dislikes? These are not the only questions of course, and a more detailed look at the girl's statement might concern the 'I' to which she is referring: people are potentially different personas when talking in different social contexts and so the particular identity adopted by the girl might change at different points in time. And exactly what does 'hate' mean? Is it 'not like'? 'Disgust'? 'Revulsion'? And just what might she understand by science? Biology? Chemistry? Physics? Geology? All of these? Epidemiology? Meteorology? Etymology? Ichthyology? Or any of countless other 'ologies'. Given the narrow confines of a doctoral study, it is possible to explore only a limited few of these questions.

To begin to answer educational questions like these implies the presence of a theoretical framework. So, for example, if the 'research spotlight' fell on the girl's age, then this falls within a body of work in science education that sees primary-age children as enthusiastic about science, but then provides evidence that many adults in the general population also express strong interest in science too through watching TV programmes, visits to museums, zoos, galleries and the like – and so 'hate' of this kind might really be a function of the intervening period – of adolescent teenage years. Equally, there is an extended body of work to say that some teachers can be inspirational, the family can be powerfully influential, that socio-economic status is significant, that gender is an important dimension and cultural heritage is paramount. There is work, too, on individual 'science identity', the role of affect and emotions, the power of role models, the presence of 'science self-efficacy' and so on.

So what does it mean to have a theoretical framework? Theories can be large or small, local or general, and are expressed in order to understand, explain – and sometimes make predictions about – particular issues. Having a framework entails shaping the research, from beginning to end, through the window of one specific theory or, perhaps, a cluster of closely associated and 'congruent' theories. Using my example, if I decide through my reading of science education literature that snappy disaffection with school science is a singularly teenage matter, then I might begin sharpening focus to evaluate theories of adolescent development, on brain growth, on the power of peer groups, on rebellious social attitudes and so on. Theory-driven thinking informs the selection of the questions at the beginning of the research, how those questions are then played out, what direction the literature review takes, how the empirical data are generated, the shape of the data analysis and the eventual conclusions and implications at the finale. The theoretical framework is the fundamental organising structure that supports the assumptions, rationale, purpose, the core statement, the essential critique and the bounding limits of the research. Put crudely, one certain way to invite major revisions, or court outright disaster, for a doctoral thesis is to have a poorly framed, fumbling, confused, ill-informed theoretical basis to the work. An all-too-common shortcoming is to mention briefly a few likely theories and theorists (a hint of Vygotsky, a sprinkle of Piaget, a few citation of Bandura) at the start of the thesis and never return to these throughout the remainder of the work. The need to articulate a theoretical framework for your research, then, embraces the essential need to ward off failure.

WHAT IS A THEORY?

They come in all shapes and sizes and in degrees of articulation. One traditional division is between quantitative and qualitative research where theory plays a different role in each paradigm. For instance, in quantitative research that uses correlational statistics, the theory being adopted will detail the objects of the study, the variables associated with those objects, the hypotheses to be tested during the research and then the tests of significance to be used in order to validate the outcomes. Does taking a child out of school for a family holiday really impair his or her education? In theory, the more time a student spends at school, then the greater his or her educational achievement. Or, put another way, is it true that lower school attendance results in lower academic attainment? If so, is there a positive correlation between school attendance and test and exam scores? What then is the effect of a two-week term-time family break to Disneyland Paris?

In this case, using the expression 'in theory' wraps together a host of societal assumptions, policies, guidelines, strictures, customs, mores. These relate to social values of education being a 'good thing', that attendance at school is largely legally regulated, that non-attendance needs to be minimised, that attainment scores are to be maximised and so on. It is relatively straightforward to delve into the appropriate literature – and the apparent gaps – on the benefits of school attendance, fasten upon a working definition of truancy, decide which of the many output measure might be used to show attainment, gain access to school-based data for both, choose one of several statistical approaches to the analysis and then work through the outcomes of these. This is certainly one way to explore the issues involved. A qualitative study, however, would come at things differently; perhaps explore a series of cases to understand how school attendance plays out in children's lives, their ambitions, aspirations and any barriers to educational success. In either case, theory – whether loosely constructed or tightly defined – needs to be explicated and articulated so that the reader can judge the antecedents to the study, the assumptions being held, the choices and decisions being made – and can then evaluate the importance and significance of the work.

A second division can be made between 'a priori' theory and 'grounded' theory. The first is 'off the peg' theory, while the second is 'knit your own' theorising. In the first, the theory and its framework are taken from work already developed, and this is used from the very start, before any other part of the research study begins. In my own case, I was steeped very early in my PhD in the work of George Kelly's (1955) personal construct theory (PCT). My supervisors were 'PCT people', I belonged to a research group that held readings and discussions of his works, met advocates of his approaches, attended local seminars, symposia and international conferences on PCT, I wrote early working papers on how Kelly's theory related to my own interests in science education and so on. The theory provided the showcase for my thesis. In direct contrast, grounded theory was originally developed by Glaser and Strauss (1967), two sociologists unhappy with the way existing grand theories dominated sociological research. They argued that researchers need a method that allows them to move from data to theory rather than vice versa. Such data-driven theories would be 'grounded' in the context from which they emerge rather than be reliant upon pre-existing analytical constructs, categories or variables. Charmaz and Henwood (2008, p. 241) sum up the defining features of the process as follows:

We gather data, compare them, remain open to all possible theoretical understandings of the data, and develop tentative interpretations about these data through our codes and nascent categories. Then we go back to the field and gather more data to check and refine our categories.

My own (and many other people's) reservations about grounded theory centre on the scant regard it pays to researchers themselves, that – somehow – the data simply speak out loud for itself, that researchers have no unexpressed, incipient or tacit theories of their own, they amount to non-theoretical 'blank slates'. Critics of positivism, however, have made a convincing case that *all* observations are made from a particular perspective, and they are all situated- and standpoint-specific: researchers are actually integral to the research that is taking place. People have assumptions and predilections that direct their gaze, and these assumptions need – as best as possible – to be made clear and explicit. This is because theory guides what counts as data in the first place, where to look for it, what it looks like when it is 'found', how it might be interpreted, what suitable codes and categories might be used and what forms of analysis might be appropriate. Social constructionists like Charmaz (2006) have made strong attempts to tackle some of these issues, and there is some good reading to be done if you are tempted to follow this direction. In the remainder of this chapter, however, I am going to pursue the need for an overt and explicit theoretical framework that shapes your work – if not from the very start, then quite soon after diving into the literature that surrounds your topic. From this perspective, then, theory-driven thinking forms the 'DNA' for your thesis; it shapes the core internal structure of your work from beginning to end.

GETTING A THEORETICAL FRAMEWORK

Lysaght (2011) makes the point that:

> A *researcher's choice of framework is not arbitrary but reflects important personal beliefs and understandings about the nature of knowledge, how it exists (in the metaphysical sense) in relation to the observer, and the possible roles to be adopted, and tools to be employed consequently, by the researcher in his/her work. (p. 572)*

The theories that I adopt to conduct research will vary from those of others. They derive from my own views of human nature, my personal beliefs, philosophies and predilections. I am prone to write under a humanistic flag although, while humanism forms a backdrop to much of my work, it does not always feature in the headlines of my writing. It is a broad philosophical direction rather than the key focus of my work. My own preferences, too, lie with psychological theories rather than sociological ones. I am not against social theories in principle, simply that my own interests lie in 'getting up close' to people, listening to their stories, discussing their ideas in some depth, trying to make something of their accounts. This is where I get my 'research buzz'. So, my research instinct is commonly to head for smaller samples of people with whom I can talk, generate discursive and narrative approaches to data and employ thematic forms of analysis.

Layers

CLA is a tactic used to probe issues through a structured approach to critical inquiry (Haigh, 2016). It was developed initially within Futures Studies as a relatively straightforward approach to exposing layers of meaning within any situation or discourse (Inayatullah, 1998). In this instance, I use CLA to explore the development of a research framework around the example with which I began, attitudes to science education, because this allows me insights into the narrative structures that underpin much of the work I enjoy doing. It is an approach that particularly emphasises metaphor (again), language and root cultural myths and fosters the suggestion that both the future and the past are created by the root narratives of the present (Milojevic, 2005). CLA is not the only way for you to excavate ideas for yourself, though its virtue here is one of explication, giving me the opportunity to clarify ideas of both theory and framework. Adopting a process such as this might enable you in formulating theory and framework for your own research.

CLA explores a sequence of four layers, which represent the multiple dimensions of social reality and their operation at different epistemological levels (Inayatullah, 2012). These four layers are (i) *Litany*, (ii) *Systemic Causes*, (iii) *Worldview* and (iv) *Metaphor and Myth*. CLA is frequently represented as an iceberg where only the small upper section is visible above the surface – analysis proceeds downwards from surface appearances towards causal depths that are commonly subconscious.

Litany

Litany is the upper, most visible, layer of surface appearances and events. This layer comprises popular talked-about understandings, the 'word on the street', the conventional wisdoms and traditions that are represented in conversations, gossip, various media and which often interact with official, politically mediated, views of reality. These are a relatively short-lived accounts and last in the region of weeks or months. So, using my example from above, it is not uncommon for young people, girls and boys, to talk about their aversion to school science. As you are reading this, you might even recognise it in yourself. The Relevance of School Science (ROSE) project was set up in the United Kingdom by Edgar Jenkins (2006) at the University of Leeds and leaned heavily on a previous study (*Science and Scientists*) in Norway established by Camilla Schreiner and Svein Sjøberg (2004). Both studies were questionnaire based and explored the relevance of school science education from the perspective of students. The broad outcomes were that most students agreed that science and technology are important for society and were optimistic about the contribution these made to everyday life through health (curing diseases such as cancer), making life easier and more comfortable. This was not, however, reflected in their opinions of school science. While the subject was regarded as 'relevant' and 'important', most boys (and rather more girls) responded that they simply did not like it – science was for other people and not for them (Jenkins & Nelson, 2005).

At this level of litany, the school-yard conversations on science, the 'pass-me-down' perspectives of others, the general stereotypes of 'mad' scientists, the 'boffin' status of Einstein or Stephen Hawkins, the gawky physics teacher, dull science lessons all combine to create an image of science that contrasts sharply with the resplendent aura conjured by the musician, artist, actress, fashion designer and celebrity chef. This level of teenage discourse very much set the scene for my own work with colleagues that pushed deeper into the reasons young people they might hold such views (Salehjee & Watts, 2015, 2019).

Systemic Causes

This layer aims at articulating the social, economic, cultural and environmental drivers of particular situations and their interactions.

It is expressed in terms of system interconnection, technical explanation, socio-cultural and policy analysis. In search for causal motivations, it analyses, engages and critiques different theories, ideologies and institutions using the language of trends, forces, flows and processes. Its timescale is often expressed in terms of years or a few decades.

In my own work, the blame for anti-science attitudes is commonly heaped upon a wide range of social systems and institutions, from the opportunities for overt stereotyping afforded by social media and Internet websites, to the actions of teachers, schools, parents and family. For example, Archer et al. (2012, 2013, 2016) use Pierre Bourdieu's (1977) work to link young people's science experiences to something they call 'science capital'. Having high science capital entails having resources available such as affirmative role models, positive parents, good schools and inspirational teachers. Having low science capital, of course, signals the opposite – each of the constituent parts of society is seen to fail quite markedly in the proper provision and management of young people's behaviours. Low science capital leads to an impoverished view of science and what might be achieved through science education. In my view, these writers overemphasise the idea of extensionality – the role of social forces – over intentionality, the internal motivational drive and ambitions of individuals. My own worldview incorporates a greater level of self-determinism than this – more a case of 'I am what I make of myself' rather than 'I am what others make me'.

This kind of structural causation moves away from individual and small group performative analyses to consider instead establishments and organisations, policies and practices in which the institutions of class, politics, religion, establishments and organisations are held responsible – in this case for schools and schooling. Science, technology and engineering at a national level are seen to have a manpower shortage and so science education is considered instrumental in maintaining a 'STEM pipeline' of suitably qualified workers. It is at this level of analysis that you read the available policy documents in the UK, government guidance, the work of major organisations such as Economic and Social Research Council (ESRC) and National Foundation for Educational Research (NFER) research, the Wellcome Foundation, the Sutton Trust, the Office for Standards in Education (Ofsted), local authority decrees and so on. The *British Educational Research Journal, Educational Review* and similar significant journals are very useful analyses and critiques at this level.

Worldview

The Worldview layer can be seen as a largely subconscious ground of culturally mediated presumption and discourse. It engages discourse analysis; it explores cultural values and aspirations, language with its strata and meta-functions (Martin & Rose, 2003), traditions, religious beliefs and the kind of broad civilisational consensuses that define culture, class, nationality and systems of socio-political organisation. At this level, science is simply taken as a 'good thing'. The developed as opposed to the underdeveloped world is commonly measured by concentrations of industrialisation, and high levels of scientific and technological achievement commonly imply high levels of national prosperity. As Steven Pinker describes in *Enlightenment Now, the Case for Reason, Science, Humanism and Progress* (2018), with rare exceptions, most of the wonders and marvels of humankind are long-term, constructed things. Progress and development come bit by bit.

Returning to science education at this level, we have the Programme for International Student Assessment (PISA) study. This is a triennial international survey under the auspices of the Organisation for Economic Co-operation and Development (OECD) that aims to evaluate education systems worldwide by testing the skills and knowledge of 15-year-old students in science, mathematics and reading. Much of PISA's methodology follows the example of the Trends in International Mathematics and Science Study (TIMSS, began in 1995), which in turn was much influenced by the United States' National Assessment of Educational Progress (NAEP). These kinds of international measures allow countries to be ranked in order of achievement, so that comparisons can be made between countries.

The use of PISA/TIMMs data, with its three-year assessment cycle, is clearly part of the visible world of science education (above the surface level of the iceberg). However, what commonly lies hidden in national education policies is a shift of attention to short-term (three-year) fixes designed to help a country quickly climb the rankings, despite research showing that enduring changes in education practice take decades, not a few years, to come to fruition. Moreover, the rush in many countries to more and more testing leads to an increasing tendency (despite serious reservations about its validity and reliability) to label young people. In my view, the new Pisa regime, with its continuous cycle of global testing, harms young people and impoverishes school classrooms, as it inevitably involves more and longer batteries of multiple-choice testing, more scripted commercially made lessons, and therefore entails less autonomy for teachers and students. From this perspective, Pisa has further increased the already high stress level in schools, which endangers the well-being of students and teachers.

In adopting that position means that I have not only read the PISA documents that have been produced along with many of the related journal papers and articles around the use of PISA data, the policy documents of several countries, but I have also formed opinions about it all. At the heart of my comments above lie a view of 'learner autonomy' that pervades my work, and this often forms the kernel of my critiques of such worldviews. The OECD is not particularly interested in individual students. As an organisation of economic development, it is naturally biased in favour of the economic role of public (state) schools. But – in my view – preparing young men and women for gainful employment is not the only, and not even the main goal of education, which has to prepare students for participation in democratic self-government, moral action and a life of personal development, growth and well-being.

It is by reading, discussing, arguing, writing that you begin to unearth common assumptions, beliefs and understandings, begin to formulate your own opinions at this level, to articulate your initial theoretical assumptions and therefore the likely choices and consequential decisions you then need to make in your study. Asking yourself the 'why?' question many times in a row often pushes you to think at deeper and deeper levels. 'I think that …', 'Why?', 'Well because …', 'Why?' – and so on. The CLA levels I am using here are just one way for doing this.

Metaphor and Myth

This is the deepest of the four layers, one of myths, meta-narratives and metaphors, with all their unconscious emotive dimensions. George Lakoff and Mark Johnson (1980) argue that, rather than being solely a literary device, metaphors permeate human thought and action. In sum, they maintain (Lakoff & Johnson, 1999) that myths and metaphors are things of extraordinary power; they shape the way the world is conceived, they subconsciously direct thought and they shape both attitudes and behaviours. Our whole conceptual system is metaphorical in nature. Moreover, as Lakoff and Turner (1989) have noted, 'because [metaphors] are used so automatically and effortlessly, we find it hard to question them, if we can even notice them'. This is why exploring the myths and metaphors that both underpin and provide underlying narrative frameworks is a most important form of deep inquiry. Some of the answers to the questions above lie in what Lakoff and Johnson call the 'cognitive unconscious', the 'hidden hand' that shapes conscious thought and action. So, for example, if a young person fails to understand a particular explanation in science, he or she might say that it 'goes over my head'. This is more than just an idle saying because we have an unconscious image of an object passing over the top of our head that we do not recognise. The young person might actually wave his or her hand above their head – or whistle as they say it – emphasising the speed of the issue and their inability to follow it. Grady's (1997) theory of primary metaphors is that very early in life we pair hundreds of subjective experience and judgement with physical, sensorimotor experiences. Some examples might be important is big ('I have a big day tomorrow'); happy is up, unhappy is down ('I'm really feeling down today'); affection is warmth ('she greeted me very warmly'); intimacy is closeness ('My sister and I are very close'); and states are locations ('I'm in a bad place, I'm close to the edge'). The point here is that the vast majority of our cognition is unconscious, and yet this unconscious metaphoric cognition importantly determines how we talk about things, how one sees the world. Roald Hoffman (2006) argues that metaphors play a role in helping scientists generate hypotheses, theories and experiments and he advocates using these devices in communicating with scientists and non-scientists alike:

A naked metaphor clearly shows the analogy's limitations,
its capacity for misinterpretation and its productive exten-
sions. It aids its creator as well as its audience. (p. 406)

Metaphors are ubiquitous in science. Most biologists are familiar
with Richard Dawkin's 'blind watchmaker' and 'selfish gene'. Richard Mayer from the University of California at Santa Barbara quotes
a well-known scientific textbook that explicitly compares electricity
to water flowing in pipes to explain Ohm's Law in physics:

To understand this idea, compare the pictures of pipes.
[Pictures show water coming out of a narrow pipe and
water coming out of a wide pipe.] The only difference in
the pipe is their diameters. The pump pushes water equally
in both cases. But more water passes through the pipe with
the large opening. The larger pipe offers less resistance to
the flow of water than the smaller pipe. In a similar way,
more current flows through a conductor with less resistance
than through a conductor with more resistance. (Mayer in
Ortony, 1993, p. 562)

In this metaphor, voltage is water pressure, current is the volume of
water flow, etc. These are the ways in which the metaphor 'fits'. However, if one bends a pipe, the flow of the water is impeded, whereas
bending a wire has no impact on the flow of electricity. As a second
example, the idea that DNA makes proteins is a popular metaphor
that has introduced the wrong idea about the relation between DNA
and protein synthesis. Proteins are the result of their genetic code plus
numerous other cell elements unrelated to DNA. In this way, the 'making metaphor' fails to fit. Drawing your attention to your own potential metaphorical thought and asking you to evaluate those metaphors
you use is one way to foster your critical thinking.

It is worth mentioning too, the role of myths in science. There is a
general and universal scientific method. Not so, and philosophers of
science from Thomas Kuhn to Paul Feyerabend have challenged this
pervasive myth: scientists tackle problems in many-varied ways. Science
and its methods provide incontrovertible truths. Again, not so: accu-
mulated evidence can provide support, validation and substantiation
to a theory or a law, but – as Karl Popper (1968) has pointed out – this

will not make a theory either 'forever' or 'true'. The imperative here, then, is that you need to look deeper into your chosen area of study to understand how myths, traditions, neologisms come about in the first place and why they become so prevalent and persistent.

To summarise this section is to restate the need to look carefully and thoughtfully at your reading. In any piece of research, what are the assumptions being made? What are the policies that have been chosen for discussion? What worldviews are apparent? What analogic and metaphoric language is being used? What myths abound? Your 'take' on these issues will be important. A theoretical framework helps you to focus on particular viewpoints, issues, ideas, concepts, definitions and variables. Using a 'levels' approach such as CLA is just one means of doing this. In the next section, I give a case study taken from recent research on classroom questioning (Pedrosa-de-Jesus, Moreira, & Watts, 2019). This case includes mention of 'logic chains' that inform each of the central ingredients of the work and of the 'decisions trains' that were take along the way through the research study.

A case study: a theoretical approach to student-based questioning

This research explored university students' classroom, and out-of-classroom, questioning during the course of their undergraduate studies. Our interest in students' question has been long-lasting over many years, for example, from Watts and Alsop (1995) to Pedrosa-de-Jesus, Neri de Souza, Teixeira-Dias and Watts (2005) and Pedrosa-de-Jesus and Watts (2019). When students ask questions during lectures, in class sessions, tutorials or even electronically outside the confines of the campus, they are undertaking a range of intellectual tasks: constructing, connecting and clarifying information into personal knowledge systems; giving teachers and peers a window into their thinking; providing evidence of conceptual change; and authentically modelling the practice of science, a discipline based on asking questions and seeking answers (Chin, Brown, & Bruce, 2002; Cuccio-Schirripa & Steiner, 2000; Harper, Etkina & Lin, 2003). As we have argued elsewhere (Teixeira-Dias, Pedrosa de Jesus, Neri de Souza, & Watts, 2005), question-asking is central to a learner's 'enculturation' into the patterns of language and thought, discussion and criticism, that are characteristic of an academic discipline such as micro-biology or biochemistry.

At the start of the research, we chose to work within David Kolb's (1984) theory of experiential learning. Kolb describes his model of learning development as a 'cone of experiential learning', such that the base of the cone encompasses the lower levels of learning development and the apex of the cone represents their climax (Fig. 1). This indicates increasing integration of learning from experience from low to higher levels. This progression in learning is characterised by an increasing composite structure and relativity in managing the world and one's own experiences (Mainemelis, Boyatzis, & Kolb, 2002).

We made our theoretical choice for several reasons:

1. We had undertaken previous small-scale research using Kolb's learning styles, and the more we read into Kolb's broader theories of adult learning, the more we felt his theory was very compatible with the kinds of work we wanted to undertake. Students learn to ask better, 'higher quality', questions through the actual experience of asking questions, and by being in the company of others who ask questions.

2. Kolb's work has made a significant contribution to the literature on experiential learning by providing a theoretical basis for exploring this. It is an established theory that has been widely read, reread, tested and criticised, not least because of its close affinity to John Dewey's long-standing theories of experiential learning and pragmatism.

3. For Kolb, learning is less about the acquisition of content than the interaction between knowledge and experience, whereby each transforms the other. In our work, we were interested in learners' experiences of asking questions and the interaction between these experiences and any knowledge that eventually accrued from their question-asking.

4. We felt that Kolb's writing was saying something intuitively correct, that it is important (for us, at least) to base education on learners' own subjective experiences, their motivations and emotions. This 'learner-centeredness' has been a central philosophical plank to our work over decades.

While we did not use CLA in exactly the detailed way described above, we covered most of those levels of analysis through the broad suite of research projects with which we were working at the time. So, we became very familiar with the common issues surrounding the asking of questions within formal educational settings, what students thought, what teachers said. The common litany was that students – on the whole – seldom asked intelligent questions, that questions tended to be prosaic and pragmatic, that question-asking in a large forum was forbidding and 'scary' and so on. Our shared reading covered the ground thoroughly and formed the basis for numerous publications and conference papers. We were conversant with the international work on classroom questions and questioning, and what this said about student participation in lectures and tutorials. We were also aware of the ways that metaphor and myth shaped the discourse on learning through questions.

The logic chain that flowed from all this was as follows:

1. Based on Kolb's theory, we might expect that question-asking would differ by learner and by experiential setting. The same student in different experiential contexts would ask different questions; different students within the same setting would ask different questions. This required us to collect the questions asked by individual students and within a variety of settings.

2. The intellectual challenge of the learning experiences was important – the more 'engaging' the challenge, the more questions would be stimulated and asked. The university departments where we were working had initiated small-group project work around issues such as 'Blood gases and deep-sea diving', 'Self-replicating molecules', 'Catalytic converters', 'Hydrogen as a fuel', 'CO_2 and the greenhouse effect', 'Catalysts based on zeolites', 'Magnetic resonance imaging in

medicine', 'Chemistry and the forensic sciences' and the like. This project work was conducted in groups of 2, 3 or 4, in their own time (outside of formal sessions). During the life of the projects, the groups had no formal lectures but attended tutorials with their lecturers, during which students could ask questions about their topic but where the teacher would provide only sufficient guidance for the students to identify and answer their own questions.

3. We researchers were not an integral part of this process of teaching and learning. In fact, our presence in any of the settings risked altering and misaligning the dynamics at play, and so we decided to collect data as unobtrusively as possible, with minimal researcher intrusion, to be very inconspicuous 'flies on the wall'.

The process ended when each 'project team' made presentations of their work to the other students and to members of staff in the department. These presentations took place on an evening over a period of three hours – with each presentation being subjected to numerous questions from both peers and tutors. In some instances, the presentations were organised around a series of the team's own questions. The research outcomes from this body of work derived from numerous hours of observation, recording, transcription, coding, analysis, member-checking and respondent validation of our results. We decided upon a taxonomy of questions based on Kolb's theoretical concepts with 'acquisition questions' shaping the base, 'specialist questions' making the centre of the cone and 'integrative question' forming the top. We were then able to track growth and development in the frequency and quality of these students' question-asking over time, in both formal and informal learning contexts (Moreira, 2012).

DECISION CHAINS

When you defend your thesis at viva, you are, in fact, defending the numerous decisions you have made along the way – both in conducting your study and in writing the final submission. You make many of these decisions quite explicitly, often in consultation with supervisors, some though are tacit or emerge only as you mature the work. I am interested here in rational decision-making rather than – say – aesthetic judgements or affective agendas. While these certainly have their place, they lie aside of the discussion here. There are, needless to say, many theoretical models of decision-making and choice-making, I flinch, however, at theorising about theorising. I am interested in the decisions made that follow from your choice of theory, that is, using your theory framework to guide the decisions you need to make – as opposed to some sort of disjointed 'muddling through'.

When using a broadly rational model in this fashion, I am assuming that you

1. Have some sense of the possible alternatives. That is, through your reading and in discussion with your supervisors, you can see what other routes might be possible, what other research questions you might ask, different lines and genres of reading, what other ways you might have for collecting data and so on.

2. Appreciate the consequences of implementing each alternative. Some decisions you make arise from pragmatic concerns about the amount of time you have available, the quality of access you have for collecting data, the complexity of data analysis that would be needed. Other decisions rest on the route you have taken from the very beginning.

3. Have a well-organised set of preferences for these consequences. This returns us to the framework; in many respects, this is the articulation of your preferences. Making decisions has to be a balance between what is compatible with your framework and what is likely to succeed in your given circumstances.

I use the David Kolb case study to illustrate some of this. As I suggested above, the use of Kolb was not clear-cut at the start of the work: yes, we had used his Learning Styles Inventory (LSI) to explore students' approaches to learning, but we had used other theoretical methods too. We were familiar with many of the criticisms lodged against the use of LSI and, while this specific instrument faded in our thinking, our interest in his broader theory grew. One paper proved very influential written by Anne and David Kolb as a wife and husband team (Kolb & Kolb, 2005), and our research group pored over and discussed this at length. And the decision was taken to use the broader theory as the framework. Kolb had not focussed on students question per se, and so we needed to adapt what he and others were saying about experiential learning in general to the asking of questions in particular.

SUMMARY

At the end of this chapter, I am hoping that you are able to:

- See the need to articulate a theoretical framework for your research.

- Appreciate how theory-driven thinking forms the 'DNA' for your thesis, the core internal shape of your work from beginning to end.

- Begin formulating both theory and framework for your own research, perhaps using a 'layered approach' such as CLA.

- Articulate your initial theoretical assumptions and therefore the likely choices and consequential decisions you then need to make.

- Criticise other work in the field from the vantage of the theory or theories you are adopting and adapting.

- Explore the theoretical validity of your work.

- Identify the limits to your own work and the extent to which you can comment and generalise from your own research outcomes.

FURTHER READING

Lingard, B. (2015). Thinking about theory in educational research: Fieldwork in philosophy. *Educational Philosophy and Theory*, 47(2), 173–191.

In this paper, Bob Lingard reflects on a series of articles that contribute to a special edition of this journal. Specifically, he deals with the use of theory in each of the papers and, in doing so, notes some of the contributors' uses of Michel Foucault, Giles Deleuze, Pierre Bourdieu, Emmanuel Levinas and Judith Butler as scholarly references.

He reflects on the necessity of theory in educational research more generally and stresses its central role to educational research committed to generating understanding. He points out that theory should be endemic in all stages of educational research, from framing research questions, deciding the unit of analysis, methodological choices, data collection (fieldwork in philosophy), analysis and dissemination. That said, theory serves different purposes in research with different goals: quantitative correlational research demands theory to move to explanation, interpretive research requires theory to strengthen interpretation and plausibility, while critical research utilises theory to uncover the hidden as a step towards emancipation.

Wilkins, S., Neri, S., & Lean, J. (2019). The role of theory in the business/management PhD: How students may use theory to make an original contribution to knowledge. *The International Journal of Management Education, 17*(3), online.

This paper assesses the extent and nature of theory-related teaching in PhD programmes, in order to identify what (in this case Business/Management) PhD students should know and do in relation to theory in order to complete their programme successfully. The authors surveyed various stakeholders in the doctoral process (students, educators and administrators) on related aspects of doctoral education. The participants unanimously agreed that students better understand, use and develop theory if they read widely and deeply. Therefore, educators (supervisors/advisors) should encourage students to read extensively and set tasks that require students to read scholarly journals. The role of top-tier journals in the education of PhD students is important – most top-tier journals in specific fields generally publish articles that make a theoretical contribution. The authors argue here that, while students need to be taught more about theory, teaching need only raise students' *awareness* of a range of theories, with the student then responsible for following up to learn and understand the theories of relevance in greater depth. Students must attend courses that involve theory in their fields and read widely during the process of selecting the theories they use in their research.

REFERENCES

Archer, L., Dawson, E., Seakins, A., DeWitt, J., Godec, S., & Whitby, C. (2016). "I'm being a man here": Urban boys' performances of masculinity and engagement with science during a science museum visit. *Journal of the Learning Sciences*, 25(3), 438–485.

Archer, L., DeWitt, J., Osborne, J., Dillon, J., Willis, B., & Wong, B. (2012). Science aspirations, capital, and family habitus: How families shape children's engagement and identification with science. *American Educational Research Journal*, 49(5), 881–908.

Archer, L., DeWitt, J., Osborne, J., Dillon, J., Willis, B., & Wong, B. (2013). Not girly, not sexy, not glamorous: Primary school girls' and parents' constructions of science aspirations. *Pedagogy, Culture & Society*, 21(1), 171–194.

Bourdieu, P. (1977). In R. Nice (Trans.), *Outline of a theory of practice*. London: Cambridge University Press.

Charmaz, K. (2006). *Constructing grounded theory: A practical guide through qualitative analysis*. London: Sage.

Charmaz, K., & Henwood, K. (2008). Grounded theory in psychology. In C. Willig & W. Stainton-Rogers (Eds.), *Handbook of qualitative research in psychology* (pp. 240–260). London: Sage.

Chin, C., Brown, D. E., & Bruce, B. C. (2002). Student-generated questions: A meaningful aspect of learning in science. *International Journal of Science Education*, 24(5), 521–549.

Cuccio-Schirripa, S., & Steiner, H. (2000). Enhancement and analysis of science question level for middle school students. *Journal of Research in Science Teaching*, 37, 210–224.

Glaser, B. G., & Strauss, A. L. (1967). *The discovery of grounded theory*. Chicago, IL: Aldine.

Grady, J. (1997). *Foundations of meaning: Primary metaphors and primary scenes*. Unpublished doctoral dissertation. University of California, Berkeley.

Haigh, M. (2016). Fostering deeper critical inquiry with causal layered analysis. *Journal of Geography in Higher Education, 40*(2), 164–181 (Published online: March 8, 2016).

Harper, K. A., Etkina, E., & Lin, Y. (2003). Encouraging and analyzing student questions in a large physics course: Meaningful patterns for instructors. *Journal of Research in Science Teaching, 40*, 776–791.

Hoffman, R. (2006). The metaphor, unchained. *American Scientist, 94*(5), 406.

Inayatullah, S. (1998). Causal layered analysis: Post-structuralism as method. *Futures, 30*(8), 815–829.

Inayatullah, S. (2012). Humanity 3000: A comparative analysis of methodological approaches to forecasting the long-term. *Foresight, 14*(5), 401–417.

Jenkins, E. W. (2006). The student voice and school science education. *Studies in Science Education, 42*, 49–88.

Jenkins, E. W., & Nelson, N. W. (2005). Important but not for me: Students' attitudes towards secondary school science in England. *Research in Science and Technological Education, 23*(1), 41–57.

Kelly, G. A. (1955). *The psychology of personal constructs*. New York, NY: Norton (Reprinted by Routledge, London, 1991).

Kolb, D. A. (1984). *Experiential learning: Experience as a source of learning and development*. Englewoods Cliffs, NJ: Prentice-Hall.

Kolb, A., & Kolb, D. A. (2005). Learning styles and learning spaces: Enhancing experiential learning in higher education. *Academy of Management Learning & Education, 4*(2), 193–212.

Lakoff, G., & Johnson, M. (1980). *Metaphors we live by* (2003rd ed.). Chicago, IL: University of Chicago Press.

Lakoff, G., & Johnson, M. (1999). *Philosophy in the flesh*. New York, NY: Basic Books.

Lakoff, G., & Turner, M. (1989). *More than cool reason: A field guide to poetic metaphor*. Chicago, IL: University of Chicago Press.

Lysaght, Z. (2011). Epistemological and paradigmatic ecumenism in "Pasteur's Quadrant:" Tales from doctoral research. In *Official conference proceedings of the third Asian conference on education, Osaka, Japan.* Retrieved from http://iafor.org/ace2011_offprint/ACE2011_offprint_0254.pdf

Mainemelis, C., Boyatzis, R., & Kolb, D. A. (2002). Learning styles and adaptive flexibility: Testing the experiential theory of development. *Management Learning, 33*(1), 5–53.

Martin, J. R., & Rose, D. (2003). *Working with discourse.* London: Continuum.

Milojevic, I. (2005). *Educational futures; dominant and contesting visions.* Abingdon: Routledge.

Moreira, A. C. (2012). *O questionamento no alinhamento do ensinio, da aprendizagem e da avaliacao.* Unpublished PhD thesis, University of Aveiro, Portugal.

Ortony, A. (Ed.). (1993). *Metaphor and thought* (2nd ed.). New York, NY: Cambridge University Press.

Popper, K. (1968). *The logic of scientific discovery.* New York, NY: Harper Torchbooks.

Pedrosa-de-Jesus, M. H., Neri de Souza, F., Teixeira-Dias, J. J., & Watts, D. M. (2005). Organising the chemistry of question-based learning: A case study. *Research in Science & Technological Education, 23*(2), 179–193.

Pedrosa-de-Jesus, M. H., Moreira, A. C.,& Watts, D. M. (2019). Approaches to student inquiry-led learning. In M. H. Pedrosa-de-Jesus & D. M. Watts (Eds.), *Academic growth in higher education: Questions and answers.* New York: BRILL/Sense Publications.

Pinker, S. (2018). *Enlightenment now, the case for reason, science, humanism and progress.* London: Allen Lane, Penguin Books.

Salehjee, S., & Watts, D. M. (2015). Science lives: School choices and 'natural tendencies'. *International Journal of Science Education, 37*(4), 727–743.

Salehjee, S., & Watts, D. M. (2019). *Becoming a scientist.* Cambridge: Cambridge Scholars Press.

Schreiner, C., & Sjøberg, S. (2004). *Sowing the seeds of ROSE (The Relevance of Science Education) – A comparative study of students' views of science and science education (Acta Didactica 4/2004)*. Oslo: Department of Teacher Education and School Development, University of Oslo.

Teixeira-Dias, J. J., Pedrosa de Jesus, H., Neri de Souza, F., & Watts, D. M. (2005). Teaching for quality learning in chemistry. *International Journal of Science Education, 27*(9), 1123–1137.

Watts, D. M., & Alsop, S. J. (1995, June). Questioning and conceptual understanding: The quality of pupils' questions in science. *School Science Review, 76*(277), 91–95.

6

RESEARCH DESIGN AND METHODOLOGICAL APPROACHES

Kate Hoskins

INTRODUCTION

A key challenge for you as a doctoral researcher is deciding upon the research design that you will use to address your research questions and understanding how to justify your decisions about design. To enable you to make appropriate choices for your own research projects and to enable you to understand the implications of your design choices, this chapter will guide doctoral researchers through the planning stage of their research, including writing their research proposal. We first look at the distinctive features of a quantitative and a qualitative methodology, considering their relative strengths and weaknesses. Second, we examine some of the most popular research methods that you may want to use including surveys, questionnaires, interviews, focus groups, observation and ethnography. In examining each of these methods, some of the key strengths and weaknesses are discussed. Third, I provide a case study of my own doctoral research to show how I made decisions about methodology and method. The aim of the case study is to apply some of the points raised in the chapter to a research project.

At the end of this chapter, you will be able to:

- Identify the key features of a quantitative and a qualitative methodology.

- Understand the strengths and limitations of different methodologies.

- Identify the key features of research methods including surveys, questionnaires, interviews, focus groups, observation and ethnography.

- Understand the strengths and limitations of these different methods.

QUANTITATIVE METHODOLOGY

In this section, I discuss the key features of a quantitative methodology and outline uses and challenges facing social researchers taking this approach to designing their research project, data collection and data analysis. The aim of this section is to help you decide if and why a quantitative methodology might be a suitable approach for your research project.

The term methodology refers quite simply to 'a system of methods used in a particular field' (Newby, 2014, p. 47). Perhaps, the most historically dominant methodological approach on the research continuum is quantitative (Silverman, 2006), partly due to the view that through scientific, the so-called positivist research, it is possible to uncover objective, generalisable social realities (Bryman, 2008). The positivist paradigm that informs quantitative research is informed by the following key features:

- To identify universal laws and regular relationships.

- To study phenomena that are directly observable.

- To tests theories *or* seek to gather facts that will form the basis for laws.

- To work objectively and thus eliminate the effect of the researcher.

- To employ explicit and standardised procedures to all data collection to achieve consistency.

From what is labelled as a positivist point of view, the task in quantitative research is to conceptualise and measure human behaviour in terms of key variables and to discover causal relationships among these. A further aim of using a quantitative methodology is to take an objective approach to your project and to strive for neutrality throughout the data gathering, analysis and writing up stages (Bryman, 2008). If your research project is concerned with providing quantifiable data that measure viewpoints to discover causal factors informing social phenomena, then a quantitative methodology is a useful approach for you to consider.

Students can be drawn to this approach because it can be viewed as an easier data collection tool to deploy. However, there are criticisms of taking a quantitative approach to carrying out research. Very often, the links between perspectives and actions, and between behaviour and its effects, are seen as complex and uncertain, rather than reducible to any kind of universal statement about fixed relationships (Torres, 1998). Other points of view emphasise the need to grasp the forces that structure wider society if we are to be able to understand how institutions, for example, schools or colleges, operate (Brown & Lauder, 1991). There are also those who stress what they see as the constitutive role of discourse, which refers to '… ideas, attitudes, courses of action, beliefs and practices that systematically construct the subjects and the worlds of which they speak' (Lessa, 2006, p. 285), in generating not just our experience of the world but also what actually happens within it. Moreover, cross-cutting these differences are disagreements about what the product of social science research ought to be about and what should be the proper relationship between (indeed, about whether there should be any distinction between) researcher and researched.

There are also problems associated with re/presenting the social world as objective because this can lead to the view that it is decontextualised and disembodied. Much recent social science research has paid attention to local context as a way of highlighting the complexity of social interactions (see, e.g., Braun, Ball, Maguire, & Hoskins, 2011). The view here is that positivist research erases relations of power and (micro)politics from view.

Reflective questions:

If you are considering using a quantitative methodology, it is useful to consider how you would answer the following questions raised by Skeggs (1997):

(1) Can we ever be sure we have objectivity and neutrality in research?

(2) How do the relations of power in the research process influence who can speak, who legitimises and authorises that speech and whose interests are represented?

If you address these points in your methodology chapter, you can reflect on how to manage some of the key limitations associated with positivist, quantitative research design and this reflection will help you defend your work in your viva.

An alternative methodology is qualitative, and this is now discussed.

QUALITATIVE METHODOLOGY

In this section, I outline the key features of a qualitative methodology and some of the uses and limitations of applying it to social science research. Qualitative methodologies tend to focus on examining the following areas:

- Exploring phenomena, rather than testing hypotheses.

- Relatively unstructured rather than structured data.

- Smaller amounts of data are explored in greater detail.

- Analysis involves explicit, detailed interpretation of the ideas and social behaviour of human actors.

Delamont (1992, p. 7) argues that the qualitative researcher's job 'is to find out how the people you are researching understand their world'. Williams and May (1998, p. 8) describe qualitative research as primarily 'concerned with the daily actions of people and the meanings that they attach to their environment and relationships'. Using a qualitative methodology and methods allow you to access and explore, in depth, the perspectives and constructions of respondents (Usher & Edwards, 1994). Through utilising a qualitative methodology, it is possible for you to gain detailed insight into your participants' worlds through their eyes, giving their meanings and understandings of events. For those researchers not seeking to turn their participants' stories into what feminists Stanley and Wise (1993, p. 115) refer to as 'generalized mush' making reference to a quantitative methodology, a qualitative methodology can provide an account of the complexities as well as any strands of similarities between individual experiences within a group who share the same status and who potentially experience some of the same structural inequalities. The point here is that social life is complicated, contradictory and nuanced, and quantitative methodologies do not engage with these issues.

However, despite its uses, using a qualitative methodology also has a number of drawbacks and limitations. For example, Stanley and Wise (1993) argue that there is a 'mythology' around the possibility of carrying out 'hygienic research'. That is, how can the qualitative researcher be 'there', in the field with their participants in any context, 'without having any greater involvement than simple presence' (Stanley & Wise, 1993, p. 114). They, along with other key commentators (see Hammersley, 2003, for an example), argue that as a researcher, your values, views, perceptions of the world and your embodied self will influence the questions you ask in an interview or focus group, the focus of an observation, the leads and questions you follow up on, or choose not to follow up on, and the subsequent choices of data representations that you make. Opie (1992, p. 52) argues that qualitative interpretations:

> are restrictive in the sense that they can appropriate the data to the researcher's interests, so that other significant experiential elements which challenge or partially disrupt that interpretation can be silenced.

A qualitative methodology is subjective and open to multiple interpretations that will be shaped by the researcher's values, the respondents' values, the context and the particular moment in time when the research was conducted. As such, a qualitative methodology offers a snapshot in time; it is historically grounded, and the views expressed are often fluid and subject to change as the respondents construct and reconstruct their social realities sometimes in the process of being interviewed (Hoskins, 2015). Thus, the data presented will be partial and incomplete; an insight into stories in progress rather than final or conclusive accounts.

A further key issue is generalisability. Much qualitative research avoids offering any 'researcher-based' discussions of 'analytical generalisation' because it seeks to offer some 'reader-based' opportunities for generalisability, where the reader:

> on the basis of detailed contextual descriptions of an interview study, judges whether the findings may be generalised to a new situation. (Kvale, 2008, p. 127)

According to Kvale (2008, p. 127), it is the process of providing 'high quality descriptions of the interview process and products', coupled with an awareness of validity and generalisability concerns encompassing the conceptual stages through to the completion stage that lends rigour to the data collection and subsequent analysis. It is due to the

> quality of the craftsmanship in checking, questioning and theorizing the interview findings that leads to knowledge claims that are so powerful and convincing in their own right that they, so to speak, carry the validation with them, like a strong piece of art. (Kvale, 2008, p. 124)

The important point for you to remember is that you have to understand how the research design choices you make will impact on the format of the data that you collect and the associated limitations. Your job as a doctoral student is to defend the choices that you make and be able to explain how you overcame some of the limitations.

Reflective question:

If you are considering using a qualitative methodology, reflect on how you will address the issues of your own subjectivity whilst in the field. What will you do to ensure you gather valid and reliable data? How will you minimise the influence of your own subjectivity when gathering data?

Moving on, I now discuss the uses and limitations of research methods that are typically (but not exclusively) used in quantitative social science research: surveys and questionnaires. I then discuss the uses and limitations of typically qualitative research methods including interviews, focus groups, observations and ethnography. This is not an exhaustive list of methods, but they tend to be the most popular with doctoral students and that is why I have chosen them for discussion in this chapter.

SURVEYS

In this section, we consider what a survey is and when it is appropriate in social science research to use a survey. Surveys and questionnaires are often confused with each as they can seem similar in terms of purpose and execution. However, a survey gathers quite different data to a questionnaire. By understanding when we use surveys and when we use questionnaires, it can be easier to understand the differences between them. Put simply, by understanding what each method does, it is far easier to not mix them up in the future. We use surveys in social science research to gather data for the following purposes:

- To find out information about a population.

- To make inferences about ideas/behaviours/knowledge, etc. – it all depends upon what you want to know.

Surveys can be a useful and effective way to capture trends and attitudinal changes over time (Bryman, 2008; Newby, 2014). For example, peoples' views on climate change or the purpose of education. Surveys can be quantitative, for example, using Likert scales, to measure views and ideas people have in relation to, for example, climate change. But they tend to gather elements of statistical data to show trends over time. They can be qualitative and have open-ended questions that capture subjective views and opinions that people hold about, for example, climate change or views on the purpose of education, but this is less common in social science research. When we gather quantitative survey data, it can be subjected to statistical data analysis and patterns and generalisations can be developed from the findings. Surveys are formulated to gather the views held by groups of people, for example, teachers, refugees, homeowners or climate change activists, so surveys tend to be based on a particular and focussed demographic group.

There are some important points to consider when to use a survey and when not to use a survey:

- They are not an 'easy' way to collect data.

- They require careful thought so that you collect data which is valid and truthful.

Ensuring that you have enough responses to achieve statistical validity is a real challenge when undertaking a survey-based research study as most surveys are self-administered by participants (Newby, 2014). People are busy and time is precious, which makes it challenging to achieve high response rates (Punch, 2003). People tend not to prioritise completing surveys for a range of reasons that can include time and the logic of the questions themselves. Another challenge is ensuring that the responses received are accurate, reliable and truthful. Punch (2003) suggests it is better to have a shorter survey that achieves a higher response rate as the answers are more likely to be accurate. He suggests that a survey taking longer than 20–30 minutes is likely to be too long.

> *Reflective question:*
>
> Take a moment to consider the last time you completed a survey. How long did you spend reflecting on your answers? How engaging and relevant were the questions? Did you try to complete it as quickly as possible, or did you spend some considerable time reflecting on your responses?
>
> Try to use your own experiences of completing surveys to inform your design.

QUESTIONNAIRES

We now consider the distinctiveness of questionnaires and the usefulness of this method. Often confused with surveys, the aim of the questionnaire is to gather data in relation to a singular issue or concern. Questionnaires are defined by Newby (2014, p. 287) as 'structured formats that generate a response by asking individuals specific questions and with the researcher not involved'. The purpose of the questionnaire is to provide understanding of a specific social phenomenon. Questionnaires are:

- The most common survey data collection tool.

- Often printed on paper but can be verbal.

- They are increasingly being used as an online tool – using a button selection technique.

In what follows, I outline some of the different types of questions and other elements you may want to include, to exemplify how you can structure a questionnaire. The main question types are open or closed questions, scaled questions or textual questions. Most questionnaires use a formation of open, closed and Likert scaled response questions.

But what else should feature in your questionnaire? To maximise the potential of gathering data for all questions in a questionnaire, you need to include the following aspects:

- An introduction – this only needs to be a few sentences, but it is important as it must explain to your participants what the questionnaire is about, why the data are being gathered and to reassure them that their responses are confidential and will be anonymised when written up.

- Your contact details to ensure they can get in contact with you if they wish to discuss any aspect of the project and their participation.

- A thank you statement so that they know that they are appreciated.

There are a number of practical issues that need to be addressed when carrying out questionnaire-based research. Some examples of these practical issues you need to think about include how you will find out the postal or email addresses of your participants, for example, schools where they work. Consider if you need to include a stamped address envelope to ensure a good return for paper copies of your questionnaire. Ensure your questionnaire has been carefully proofread before you send it out to participants. If possible, pilot your questionnaire to check that the structure and questions are clear and identify any areas of weakness or ambiguity.

The advantage of using questionnaires to collect data is that they are cheap to administer, particularly online questionnaires. Even postal questionnaires can be relatively good value for money. The data gathered in questionnaires are standardised and can be easy to analyse as the data are directly comparable. Questionnaires are easy to anonymise which is useful from an ethical perspective.

However, there are disadvantages associated with using this method, which include the issue of incomplete data as participants can skip questions – particularly when using a paper questionnaire. Skipping questions can be more difficult when the questionnaire is online as it is possible to not let participants progress without answering each question. It is also argued that questionnaires lack nuance and so provide limited insight into complex social phenomena (Torres, 1998). A further issue is the difficulty in getting responses due to questionnaire fatigue. To address this issue, the design, layout and clarity of your questions can help a great deal. When considering if using a questionnaire is right for your project carefully consider your research question and if, how and why answering it requires questionnaire data.

We now consider qualitative research methods, starting with interviews.

INTERVIEWS

In this section, I outline the uses and limitations of using interviews to collect qualitative data.

Kvale (2008, p. 1) defines an interview as quite literally an 'interview where knowledge is constructed in the inter-action between the interviewer and the interviewee'. He also uses the metaphor of the interviewer as a traveller who is 'on a journey to a distant country that leads to a tale to be told upon returning home' (Kvale, 2008, p. 20) as a way of helping you to conceptualise and enact your role as an interviewer.

To justify her use of interviews, Spradley (1979, p. 34) argued that she wanted to:

> [...] understand the meaning of your experience, to walk in your shoes, to feel things as you feel them, to explain things as you explain them.

This sentiment captures the spirit of carrying an interview study, where the aim is always to tell participant's stories of their experiences and perspectives in a way that they would recognise as a true depiction of their lives.

Kvale (1996) suggests that when carryout any type of interview 'advance preparation is essential to the interaction and outcome of an interview' (p. 126). As such, prior to embarking on any interviews you need to spend time thematising your study by engaging in the 'formulation of research questions and a theoretical clarification of the theme investigated' (Kvale, 2008, p. 37). Kvale is referring to the need for theorised and well-thought out themes, which are informed and shaped by your research questions.

A further reason for preparation in interview-based research is to avoid so-called talk tracks. Kvale (2008, p. 70) cautions that during the interview participants can prepare 'talk tracks' to promote the viewpoints they want to communicate '[...] which requires considerable skill from the interviewer to get beyond'. Therefore, you should ensure in preparing your interview questions, these can in some instances transcend and disrupt some of the 'talk tracks' that participants may follow in the telling of their stories.

There are different types of interviews, and in what follows, I briefly define the key features of unstructured and semi-structured interviews and discuss the uses of each.

An unstructured interview refers to an interview in which there is no specific set of predetermined questions, although the interviewers have topics and points in mind that they intend to cover in the interview setting. An unstructured interview flows like everyday conversation and for those reasons, the questions used are open ended and the interview itself is informal.

A semi-structured interview is defined by Kvale (1996, p. 125) as having:

> [...] a sequence of themes to be covered, as well as suggested questions. Yet at the same time there is an openness to changes of sequence and forms of questions in order to follow up the answers given and the stories told by the subjects.

Kvale argues that the strength of a semi-structured interview is the flexibility in the process to follow-up and probe the responses provided by participants.

A structured interview refers to a questionnaire-style interview, where participants are asked a series of standardised yes/no or maybe questions and they are not invited to elaborate on their responses. A structured interview is useful in gathering directly comparable data, and this can make data analysis an easier task.

These different approaches to interviewing will yield different data and the important point to remember when deciding which type of interview to use is to consider the sort of data your research questions demand. If you are unsure, it is worth piloting an interview to see if any how it helps you gather appropriate data and address your research questions.

Limitations of using Interviews

Despite the usefulness of these three different types of interview as a forum for gathering data, there are wide-ranging criticisms of the method, of which I have selected three, on the basis that these three are arguably the most frequently encountered issues. Interviews are complex for several reasons: the first issue discussed here is that of the unequal power relations between the interviewee and the interviewer and as such 'there is a definite asymmetry of power' in the interview setting (Kvale, 1996, p. 126). Ramazanoğlu and Holland (2002, p. 13) argue that it is important for researchers to consider 'how power is implicated in the process of producing knowledge'. The question of who has power in an interview is a key issue and you must remain alert to the power tensions within the interview process. One practical way to address this issue is through remaining reflexive throughout the data collection, analysis and writing up stages to provide an accurate portrayal of your participants' stories of their experiences.

Second, there is the artificial and constructed nature of an interview in relation to the exchange itself. Drawing on Murphy, Dingwall, Greatbatch, Parker, and Watson's (1998) 'radical critique of interviews', Hammersley (2003, p. 120) argues that:

> *the radicalness of the recent critique lies in its scepticism about the capacity of interviews to provide accurate representations, either of the self or of the world.*

The argument here is centred on the constructed nature of what people say in interviews, which Hammersley (2003, p. 120) sees as being:

> *closely attuned to the local context and is driven by a preoccupation with self-presentation and/or with persuasion of others, rather than being concerned primarily with presenting facts about the world or about the informant him or herself.*

The question for you, as the researcher, is: how is it possible to present these 'artful productions (interview data)' that may be 'shaped by concerns about self-presentation or persuasion' as 'accurate representations' (Hammersley, 2003, p. 123) of your participants' stories? Should, for example, your analysis presents the 'performative character of what is said in interviews, as accurate representations' (Hammersley, 2003, p. 123)? In practice, this means that the 'interpretation of data is not merely a theoretical exercise; it also is a contextual exercise' (Ball, 1990, p. 164). This quote refers to the need to consider the context in which your interviews take place and the power relations present when you are interviewing.

The third and final limitation relates to the trustworthiness, validity and generalisability of interview data. This issue arises from the subjective rather than the objective nature of qualitative interviews. Such issues go 'beyond technical or conceptual concerns and raise epistemological questions of objectivity of knowledge and the nature of interview research' (Kvale, 2008, p. 120). Obtaining trustworthy and valid data via open-ended qualitative interviews is disputed (see, e.g., Hammersley, 2003; Kvale, 2018). Taking trustworthiness and validity as the first issue, the decisions of why, what and how you can address these issues is discussed in a wide range of literature (e.g., Bryman, 2008; Miles & Huberman, 1994; Newby, 2014; Walford, 2001; Weis & Fine, 2005). According to Kvale (1996, p. 242), achieving validity in the research process is not:

> *some final verification or product control; verification is built into the research process with continual checks on the credibility, plausibility and trustworthiness of the findings.*

Thus, it is achieved through the process of checking, questioning and theorising your data set (and the problems associated with this) and subsequent analysis (see Kvale, 2008, pp. 123–124), and as a researcher, you will need to try and maintain a 'continual process of validation' which will 'permeate the entire research process'. In practice, this means that you will need to ensure you are reflecting on your data collection and analysis throughout the research process.

Moving on, we now consider group interviews, known as focus groups, and we explore the uses and limitations of this method.

FOCUS GROUPS

Focus group interviews are quite simply semi-structured or unstructured interviews carried out in a group setting. This approach to data gathering can be used when your research is seeking to understand shared experiences amongst a group who share some of the same experiences, for example, in their work lives or home lives. The benefit of carrying out focus group-based research is the 'interaction found in a group' (Morgan, 1988, p. 12), which is particularly useful to 'stimulate people in making explicit their views, perceptions, motives and reasons' (Punch, 2009, p. 147). When undertaking research with children, focus groups can be particularly useful to encourage participants to talk about their experiences in the context and comfort of a group. In addition, carrying out focus group research can disrupt, to some extent, the power dynamics within the research process, as the participants have some opportunities to define and direct some of the information they chose to share with you as the researcher.

However, the strength of the focus group – the interaction found therein – can also be viewed as a weakness because some personalities in the group can be stronger than others, which can mean that not all perspectives and opinions are successfully shared within the group (Kamberelis & Dimitriadis, 2013). As the researcher, it will be important for you to manage the interactions in the group and try to ensure parity in responses between your participants.

A further challenge when carrying out focus group research relates to the difficulty of transcribing the interaction as it can be challenging to identify who is saying what. A way of addressing this issue is to request all participants state their name when responding to a question to achieve greater accuracy in the transcription, analysis and subsequent data representations that you make.

OBSERVATIONS – STRENGTHS AND LIMITATIONS OF THE METHOD

The next method we consider is observation. Some form of observation is often used in educational research – usually in combination with interviews. Observations tend to take place over a period of time to enable researchers to build up a picture of a social context over time. However, it is not always possible to have access to a research site for extended periods of time so you will need to work within the constraints of your context.

Observations can be covert or overt (unknown/known) and participant or non-participant (active/inactive). Each of these is now defined:

Covert participant observation is where the researcher is not known as being a researcher by the participants but is involved in what they're doing. This is quite rare in social and educational research. An example is a study by James Patrick (1973) *A Glasgow Gang Observed*. Patrick, a young schoolteacher, went undercover with the help of one of his students to investigate the goings-on of a teenage gang.

Covert non-participant observation is where the researcher is not known as being a researcher by the participants and is not involved in what they're doing. Again, it is quite rare in social and educational research. An example could be studies of crowd behaviour at a football match, the way students use social space in a library or social setting, etc. It has to be quite a populous/anonymous event, so that the researcher does not stand out.

Overt participant observation is where the researcher is known as being a researcher by the participants and is involved in what they're doing. These 'overt' practices are far more likely as an option by social and educational researchers. An example is Whyte's (1943) classic study *Street Corner Society*. Whyte spent long periods of time living in a neighbourhood in Boston mainly inhabited by first- and second-generation Italian migrants. It was considered a dangerous and crime-ridden place. Whyte spent a long time getting to know the various people there, and was eventually accepted, and took part in group activities, but it was always known that he was a researcher and was at the same time studying them.

Overt non-participant observation is where the researcher is known as being a researcher by the participants and is not involved in what they are doing. This is the most common form of observation activity and the one most commonly used with children in the context of educational research. The observer is visibly an outsider to the group, the group knows they are there and will often know why they are there. The observer tries not to get involved.

Some challenges associated with carrying out observations relate to what you observe and why. Observations can be structured or unstructured. To carry out a structured observation, the researcher begins with a list of things to observe and counts the number of times that this action, behaviour, activity or talk occurs in the context. To carry out an unstructured observation, the research makes notes on any action, behaviour, activity or talk in the context in an unstructured way. There are issues with both approaches as it can be difficult to count instances accurately in many research contexts, for example, a classroom or a hospital ward, and it can be challenging to be sure that unstructured observations capture the complexity and variety of what is going on in a given social context in any given moment in time (DeWalt & DeWalt, 2011). To address these challenges, you must give careful thought and attention to what you are going to observe and how you are going to record your observations. A pilot observation is always useful as you can try out how much is reasonable to observe in one observation session. By carefully planning the focus of your observations, you can gather useful, comparable and rigorous data.

ETHNOGRAPHY – STRENGTHS AND LIMITATIONS OF THE APPROACH

The final method reviewed in this chapter is ethnography, which has been described by Agar (1980, p. 9) as follows:

> *In ethnography [...] you learn something ('collect some data'), then you try to make sense out of it ('analysis'), then you go back and see if the interpretation makes sense in light of new experience ('collect more data'), then you refine your interpretation ('more analysis'), and so on. The process is dialectic, not linear.*

The term dialectic refers to the art or practice of arriving at the truth by the exchange of logical arguments.

There is an important difference between what Green and Bloome (1997) refer to as 'doing ethnography' compared with 'adopting an ethnographic perspective' and compared with 'using ethnographic tools'. Doing ethnography is the approach taken by many social anthropologists. Classically an anthropologist would go and live with members of another culture for long periods of time, observing them and interviewing them and collecting documentary materials. For this reason, ethnography as a method is wider than just observation, as it includes interviewing and documentary analysis. Adopting an ethnographic perspective refers to taking 'a more focused approach (i.e., do less than a comprehensive ethnography) to study particular aspects of everyday life and cultural practices of a social group' (Green & Bloome, 1997, p. 4). Finally, using ethnographic tools refers to the 'use of methods and techniques usually associated with fieldwork. These methods may or may not be guided by cultural theories or questions about social life of group members' (Green & Bloome, 1997, p. 4). It is important at the outset that you identify which method is more useful and appropriate to enable you to address your research questions.

Ball (1990) highlights some of the key challenges and limitations of working ethnographically in the following quotation:

> For the student ethnographer, the decision to choose field-work as the primary method for research is typically a plunge into the unknown. Participant observation in natural settings is probably the least well understood, most feared, and most abused of all the contemporary methods of educational research. Crucially – and this is often ignored or underplayed by methods texts and in methods courses – the choice of ethnography carries with it implications about theory, epistemology, and ontology. Ethnography not only implies engagement of the researcher in the world under study; it also implies a commitment to a search for meaning, a suspension of preconceptions, and an orientation to discovery. In other words, ethnography involves risk, uncertainty, and discomfort (p. 157).

Ball (1990) goes on to highlight that researchers must work hard in the field for extended periods of time to ensure that they gather the data they need:

> they must charm the respondents into cooperation. They must learn to blend or pass in the research setting, put up with the boredom and the horrors of the empty notebook, cringe in the face of faux pas made in front of those whose cooperation they need, and engage in the small deceptions and solve the various ethical dilemmas which crop up in most ethnographies. (p. 157)

The key challenges here relate to the difficulty of gathering data ethnographically, the time needed to build relationships that make gathering useful data much more successful and the importance of navigating a social context where you have little understanding of the everyday nuances taking place.

Despite the challenges, ethnography can provide detailed descriptions of social life and social context that is not easily found using other research methods (see, e.g., Crowe & Hoskins, 2019). Ethnography is also, according to Hymes (1996, p. 13) a useful approach in a democratic society:

> The fact that good ethnography entails trust and confidence, that it requires some narrative accounting, and that it is an extension of a universal form of personal knowledge, makes

me think that ethnography is peculiarly appropriate to a democratic society.

Now that we have reviewed methodologies and methods, it is useful to consider a real-life research case study that draws on some of the issues raised so far in this chapter.

REAL-LIFE CASE STUDY

To exemplify some of the challenges I encountered when carrying out qualitative research, I use my own doctoral research study to provide a case study of the methodology choices I made. The aim here is to share with you the decisions I made, the strengths and limitations of my choices and how I addressed the methodological limitations inherent in my own research.

My PhD examined how senior female academics (all were professors) constructed their career 'success' and how those constructions were shaped by social class, gender and ethnicity. To understand how to frame and interpret my participants' stories and experiences, I decided to take a feminist epistemological approach to my research. I followed Maynard's (1994, p. 10) view that:

Epistemology is concerned with providing a philosophical grounding for deciding what kinds of knowledge are possible and how we can ensure that they are both adequate and legitimate.

I argued in my thesis that all research is informed and shaped by the researcher's assumptions, whether or not these are made explicit. My epistemological assumptions influenced my decisions of methodological perspective and choice of methods. Denscombe (1998, p. 3) suggests that every research decision 'brings with it a set of assumptions about the social world it investigates' and that, as such, 'each choice brings with it a set of advantages and disadvantages'.

To understand how senior female academics constructed and experienced their objective career 'success', I decided to utilise a social-constructionist epistemology, which is outlined by Edwards, Ashmore, and Potter (1995, p. 436, cited in Burr, 2003, p. 92) as follows:

the epistemic sense of social constructionism rests on the notion that as soon as we begin to think or talk about the world, we also necessarily begin to represent. Talk involves the creation or construction of particular accounts of what the world is like.

This perspective views society as socially constructed through discourse and people's daily interactions with each other, and these interactions are manipulated to maintain the social and economic status quo across society (Burr, 2003). Such an approach was appropriate for my feminist research which sought to disrupt and challenge taken-for-granted norms and assumptions about women's lives and their careers.

Feminist epistemologies are concerned with challenging 'the legacy of white male hegemony which tyrannizes many forms of knowledge, knowers, and approaches to knowing' (Marshall & Young, 2006, p. 68). To do this involves problematising the familiar, the taken for granted. Yet there is no one particular feminist epistemology and much detailed discussion about what counts as feminist epistemology (see, e.g., Hekman, 1997; Smith, 1997). Indeed, as Ramazanoğlu and Holland (2002, p. 24) point out 'there is more than one feminist theory and more than one feminist epistemological position'. However, according to Ramazanoğlu and Holland (2002, p. 103), there are some key characteristics of feminist epistemology:

> *feminist knowledge encompasses movement between partial knowledges, limited experiences and specific social locations, and justifiable, accountable, reasonable knowledge of social interaction, experiences, meanings, relations and structures.*

I also recognised that my attempt to 'tell "better stories" of gendered social realities' (Ramazanoğlu & Holland, 2002, p. 3) was fraught with challenges, problems and obstacles that had to be grappled with. For example, feminist researchers are:

> *under increasing pressure from the wider academic community to justify their knowledge in terms of, for example, rationality, validity, rules of method, control or subjectivity and political bias. (Ramazanoğlu & Holland, 2002, p. 3)*

According to Lather (1991, p. 71, italics as original) social constructionism is central to feminist research. She argues:

> *To do feminist research is to put the social construction of gender at the centre of one's inquiry .... The overt ideological*

goal of feminist research in the human sciences is to correct both the invisibility and distortion of female experience in ways relevant to ending women's unequal social position.

Thus, feminists' concern with giving expression to women's voices can 'be seen as part of a broad trend towards contextualizing social life through an appreciation of individual experiences' (Coffey & Delamont, 2000, p. 61). Drawing on a qualitative methodology facilitated my efforts to understand the nuances and differences of how my cohort experienced and constructed their engagement with having, what might be described as, objectively successful careers.

Yet despite its usefulness, I want to finish the case study by outlining a couple of the limitations of my chosen epistemological and methodological approach to the data gathering and analysis and how I addressed these in my research. The first criticism is one levelled at feminist researchers who, it has been argued, may sometimes focus on experiences related to gender at the exclusion of other factors such as class, race, nationalism, sexuality and age (Ramazanoğlu & Holland, 2002). Thus, within this viewpoint, women's lives are liable to be reducible to a narrow and one-dimensional identity. However, my research did, with some success and failure, engage with social class background, gender and race in an attempt to offer a thorough and detailed account of how the respondents' identity shapes their experiences and constructions of career success.

The second criticism, again related to undertaking research informed by a feminist perspective, is the blurring between English-language feminism and its brushes with post-modernism and post-structuralism, which has resulted in questions being asked about power relations and 'the foundations of feminist knowledge and methodology' (Ramazanoğlu & Holland, 2002, p. 4). My research took a post-modern approach where facets of identity (gender, class and race) were not 'abandoned' but interrogated, which:

means that their histories should be questioned, the constitution and crossings of their boundaries examined, and their multiplicities enabled, in order to show what makes some identities powerful in relation to others, and how this power is exercised. (Ramazanoğlu & Holland, 2002, p. 92)

As such, I questioned the aspects of my respondents' identities I set out to examine to consider how power is mediated through aspects, or combinations of aspects, of identity which result in unequal distributions of power between people.

The aim of this case study has been to show you how epistemology and methodology informs research design, how all epistemological and methodological approaches have flaws and how to go about addressing these flaws. To begin the process of designing social science research, you must first understand your epistemological position. You must then decide upon an appropriate methodology and ensure that the methods used will enable you to gather relevant data to address your research questions.

SUMMARY OF THIS CHAPTER

In this chapter, I have outlined the key features of different methodologies and methods used in social science research. The aim has been to help you understand how design decisions influence the sort of data that you can gather. From reading this chapter, the main points for you to take away and reflect on are:

- How do your research questions inform the type of methodology and method(s) that you will use?

- How will you address any of the research methods' weaknesses in the process of gathering and analysing your data?

- How will you defend your choice of methodology and method(s) in a viva?

When you can answer these questions convincingly, then you have made significant progress in your work, so well done! Remember, in social science quantitative or qualitative research, it is important to ensure that you understand the strengths and limitations of the methodology and methods you are going to use and to work with your supervisory team so that you can explain to them how you will address any shortcomings.

This chapter has covered some of the most common methods used in social science research, but of course there are others. In a short chapter it is difficult to cover all of the useful methods, particularly those related to new technologies. As such, I finish this chapter by signposting some further reading that you might find useful.

FURTHER READING

In this section, I outline two useful readings for you to follow up on and briefly summarise the value of the reading. The first useful reading to follow up on is:

Hines, C. (2005). *Virtual methods. Issues in social research on the internet*. Berg: Oxford.

This reading will introduce you to some of the key issues associated with carrying out research in online spaces. The chapters in this edited book each provide a detailed exploration of the pro-research design and methodological approaches, problems and opportunities surrounding internet-based research. If you are planning a research project involving the Internet, you will find this book an essential guide.

Punch, K. (2009). *Introduction to research methods in education*. London: Sage.

This book provides a thorough and balanced look at the variety and complexity of methods that can be used in education. Whilst the focus is on educational contexts, the book is written in a way that makes it relevant to all social science researchers, regardless of their subject area.

REFERENCES

Agar, M (1980). Getting better quality stuff: Methodological competition in an interdisciplinary niche. *Urban Life*, 9(1), 34–50.

Ball, S. J. (1990). Self-doubt and soft data: Social and technical trajectories in ethnographic fieldwork. *International Journal of Qualitative Studies in Education*, 3(2), 157–171.

Braun, A., Ball, S., Maguire, M., & Hoskins, K. (2011). Taking context seriously: Towards explaining policy enactments in the secondary school. *Discourse: Studies in the Cultural Politics of Education*, 32(4), 585–596.

Brown, P., & Lauder, H. B. (1991). Education, economy and social change. *International Studies in Sociology of Education*, 1(1–2), 3–23, doi:10.1080/0962021910010102

Bryman, A. (2008). *Social research methods* (3rd ed.). Oxford: Oxford University Press.

Burr, V. (2003). *Social constructionism* (2nd ed.). East Sussex: Routledge.

Coffey, A., & Delamont, S. (2000). *Feminism and the classroom teacher: Research, praxis and pedagogy*. London: RoutledgeFalmer.

Crowe, N., & Hoskins, K. (2019). Researching transgression: Ana as a youth subculture in the age of digital ethnography. *Societies*, 9(3), 1–11.

Delamont, S. (1992). Old fogies and intellectual women: An episode in academic history. *The Women's History Review*, 1(1), 39–61.

Denscombe, M. (1998). *The good research guide: For small-scale social research projects*. Milton Keynes: Open University.

DeWalt, K. M., & DeWalt, B. R. (2011). *Participant observation: A guide for fieldworkers*. Plymouth: AltaMira Press.

Edwards, D., Ashmore, M., & Potter, J. (1995). Death and furniture: The rhetoric, politics and theology of bottom line arguments against relativism. *History of the Human Sciences*, 8, 25–29.

Green, J., & Bloome, D. (1997). Ethnography and ethnographers of and in education: A situated perspective. In J. Flood, S. B. Heath, & D. Lapp (Eds.), *Handbook of research on teaching literacy through the communicative and visual arts* (pp. 181–202). New York, NY: Macmillan Publishers.

Hammersley, M (2003). Recent radical criticism of interview studies: Any implications for the sociology of education? *British Journal of Sociology of Education*, 24(1), 119–126.

Hekman, S. J. (1997). Reply to Hartsock, Collins, Harding and Smith. *Signs*, 25(21), 399–402.

Hines, C. (2005). *Virtual methods. Issues in social research on the internet*. Berg: Oxford.

Hoskins, K. (2015). Researching female professors: The difficulties of representation, positionality and power in feminist research. *Gender and Education*, 27(4), 393–411.

Hymes, D. (1996). *Ethnography, linguistics, narrative inequality: Toward an understanding of voice*. London: Taylor & Francis.

Kamberelis, G., & Dimitriadis, G. (2013). *Focus groups: From structured interviews to collective conversations*. London: Routledge.

Kvale, S. (1996). *Interviews: An introduction to qualitative research interviewing*. Thousand Oaks, CA: Sage.

Kvale, S. (2008). *Doing interviews*. London: Sage.

Kvale, S. (2018). *Doing interviews*: London. Sage.

Lather, P. (1991). *Getting smart: Feminist research and pedagogy with/in the postmodern*. London: Routledge.

Lessa, L. (2006). Discursive struggles within social welfare: Restaging teen motherhood. *British Journal of Social Work*, *36*(2), 283–298.

Marshall, C., & Young, M. D. (2006). Gender and feminist methodology. In C. Skelton, B. Francis, & L. Smulyan (Eds.), *Sage handbook: Gender and education* (pp. 63–78). Thousand Oaks, CA: Sage.

Maynard, M. (1994). Methods, practice and epistemology: The debate about feminism and research. In M. Maynard & J. Purvis (Eds.), *Researching women's lives from a feminist perspective* (pp. 10–26). London: Taylor & Francis.

Miles, M., & Huberman, M. (1994). *Qualitative data analysis* (2nd ed.). London: Sage.

Morgan, D. L. (1988). *Focus groups as qualitative research*. Thousand Oaks, CA: Sage.

Murphy, E., Dingwall, R., Greatbatch, D., Parker, S., & Watson, P. (1998). Qualitative research methods in health technology assessment: A review of the literature. *Health Technology Assessment*, *2*(16), 1–260. Retrieved from http://www.hta.nhsweb.nhs.uk/execsumm/summ216.htm. Accessed on August 2018.

Newby, P. (2014). *Research methods for education*. London: Routledge.

Opie, A. (1992). Qualitative research, appropriation of the "other" and empowerment. *Feminist Review*, *40*, 52–69.

Patrick, J. (1973). *A Glasgow gang observed*. London: Eyre Methuen.

Punch, K. (2003). *Survey Research: the Basics*. London: Sage.

Punch, K. (2009). *Introduction to research methods in education*. London: Sage.

Ramazanoğlu, C., & Holland, J. (2002). *Feminist methodology: Challenges and choices*. London: Sage.

Silverman, D. (2006). *Interpreting qualitative data: Methods for analyzing talk, text and interaction*. London: Sage.

Skeggs, B. (1997). *Formations of class and gender: Becoming respectable*. London: Sage.

Smith, D. E. (1997). Comment on Hekman's "Truth and method: feminist standpoint theory revisited." *Signs*, 22(21), 392–397.

Spradley, J. (1979). *The ethnographic interview*. Belmont, CA: Wadsworth Thomson Learning.

Stanley, L., & Wise, S. (1993). *Breaking out again: Feminist ontology and epistemology*. London: Routledge.

Torres, C. A. (1998). *Education, power and personal biography: Dialogues with critical educators*. New York, NY: Routledge.

Usher, R., & Edwards, R. (1994). *Postmodernism and education: Different voices, different worlds*. London: Routledge.

Walford, G. (2001). *Doing qualitative educational research: A personal guide to the research process*. London: Continuum.

Weis, L., & Fine, M. (2005). *Beyond silenced voices* (2nd ed.). Albany, NY: SUNY Press.

Whyte, W. F. (1943). *Street corner society: The social structure of an Italian slum*. Chicago, IL: The University of Chicago Press.

Williams, M., & May, T. (Eds.). (1998). *Knowing the social world*. Buckingham: Open University Press.

7

ANALYSING AND INTERPRETING DATA

Jim Crawley

INTRODUCTION

With appropriate, carefully planned, high-quality data analysis and interpretation, you will almost always get the best from your data and will take significant steps towards the answer/s to your research question/s and meeting your research objectives. Researchers usually find the process of analysing and interpreting the data they have gathered one of the most rewarding parts of the whole experience. This stage of your research should be exciting, informing, absorbing and fulfilling. From the moment your first piece of data has been collected, analysis and interpretation start to take place, even if at that early stage this takes place informally and mainly in your head. The early analysis and interpretation of data will give you a strong impression of the success (or otherwise) of the research to date. As the process continues, the stories from your data unfold. When data analysis is successful, the stories unfold naturally and clearly, and they will illuminate and bring your findings to life as you have planned, intended and hoped.

There are, of course, also challenges with analysing and interpreting data. You may, like many researchers before you, feel weighed down under the pressure of analysing large (or small) quantities of complex data, and the stage of your research which was supposed to lead smoothly to your discussion and conclusions becomes a difficult situation where alterations, additions, shifts of emphasis and even changes of direction may need to be made. However well you prepare and organise for data analysis and interpretation, part of the excitement of carrying out research is that it can never be entirely predictable. It is highly likely that you will encounter at least some level of complication with this stage of research in just the same way as you may with others but resolving questions, reducing uncertainties and solving problems successfully with your data analysis and interpretation is an important step on the way to completing your thesis. Engaging in critically analytical discussions and revealing interesting and enlightening conclusions is a central part of doctoral work which will lead your thinking into coherence and originality, and it is through the stage of analysing and interpreting data that this will largely happen.

Analysing and interpreting data is therefore at the heart of every piece of research, and succeeding with this stage is crucial.

A chapter such as this can only scratch the surface of the multitude of approaches, methods and techniques which can be involved in analysing qualitative, quantitative and mixed-methods research. The focus therefore is to provide a selection of what is needed to help you to bring your data to life and get the most from it. A range of ways in which the data analysis and interpretation process is supported will be explained, explored, discussed and critiqued. Steps and structures to assist you in engaging with your data with care, accuracy, rigour, imagination and reflexivity will be considered, and advice on overcoming problems with both analysis and interpretation will be included. Further reading will also be provided to take your understanding and use of data analysis further.

At the end of this chapter, you should be able to:

- Identify and select practical, flexible, valid, socially responsible and fit for purpose types of data analysis to help answer your research questions.

- Interrogate, collate, find connections, bring together and make sense of your data through analysis and interpretation.

- Discuss your data and signpost conclusions from the analysis and interpretation stage/s which will contribute towards answering your research question/s.

- Evaluate the effectiveness of your analysis and interpretation in your research.

KEY DISCUSSIONS AND DEBATES ABOUT DATA ANALYSIS AND INTERPRETATION AND WHY THIS STAGE IS SO IMPORTANT

As with most other areas of education, and indeed many areas of research, there are numerous ideas, discussions and debates about the nature and purpose of data analysis and interpretation. This section of this chapter introduces a selection of key principles relating to planning for and engaging with data analysis and interpretation from a number of authoritative writers and thinkers.

Key Questions:

(1) What are the key discussions and debates about data analysis and interpretation and why is this stage of your research so important?

(2) What types of data analysis are available and how do you decide which to use?

(3) How do you develop your analysis and interpretation into sufficient and substantial discussion and conclusions?

(4) How do you evaluate the quality of your data analysis and interpretation?

PRACTICALITY, CLARITY AND VALIDITY

Bryman (2012, p. 13) argues that

> *data analysis is a stage that incorporates several elements. At the most obvious level, it might be taken to mean the application of statistical techniques to the data that have been collected.*

He readily accepts, however, that 'alternative approaches are sometimes taken' and that 'there are other things going on when data are being analysed.' Atkins and Duckworth (2019) also emphasise the practicality of this stage whilst emphasising its importance within the intentions and objectives of the research when stating

> the importance of analysis or 'the separation of something into its component parts' (Denscombe, 1998, p. 239) is a critical activity which should provide a credible response to the questions posed within the study. (p. 132).

This striving for practicality, clarity and validity

> demands that any analysis is conducted in a systematic and structured way which recognises issues such as bias or threats to the validity of the study, in order to develop and sustain a rigorous and credible argument. (Atkins & Duckworth, 2019, p. 132)

Arthur, Waring, Coe, and Hedges (2012) propose a means of helping to ensure that data analysis and interpretation provides the best quality evidence possible, by advising all researchers to ask three key questions when evaluating the quality of the research. These are adapted below as reflective questions.

Reflective questions

1. Are the aims and objectives of the research clear and explicit?

2. Does the evidence support the claims?

3. Could a different analysis and interpretation of the data have been interpreted or analysed differently, and could this have led to different conclusions?

Practicality, clarity and validity, contained within a structure which supports systematic and structured evaluation, are highly important principles in data analysis and interpretation.

FLEXIBILITY, ADAPTABILITY AND FITNESS FOR PURPOSE

Supporting the practicality, clarity and validity of the research can be addressed in many ways, and this often requires flexibility and adaptability on behalf of the researcher in relation to the analysis and interpretation of data. As Cohen, Manion, and Morrison (2017, p. 130) outline

> *there are no blueprints for how and when to conduct and write-up the data analysis. Each piece of research suggests its own most suitable designs, and these may be iterative and emergent, with several stages which move from quantitative to qualitative data and vice versa and their consequent own suitable ways of presenting the data analysis and the timing of these.*

What links these elements together is the 'fitness for purpose and legitimacy' of the data analysis which 'must be appropriate for the kinds of data gathered'. Overall then 'fitness for purpose is complemented by the need for clarity, relevance and ease in understanding the data and how they answer the research question' (Cohen et al., 2017, p. 371).

Within this clarity and fitness for purpose, it is also important to remember that the researcher has immense control over their data analysis and which statistics or details to include or use, and what they may or may not reveal. Remembering Arthur et al.'s (2012) three questions stated above can also be very helpful in ensuring flexibility, adaptability and fitness for purpose remain at the forefront of your data analysis and interpretation.

THE CHANGING WORLD WE LIVE IN

The key principles so far considered in this section have been situated in the more practical aspects of research, but researchers should not forget that research is taking place in a changing world, and that it can contribute to helping that world change into a better place. Recognition of the importance of situating research within its societal context is another strongly argued principle of data analysis and interpretation. Atkins and Duckworth (2019, p. 16) argue that educational research should explore 'understandings of social justice and equity' and 'the contribution that research for equity and social justice can make to new emerging methods and methodologies'. In terms of analysis within socially just research, this should involve 'self-analysis, but also practical social-practice analysis' and that the knowledge produced can affect 'human reality' (Atkins & Duckworth, 2019, p. 38). Cohen et al. (2017, p. 54) suggest that researchers should 'be concerned with the political consequences of their research (e.g. consequential validity), not only the conduct of the research and data analysis itself. They continue to argue that research must lead to change and improvement' and that it 'is a political activity with a political agenda'.

This concern to contribute to a changing world can extend research into greater participation of the research subjects in all aspects of the research, including data analysis, and it can also have profound benefits for the researcher. It also brings additional challenges in terms of validity and fitness for purpose as it can change how and if we

> *approach the study honestly and openly. Exploration of personal beliefs makes the investigator more aware of the potential judgements that can occur during data collection, analysis and generation of knowledge based on the researcher's belief system rather than on the actual data collected from participants. (Atkins & Duckworth, 2019, p. 78)*

This brief exploration of some key guiding principles associated with data analysis and interpretation has suggested that practicality, clarity and validity combined with systematic but flexible structures and adaptability should ensure your research is fit for purpose. Reinforcing this with an enhanced societal awareness of the potential for a contribution to a changing world of education and enhanced social justice will also enhance analysis and interpretation of your data, and the ways in which you carry them both out. If these principles are kept to the fore of your research, it should lead you confidently on to drawing conclusions from your data.

WHY IS DATA ANALYSIS AND INTERPRETATION SO IMPORTANT?

As Ashley (2012, p. 36) states, data analysis 'should not be a process that is only thought about and carried out after data collection has occurred. Instead the analysis of data is central to the research process'. This stage is of central importance to the research process, because it is the stage where data can be 'meaningfully analysed to build descriptions and explanations that answer the research questions'. As mentioned earlier in this chapter, data analysis and interpretation needs to be carried out in a systematic and structured manner to ensure it is fit for purpose. If this is not the case, the success of your research is undermined and threatened. As Hambleton (2012, p. 241) asserts, there are many steps in research, and 'some of the steps, if completed poorly, can be corrected'. Some steps however, such as incomplete audio recording of interviews, failures of transcription or smaller amounts of data from participants than planned can be 'impossible to fix without collecting more data'. Hedges (2012) outlines what he refers to as 'threats to data analysis', and these are included as reflective questions below.

Reflective questions – is your data analysis threatened by …?

1. 'Unreliable data elements – problems with fieldnotes, observation records, measurements often due to poor planning and organisation.

2. Incorrect analysis – limited verification of data, improper statistical methods relying on memory, inaccurate summaries.

3. Incorrect data elements – focussing/selecting on the wrong participants; deceit, overinterpretation or bias from participants.' (p. 28)

These threats to data analysis can leave the researcher with results which are not

> adequate to draw conclusions or if the analysis is not organised to permit drawing valid conclusions even if the materials collected are sufficient to do so then the conclusions drawn from the research design will be invalid. (Hedges, 2012, p. 28)

Quite simply, data analysis and interpretation is so important because if it is inadequate, it is likely that the whole of your research will also be inadequate.

WHAT TYPES OF DATA ANALYSIS ARE AVAILABLE AND HOW DO YOU DECIDE WHICH TO USE?

This section of this chapter includes a small selection of types of data analysis and considers each by asking these three questions. What is it? Why should you use it? What problems can be associated with it? The four included examples of types of data analysis can never represent fully the whole range, but they do contain viable and workable processes and procedures which will provide you with valuable insights when planning your own data analysis and interpretation. As you will see, they do have similarities as well as differences, so the choice of which data analysis type to use is not always entirely straightforward. They are Thematic Analysis, Grounded Theory, Computer-Assisted Qualitative Data Analysis (CAQDA) and Mixed-Methods Analysis.

Thematic Analysis

What is it?

Thematic analysis, as the title suggests, is a type of data analysis where themes which emerge from the research are identified as the key elements of analysis. Clarke and Braun (2018) liken themes to 'key characters in the story we are telling about the data' and suggest that each theme 'has an "essence" or core concept that underpins and unites the observations, much like characters'. Denscombe (2014) adds that analysis moves from identifying possible patterns or potential themes in the data to connecting those patterns as emerging themes and then to testing the viability and validity of those themes. As the themes emerge, they are written up as part of the analysis. The researcher will almost certainly move backwards and forward through these stages until they are satisfied that the key themes have been identified and written up successfully.

Why should you use it?

Thematic analysis is not directly associated with any theoretical framework (e.g. in the way that Critical Analysis is). It can therefore be used across and within different theoretical frameworks and can also be used to do different things within them (Braun & Clarke, 2006). Making explicit the theoretical framework/s you are using within your research is still an essential part of your thesis, but thematic analysis has a strong level of flexibility and adaptability whilst it is also structured and systematic. As a result, it can be fit for purpose when used in a range of qualitative research studies. Focussing on patterns and themes can also assist when seeking to place your results in relation to other research and existing theories which you will have identified in your literature review.

What Problems can be Associated with it?

Braun and Clarke (2006) also identify challenges which can present themselves with thematic analysis. These include the following:

- *Failure to analyse the data* – you can become so engaged with collecting extracts of your data that you almost get trapped in individual themes and do not extract the connections and differences between themes in ways which lead to a deeper interpretation of the data.

- *Taking data headings as your themes* – you may take the headings or section titles of data (e.g. interview questions or survey questions) and use them as your themes rather than analyse themes across the full data set.

- *A weak or unconvincing analysis* – this can happen when you do not select enough examples from the data in order to provide a convincing analysis for the external reader.

- *When analysis and interpretation are not consistent with the data* – the use of unconvincing examples which are not consistent with the theoretical frameworks you are using.

These problems can also occur with other types of analysis.

Grounded Theory

What is it?

Cohen et al. (2017) provide a helpfully clear explanation of grounded theory as follows:

> *Grounded theory ... is not predetermined, but, rather, emerges from, and is consequent to, data [...] it is grounded in data and rises up from the ground of data: a 'bottom-up' process. It seeks to generate rather than simply to test an existing theory.*

They make it clear that data collection and analysis take place simultaneously during grounded theory research and add that grounded theory

> *identifies key features and relationships emerging from data and categories and then proposes a plausible explanation of the phenomenon under study by drawing on the data generated, ensuring that the theory explains all the data without exception. (Cohen et al., 2017, p. 178)*

Grounded theory can be used to 'clarify concepts or produce new theories' and 'explore a new topic and produce new insights' (Denscombe, 2014, p. 26).

Why should I use it?

Grounded theory is seen as not only systematic and structured but also flexible and creative (Waring, 2012). Theory develops from the start of the process and is to the forefront at every stage. It is argued to be 'an orderly, methodical and partially controlled way of moving from data to theory' (Cohen et al., 2017, p. 1293). The 'intention of grounded theory is to build and generate theory rather than to test an existing theory, providing researchers with tools to generate this theory through data analysis' and 'to weigh up alternative explanations' (Cohen et al., 2017, p. 1294). Grounded theory is popular and used extensively in educational research.

What are the Problems Associated with it?

Grounded theory has been considered somewhat too open at times in terms of the place of theory, and the emphasis on developing new theory in a creative manner has been argued to not take enough account of existing theory. This criticism and the assertion that grounded theory lacks rigour can be offset by taking a carefully systematic approach and by remaining sensitive to other theories whilst concentrating on the development of new theory. Because the grounded theory researcher is 'basing an investigation upon whether certain theories do or do not work, the researcher embarks on a voyage of discovery' (Denscombe, 2014, p. 157). This can prove difficult when sampling and planning research as you can get carried away by the voyage of discovery and not remain systematically focussed on answering your research question/s. However carefully grounded theory research is planned and carried out, it can be unpredictable. Although most unpredictability is manageable, this could be a challenge for some researchers.

CAQDA

What is it?

CAQDA is exactly what the title suggests, and that is making use of computer technology to assist with analysing data. There are many apps, pieces of software, specialist and generalist programmes available, and some, such as NVivo and SPSS, are extremely popular. Routinely used software such as MS Word and MS Excel can also be helpful in identifying and testing out patterns within data analysis and interpretation, and simple techniques such as word searches can be extremely illuminating. Devices available in public organisations such as microfiche readers can also be a means of accessing some sets of data. It is also possible to share data analysis across teams of researchers successfully. The capacity of current technology to be used to assist data analysis has opened up a number of new possibilities for researchers.

Why should I use it?

When you have large amounts of data, and when you are looking for possible connections between that data, CAQDA can be particularly helpful. Other practical advantages include the reduction of transcription time and the capacity to store large quantities of data securely and with good access; capacity to transfer and share files with ease; once data has been collected using software, indexing and categorising can be carried out, developed, changed and scrutinised. Gibbs (2012) suggests three questions to ask about whether to use CAQDA, which are as follows:

Reflective questions

1. Do you have enough data to make it worthwhile?
2. Will the software you are considering genuinely support your research and data analysis plans?
3. Can you carry out your analysis successfully without the use of CAQDA?

What are the Problems Associated with it?

Gibbs (2012) also helpfully outlines some of the problems which can be associated with CAQDA. When analysing data with technology, this can sometimes create a distance between you and the data which would not be there with other data analysis types. Access to and reliability of technology have both improved significantly in recent years, but this can still be an issue in your research. When teaching with technology, it is often advised to have a 'plan b' just in case. This is the same when using CAQDA. Regulations for data protection and privacy can complicate the arrangements and processes of analysis. Because technology has made the creation of visually interesting data analysis easy, it can be tempting for researchers to include excessive numbers of charts, graphs and visualisations because they can rather than because they need to. It is also sometimes the case that because creating an online survey is so simple and some of the analysis of data is done for you, researchers can use CAQDA when it is not necessarily the best type of data analysis to use. Finally, as Denscombe (2014, p. 372) reminds us, computers '*do not actually do the analysis* – the researcher still needs to decide the codes and look for the connections within the data'. Technology can be a great help but still needs to be considered a tool to help the researcher and nothing more.

Mixed-methods Analysis

What is it?

Denscombe (2014, pp. 205–206) proposes 'three characteristic features' of mixed-methods research and analysis, and these are a 'preference for viewing research problems from a variety of perspectives', 'the combination of different types of research within a single project' and 'the choice of methods based on "what works best" for tackling a specific problem'. The mixture of methods facilitates collection of a variety of types of data, both qualitative and quantitative, and the analysis should produce results which connect, converge and triangulate findings in a complementary manner. It is not the refuge of those who cannot decide on a singular type of analysis but a conscious emphasis on comparison across types and methods.

Why should I use it?

Mixed methods should result in findings which produce a high level of confidence, as findings from one method are checked against findings from a different one. This can both confirm and challenge the results of analysis and interpretation. Data types can be compared in sequence, and this can help findings to emerge in a systematic and structured manner. It is possible to add further methods and types of analysis as your research progresses if you need them, and this can again further illuminate the data and help it converge. You have a high degree of flexibility without any loss of systematic, structured analysis, and you can move clearly towards fitness of purpose of the types of analysis as the research progresses. As Bryman (2012, p. 649) suggests, mixed-methods research 'may provide a better understanding of a phenomenon than if just one method had been used'.

What are the Problems Associated with it?

Using multiple methods demands an increased level of data analysis skills for you, the researcher, as you need to become proficient in all the methods and types of analysis. Data analysis can be more complex, and the additional comparing and contrasting data is likely to be more demanding than just using one method (Denscombe, 2014).

It is also always possible that the mixture of types of analysis may not confirm or corroborate your findings as planned. They could even cast doubt on them. Mixed methods are sometimes seen as so open and flexible that they can be less reliable than other types of data analysis, but they work best when meeting our earlier rules of being used with practicality, clarity and validity; flexibility, adaptability and fitness for purpose; and a recognition of research in a changing world.

DEVELOPING YOUR ANALYSIS AND INTERPRETATION INTO DISCUSSION AND CONCLUSIONS

From the first moment your first piece of data is gathered, however you have gathered it, you will start to analyse it, as has already been said at the start of this chapter. It can be one answer to one question in an interview, as you are listening to the answer. It can be hundreds of online questionnaire results. It can be the first minute of an observation. Your mind naturally wants to make sense of the data, engage with it, make connections with other pieces of data and link them together. How successfully you then move forward with your data analysis and interpretation can depend to a large degree on how well you have planned the whole research process. Ashley (2012, p. 37) argues that

> *carefully planning your data collection and analysis can prevent you making a common research error – collecting more data then you will have time to analyse. Planning can help you remain focused on collecting data that directly addresses your research questions and helps you keep in mind what you will be doing with this data in terms of analysis.*

Cohen et al. (2017, p. 1173) emphasise that data analysis and interpretation is about

> *distilling from the complexity of the findings, the key points of the phenomenon in question, reducing complexity without violating it, catching the essence of the issue or the situation, enabling the researcher to identify, for example, patterns, key issues, causal processes and sequences.*

Denscombe includes an analysis of how the different stages of your research are written and this should be helpful when you are developing your own analysis and interpretation into discussion and conclusions. An abridged version (Denscombe, 2014, p. 433) with some parts formatted as reflective questions, and comments, is below.

Reflective questions

Findings

1. Do the findings tell us what your research has found out as simply as possible?

Judging how much of your findings you include, and maintaining a balance between enough, too little and too much is not straightforward. It is a question of judgement, and this part of your thesis will go through several edits. It will help if you compare your analysis with other already written up pieces of research, which use similar methods and types of analysis. Your supervisory team should also be helpful in supporting you to make the judgement about the sufficiency of your data.

Analysis and discussion

2. How does the analysis lead to discussion and conclusions?

'The findings are reviewed and interrogated to see what they imply. This then leads on to a discussion that connects the emerging ideas to the theories and ideas, issues and problems' (Denscombe, 2014, p. 433) which you will have synthesised from your literature review. You make sense of the findings by comparing the connections, themes and theories from your study with those from your literature review through critical analysis and discussion and drawing out ideas and initial conclusions from this process.

Conclusions and recommendations

3. How do you draw your threads of research through into
   conclusions and recommendations?

Finally, you draw together the threads of the research and your
initial conclusions and build them into more clear and full conclusions, which you support from your data analysis and discussions.
If you wish to suggest some ways forward in the field which you
have been researching, these can build into recommendations.

As data analysis and interpretation continues, one thing which is
very important is drawing together the connections within the data
into a write up which develops your conclusions systematically, rigor-
ously, imaginatively and clearly. This is a highly sophisticated writing
task. Bryman (2012, p. 685) states that 'writing up your research is not
simply a matter of reporting your findings and drawing some conclusions'. He argues that 'above all you must be persuasive. This means
you must convince your readers of the credibility of your conclusions.'
Data analysis and interpretation is the essence of the way in which you
'persuade your readers that your findings and conclusion are significant and that they are plausible' (Bryman, 2012, p. 686).

EVALUATING THE QUALITY OF YOUR DATA ANALYSIS
AND INTERPRETATION

First, before considering what other writers have to say about this
final part of section one, the recommended key principles of all
data analysis and interpretation from the start of this chapter are
used to help you consider some important questions.

Reflective questions:

Practicality, clarity and validity

1. Has the process of data analysis and interpretation gathered
   enough clear and valid data as planned?

2. Has the data analysis and interpretation yielded a strong range of connections, themes, theoretical concepts and ideas?

3. Does your analysed data and interpretation relate well to your research aims and objectives?

Flexibility, adaptability and fitness for purpose

4. How well have you been able to adapt and change the process of data analysis and interpretation if you needed to, and has this been successful?

5. Are you satisfied your data analysis and interpretation has supported critically analytical discussion and conclusions which have been fit for the purpose/s stated in the research question?

The changing world we live in

6. Has your data analysis and interpretation taken appropriate account of the societal context of the research and your own and your subjects professional and life situations?

If the answer to any of these questions is 'no' as you near the end of your research, it's safe to say you should be worried! The best way to avoid that being the case is to ask the questions regularly as you carry out the data analysis and interpretation.

Coe (2012, p. 12) lists 26 questions to assist 'in evaluating the quality if a piece of research'. An adapted version of the questions which have relevance to data analysis and interpretation are listed below. Some also feature separately in other parts of this chapter.

Reflective questions:

1. Does the research address the research questions/aims?

2. Is the interpretation of data supported with convincing validity?

3. Does the data support any claims made?

4. Are the claims generalised and how far is that justified?

5. 'if the data had been interpreted or analysed differently, could this have led to different conclusions?' (Coe, 2012, p. 12).

A well-known and well-used set of criteria to evaluate qualitative research are those produced over 30 years ago by Lincoln and Guba (1985). Many qualitative researchers have found them helpful. This part of section one closes with Bryman's (2012) clear summary of Lincoln and Guba's concept of 'trustworthiness' which has four aspects as follows and which he explains as paralleling quantitative research criteria:

> *Credibility, which parallels internal validity – that is, how believable are the findings?*
> *Transferability, which parallels external validity – that is do the findings apply to other contexts?*
> *Dependability, which parallels reliability – that is are the findings likely to apply at other times?*
> *Confirmability, which parallels objectivity – that is, has the investigator allowed his or her values to intrude to a high degree? (Bryman, 2012, p. 49)*

Your data analysis and interpretation is the core evidence for evaluating the quality of your research, and section two of this chapter now continues to provide a case study as an example of the experiences and reflections of a doctoral researcher when they were engaged in their own data analysis and interpretation.

CASE EXAMPLE OF DOCTORAL STUDENT

This section of this chapter is based on an interview with a doctoral student working in the Further Education and Skills sector in England, who has kindly given her permission for the use of her interview as an example of the experience of a doctoral student when engaged in the data analysis and interpretation stage of their research. The text is based on Catherine's responses in the interview to a series of questions with quotes where appropriate.

Dr Catherine Manning is Head of Teaching, Learning and Assessment at the Education and Training Foundation, which is the government-backed, sector-owned national support body for the Further Education and Skills sector. Her doctoral thesis is titled 'Mentoring for student teachers in Post-Compulsory Education in England and Norway: Judgemental and developmental Approaches'.

The research studied mentoring for student teachers in the Further Education and Skills sectors in England and Norway. The study sought to generate further understanding of what were identified as 'judgemental' and 'developmental' approaches to mentoring and drew on both a qualitative and comparative research design.

> *Twelve mentoring pairs participated (six from England and six from Norway). These pairs were recruited through three universities in England and two in Norway. Each mentor and mentee took part in two semi-structured interviews. In addition, each mentoring pair completed two audio recordings of mentoring meetings. (Manning, 2018, p. 2)*

Three derivative versions of mentoring were identified:

- A hybrid of judgemental and developmental mentoring.

- A restricted version of developmental mentoring.

- A more extensive version of developmental mentoring.

None of the approaches were found to be realising the full potential of mentoring to support the student teachers' learning and growth. The study recommended that in the future judgemental and developmental approaches might be viewed as 'archetypes' of mentoring. Additional recommendations for policy, practice and research are offered, and a 'personalised' mentoring approach is proposed.

What Types of Data Analysis Did you Use in Your Study, and Why?

Catherine used 'two types of thematic analysis' in her study. One type created profiles of mentoring pairs of participants in the study which were like 'portraits' or 'mini stories'. The other type was a 'cross case' thematic analysis across all 12 mentoring pairs. The results of the analysis were featured in three findings chapters in her thesis. As this was a qualitative study 'thematic analysis came up early on as the most logical approach to use'. Catherine's university had encouraged a study involving 'narrative research', and a supervisor recommended a piece of writing by Kelchtermans (1993) as it related to the research topic, 'and the methods that he used'. This approach to thematic analysis was considered to be a 'vertical and horizontal approach to data analysis'. Further reading on and reflecting about thematic analysis reinforced this as the choice for data analysis and interpretation. Not to underestimate the pressure and sometimes uncertainty that can be involved in this level of study, Catherine also emphasised that making what felt like a good choice of data analysis was 'something to hold on to in an uncertain time'.

When Did the Process of Analysing and Interpreting the Data from Your Study Begin?

For Catherine, the process started informally 'as soon the interviewee started responding to my questions', and 'my brain was starting to make connections'. For Catherine, it was important to pay some attention to those initial analytical thoughts, but not to go too far with that because 'you might start to draw conclusions too early and you want to remain as open as possible to where the data might take you'. As the data gathering and analysis proceeded, Catherine did start to identify connections and 'instances' which were beginning to emerge and used these to help frame and inform interview questions. Fuller data analysis did not take place until all the data had been collected, transcribed and put into NVivo that the 'formal stage of data analysis' took place. The key message from Catherine in relation to this question is that the informal analysis of data early on and throughout the process is important, and it can indeed generate some excellent insights. The key emphasis, however, is that care needs to be taken to ensure the full, systematic and rigorous analysis of all the data is at the heart of the process, and that informal responses to data can take the researcher down some difficult paths.

Could you Describe the More and Less Successful Aspects of Your Data Analysis and Interpretation?

Catherine had a large amount of data (69 transcripts) and coding such a large quantity proved challenging 'given that I was relatively new to education research'. To address this problem, Catherine chose to take data from one mentoring pair and get 'in deep with that data' to extract commonalities and differences. This proved successful. The coding and analysis of the larger quantity of data was more of a challenge, as a very large number of codes were generated across all of the data. At the end of the first full data analysis, the codes needed to be revisited and 'moderated' to reduce overlap and reinforce deeper thematic connections. This was a challenge Catherine believed she met, but it was a very large undertaking for what was a relatively small research project.

Could you Recommend any Particular Resources which Helped with Your Data Analysis and Interpretation?

NVivo is a qualitative data analysis computer software package which Catherine made use of in the data analysis and interpretation stage. Catherine found it a 'really helpful' tool and emphasised that 'it is only as good as what you put into it'. NVivo assisted with 'the organisation of the data' and from Catherine's perspective 'I don't know how I would have analysed that amount of qualitative data unless I had something like NVivo'. As has been already suggested in this chapter, and as reinforced by Catherine's experience, CAQDA does not, however, write your thesis for you, but it can be of significant assistance. In terms of the challenge of learning to use such software, Catherine had watched online tutorials and used a degree of trial and error before developing full confidence in NVivo, but felt it was straightforward to use overall. Catherine would therefore recommend that educational researchers could find NVivo useful.

Catherine also felt Miles and Huberman's (1994) text on qualitative data analysis was helpful in planning and executing her data analysis and interpretation and could be recommended.

What would Change About Your Data Analysis and Interpretation if You Were Carrying Out the Research Now?

Catherine felt that 'I would have thought more carefully about the data analysis process when I was designing the data collection tools', and that this would have been helpful in aligning the data analysis and interpretation stage more closely to the research question.

On reflection, Catherine also suggested that practising the data analysis approach by taking 'extracts of data from a number of pairs' to code them in order to 'get a sense' of interpretation and themes before 'going ahead with the rest of it'. This is another very important point about data analysis, as it would almost certainly save time (Catherine took 'six- or seven-weeks full time' for this stage) and reduce repetition and overlap of codes, themes and ideas. It is also important, however, to remain open and ready to identify different and possibly conflicting themes as the full range of data sets are analysed. Selecting the sample for piloting your data analysis would be crucial.

What Advice would you Give Other Researchers About the Data Analysis and Interpretation Element of their Research?

First, Catherine felt that 'reading widely about the data analysis processes that other people had undertaken' and 'just focussing on the data analysis in particular' in other studies would be helpful.

Second, Catherine suggested that reading a wide range of publications on data analysis and interpretation, including those from different fields, and some which are not necessarily completely current was 'really helpful' for her and could be for other researchers.

Third, 'you don't have to be doing something new with your data analysis. You can rely on tried and trusted methods'. Researchers should not feel pressured to be original in terms of data analysis methods.

Fourth, 'don't be put off by other people's views about data analysis' and 'find your own way of doing it in a way that works for you and the study'. There will be a point at which your confidence in your approach will become justified, so it is important to sustain your efforts until the point at which you do become satisfied of where your data analysis and interpretation is leading. As Catherine concluded, 'you will get your reward.'

As a final piece of advice for other researchers, Catherine suggested that pairing with another research student with whom you could get together 'in a relaxed and informal way' and compare notes and ideas on sections and aspects of each other's data analysis and interpretation (and indeed other parts of their research) could be a very helpful, confidence building experience for both. This is an idea the author of this chapter would strongly endorse.

SUMMARY OF THIS CHAPTER

- *Analysing and interpreting data is at the heart of every piece of research and succeeding with this stage is crucial* – practicality, clarity, validity and adaptability combined with systematic but flexible structures will prepare you well for analysis and interpretation which is fit for purpose.

- *Contributing to a changing world* – extending research by ensuring reference to social justice in a changing world has profound benefits for the researcher and the participants, including greater involvement in data analysis and interpretation. It does also bring additional challenges in terms of validity and fitness for purpose as the ways we 'approach the study honestly and openly'.

  Exploration of personal beliefs makes the investigator more aware of the potential judgements that can occur during data collection, analysis and generation of knowledge based on the researcher's belief system rather than on the actual data collected from participants. (Atkins & Duckworth, 2019, p. 78)

- *The central importance of data analysis and interpretation* – threats to data analysis can leave the researcher with results which are not adequate to draw conclusions can result in the conclusions drawn from the research being invalid. If data analysis and interpretation is inadequate, the whole of your research could be inadequate.

- *There are many choices of types of data analysis and interpretation* – the chapter includes four types of data analysis and interpretation which are thematic analysis, grounded theory, CAQDA and mixed-methods analysis. The most important choice is associated with selecting data analysis types which will answer your research question/s best. Different researchers researching the same field may well select different types of data analysis from each other, as there is rarely one type which is the only type which would be fit for purpose.

- *You need to draw together connections within the data into a write up which goes beyond simple writing up* – 'you need to convince your readers of the credibility of your conclusions' and 'persuade your readers that your findings and conclusion are significant and that they are plausible' (Denscombe, 2014, p. 686).

- *Evaluating the quality of your data analysis and interpretation can be carried out in many ways* – there are numerous frameworks, theories and structures for evaluating research overall, and data analysis and interpretation. Within the context of this chapter, it is suggested that this is a matter of selecting from the many available a number of questions to ask of your data analysis and interpretation, and this chapter provides a good range of those.

FURTHER READING

Arthur, J., Waring, M., Coe, R., & Hedges, L. V. (Eds.). (2012). *Research methods and methodology in education*. London: Sage.

This book is very useful for all aspects of research and includes contributions from 49 separate authors, many of whom are leaders in their field. Its aim is to 'provide students with the theoretical understandings, practical knowledge and skills which they need to carry out independent research' (Arthur et al., 2012, p. 3). It has a particularly substantial section on data analysis which is the main reason why it is recommended for this chapter. There are 14 chapters in the 'analysis methods' section of this book, and although some of them are complex and obscure, there is much in this section of this book to help all researchers in their data analysis and interpretation.

Bryman, A. (2012). *Social research methods* (4th ed.). Oxford: Oxford University Press.

As Bryman (2012, p. xxxi) indicates, this book

> *covers a wide range of research methods, approaches to research and ways of carrying out data analysis, so it is likely to meet the needs of the vast majority of students.*

This book is not a specialist publication for education but has much to recommend for any researcher carrying out social research. It includes experiences from real student researchers and much helpful and clearly explained content relating to data analysis and interpretation.

The book recommended here is the fourth edition, but the fifth edition has a bank of online resources at https://global.oup.com/uk/orc/sociology/brymansrm5e/

Cohen, L., Manion, L., & Morrison, K. (2017). *Research methods in education* (8th ed.). London: Routledge.

The edition of this book recommended here is the eighth, which gives an indication of its popularity. It is huge (over 1,500 pages) and the authors have considerably updated the text and

> *whilst retaining the best features of the former edition, the reshaping, updating and new additions undertaken for this new volume now mean that the book covers a greater spread of issues than the previous editions, and in greater depth, catching the contemporary issues and debates in the field. (Cohen et al., 2017, p. 40)*

Part 5 'data analysis and reporting' has 14 chapters and contains good advice, examples, theory and practice in these chapters, as in the whole book.

Denscombe, M. (2014). *The good research guide* (5th ed.). Maidenhead: Open University Press.

This book is somewhat more modest in its aims than the others recommended as further reading and is aimed at 'project researchers' who are 'undertaking small scale research projects'. It aims to

> *present these 'project researchers' with practical guidance and a vision of the key issues involved in social research. It attempts to provide them with vital information that is easily accessible, and which gets to the heart of the matter quickly and concisely. (Denscombe, 2014, p. 21)*

It is genuinely readable and accessible for the most part and certainly to a greater degree for more of its somewhat fewer pages (a mere 460) than the other texts here. It provides some particularly helpful advice and examples about data analysis and interpretation in its chapter 3 'data analysis' and can be recommended as at least the starting point for many other topics about social research.

REFERENCES

Ashley, L. D. (2012). *Planning your research*. In J. Arthur, M. Waring, R. Coe, & L.V. Hedges (Eds.), *Research methods and methodology in education* (pp. 31–40). London: Sage.

Atkins, L., & Duckworth, V. (2019). *Research methods for social justice and equity in education*. London: Bloomsbury.

Braun, V., & Clarke, V. (2006). Using thematic analysis in psychology. *Qualitative Research in Psychology*, *3*(2), 77–101.

Bryman, A. (2012). *Social research methods* (4th ed.). Oxford: Oxford University Press.

Clarke, V., & Braun, V. (2018). Using thematic analysis in counselling and psychotherapy research: A critical reflection. *Counselling and Psychotherapy Research*, *18*, 107–110. https://doi.org/10.1002/capr.12165

Coe, R. (2012). The nature of Educational Research – Exploring the different understandings of educational research. In J. Arthur, M. Waring, R. Coe, & L. V. Hedges (Eds.), *Research methods and methodology in education* (pp. 5–14). London: Sage.

Cohen, L., Manion, L., & Morrison, K. (2017). *Research methods in education* (8th ed.). London: Routledge.

Denscombe, M. (1998). *The good research guide*. Maidenhead: Open University Press.

Denscombe, M. (2014). *The good research guide* (5th ed.). Maidenhead: Open University Press.

Gibbs, G. R. (2012). Software and qualitative data analysis. In J. Arthur, M. Waring, R. Coe, & L. V. Hedges (Eds.), *Research methods and methodology in education* (pp. 251–258). London: Sage.

Glaser, B. G. (1992). *Basics of grounded theory analysis*. Mill Valley, CA: Sociology Press.

Hambleton, R. K. (2012). Measurement and validity. In J. Arthur, M. Waring, R. Coe, & L. V. Hedges (Eds.), *Research methods and methodology in education* (pp. 241–246). London: Sage.

Hedges, L. V. (2012). Design of empirical research. In J. Arthur, M. Waring, R. Coe, & L. V. Hedges (Eds.), *Research methods and methodology in education* (pp. 23–30). London: Sage.

Kelchtermans, G. (1993). Getting the story, understanding the lives: From career stories to teachers' professional development. *Teaching and Teacher Education*, 9(5), 443–456.

Lincoln, Y. S., & Guba, E. G. (1985). *Naturalistic inquiry*. Beverly Hills, CA: Sage Publications, Inc.

Manning, C. (2018). *Mentoring for student teachers in post-compulsory education in England and Norway: Judgemental and developmental approaches*. PhD. thesis, University of Brighton, Brighton.

Manning, C. (2019, October 4). Skype Interview, 4th October, 2019.

Miles, M. B., & Huberman, A. M. (1994). *Qualitative data analysis* (2nd ed.). London: Sage.

Waring, M. (2012). Grounded theory. In J. Arthur, M. Waring, R. Coe, & L. V. Hedges (Eds.), *Research methods and methodology in education* (pp. 297–307). London: Sage.

8

GETTING OVER THE FINISHING LINE

Iona Burnell and Gerry Czerniawski

INTRODUCTION

Having carefully drafted and constructed the various chapters and sections of your thesis, you may now be thinking about making finishing touches in readiness for submission. Within this chapter, we will cover the abstract, introduction, what to check when proofreading, various ways of presenting findings, using headings and subheadings, the metaphorical 'golden thread' that links the thesis together in a cohesive manner and ensures that the end product possesses the 'doctoralness' that is needed for work at this level.

The advice given by your supervisor(s) is of utmost importance when you are preparing your thesis for examination. From this chapter, you will benefit from our own experiences as doctoral examiners, those of other researchers, and how theses from previous educational research projects have been effectively written up and submitted.

At the end of this chapter, you should:

- Be fully aware of why the 'golden thread' of your thesis is so important to your examiners.

- Be able to improve signposting the clarity and coherence of your thesis.

- Present a thesis that helps to reduce the amount of potential questions examiners ask in your viva.

MANAGING YOUR EXAMINERS' FIRST IMPRESSIONS OF THE THESIS

Once you have submitted your thesis, you may have two or three examiners (depending on institutional arrangements). One may have been chosen, not because of their expertise in your particular field but possibly because of expertise with a particular methodology or theoretical and conceptual framework. Knowing this immediately helps you to understand the importance in not assuming examiners always have prior knowledge of your field, and what that means for the clarity of your writing. The rigour and quality of work that is required at level 8 (the level associated with doctoral-level writing) is the same for all doctoral programmes. As outlined in Chapter 1, the word count for the professional doctorate thesis may differ from the traditional PhD thesis, and the professional doctorate may contain an element of professional practice, not found in all PhDs.

The examiners have chosen to examine your thesis. They have been approached by your supervisors, have looked at your topic and made a decision to take it on. This means that prior to them reading your thesis, they are, initially, 'on your side', have an interest in your research, and, under the right circumstances, want you to pass. The examiner may read your thesis on a train, a plane, a beach, at night, at the weekend and they won't necessarily read it all at once or in the order that it has been presented. They may, for example, look at the introduction and conclusion first, the abstract, the references, the contents page or the findings and not necessarily in that particular order. The examiners will make checks for scholarliness and scholarly conventions. For example, you need to ensure you have included relevant references to books and journals and that these are current and up to date. If references are not up to date, you may start to lose the trust of the examiner in relation to the quality and doctoralness of your thesis. This could mean, for example, the extent to which they feel there is sufficient evidence to show that the thesis contributes new knowledge to the field. Examiners are looking for proof that you deserve your doctorate, so keep them interested and make sure they don't lose faith in your scholarly authority.

Your university will have their own criteria against which your thesis will be examined. In addition to these, the examiners will award your doctorate in recognition of the following points: (1) your doctorate, once awarded, conveys international recognition that you are a national expert in your field; (2) you have the potential to start examining others' doctoral theses (EdD or PhD) even though in some cases you may not be a substantive expert in that field; and (3) you are contributing original knowledge to the discipline and subject area through your research and findings.

Golding, Sharmini and Lazarovitch conducted an analysis of 30 articles including examiner reports and recommendations, rankings of thesis quality by examiners and qualitative data from examiners participating in their research. They derived a number of general conclusions about what examiners do during the process of examining a thesis. Some of these conclusions about what examiners tend to do include:

- expect a thesis to pass

- judge a thesis by the end of the first or second chapter

- read a thesis as an academic reader and as a normal reader

- be irritated and distracted by presentation errors

- favour a coherent thesis

- favour a thesis that engages with the literature

- favour a thesis with a convincing approach

- favour a thesis that engages with the findings

- require a thesis to be publishable (Golding, Sharmini, & Lazarovitch, 2014, pp. 566–567)

As Golding et al. state, examiners will read the thesis both as an expert/academic from the discipline/subject area and as a normal reader. Remember, they too have been through the doctoral process and many examiners will have published widely within the field the thesis is situated. What is meant by 'normal reader' is simply somebody who is reading an extended text and expects that text to be well laid out, cohesive, coherent and presented in a clear and logical way. Just like any reader of any text, for example, a newspaper, a novel, a research paper, etc., you may also have to make very clear certain aspects of your educational practice that the examiner may not be familiar with. After all, something that is obvious to you about your daily work practices within, for example, your educational institution such as the school where you conducted fieldwork, may not necessarily be obvious to the examiner when they are reading your thesis, especially if they do not share that background.

Your doctoral thesis does not have to be perfect, but it does have to be perfectly presented. You can acknowledge in the conclusion, setting out what you learned, and how you might have done it differently, the implications of that are that it is not flawless, and that is OK. Don't try to pretend it is a work of perfection. The examiners have also gone through the doctoral process and they will know that research rarely goes to plan. Research is never problem free, and they will expect you to acknowledge this. Think of the process as an apprenticeship and that you are worthy of your training. Thomson and Walker (2010) point out that 'in Australia, as in much of Europe, it is only recently that doctoral studies have begun to be widely referred to as "research *training*"' (p. 299). However, while the idea of a doctoral student being in training may be a reassuring one for many, you are still expected to demonstrate the levels of rigour, originality and 'mastery' associated with doctoralness. Thomson and Walker (2010) also argue that 'to succeed, students will have to show they have mastered the norms of what it is to do good research in their field' (p. 299).

THE GOLDEN THREAD

The 'golden thread' is the central argument of the thesis. It pulls through the whole thesis and creates cohesion and synergy – the title, abstract, contents page, introduction, methodology, literature review, findings and conclusion – all well linked back to each other. That golden thread should be explicit at every stage; present not just in the introduction and conclusion, but when you set up a new heading and sub-heading within each and every chapter.

Over the course of your EdD programme, you will have become familiar with the literature that is relevant to your topic and with who the 'big names' are within the various fields that you engage with in your thesis. Following the conventions of referencing is expected but avoid, for example, repetitive 'Jones said this, Smith said that'; examiners are interested in the field of research, the debates, the contestations and the theories and concepts that underpin your research. These are all part of your golden thread and should be consistently present throughout the thesis. Remember – Golding et al. (2014) state that:

> *A thesis is crafted into a coherent whole by threading an argument through it for the examiners to follow – connecting the research question with an answer, connecting various subsidiary conclusions and connecting these conclusions with the supporting data, evidence and reasons, and with the background literature. (p. 569)*

This coherence is particularly important for examiners who do not, for whatever reason, possibly due to work/family commitments, read the thesis in one sitting. If they read chapter one on Sunday, and don't get a chance to return to the thesis until Thursday, a lack of coherence will make the examiner's job so much harder.

Reflective exercise:

Search for question marks in the thesis. Get rid of unwanted and/or rhetorical questions; there is no need for these. The only questions you need are the research questions, and any questions that you are asking in interviews, questionnaires, etc.

FIRST IMPRESSIONS COUNT

'Even though examiners expect a pass, first impressions can change their mind', according to Golding et al. (2014, p. 568). They go on to explain that within the first two chapters of the thesis, and by skimming the abstract, contents page, introduction and conclusion, a preliminary judgement is made about the quality of the thesis.

Carter (2008) cited in Golding et al. (2014) query whether you are going to present the examiners with a 'treat' or an 'endurance test'. Perfect presentation, with everything in the right place, proofread, no spelling, grammar, punctuation errors, consistent font and type and the appropriate referencing style – according to the university where you are studying, are all conducive with the 'treat'. As we have previously pointed out, and asserted by Golding et al. (2014),

> *They read with academic expectations and the expectations of a normal reader. Like any reader, thesis examiners get annoyed and distracted by presentation errors, and they want to read a work that is a coherent whole. (p. 563)*

Therefore, it is crucial that the examiner's first impression is a very good one.

We previously stated that your doctoral thesis does not have to be perfect, but it does have to be perfectly presented. Murray (2011) in her book *How to Write a Thesis* discusses the notion of 'good enough' as 'reaching an adequate standard for submission' (p. 269). What you should be preparing for at this stage is damage limitation at the viva. In other words, hoping to rule out all of the additional questions that the examiners might have wanted to ask had you not managed to answer them in the actual thesis.

Reflective exercise:

Send the abstract and introduction to a few of your critical friends. Asking critical friends to read and give feedback on your abstract and introduction will also ensure that both are accessible to lay readers.

Whether or not they work in education, anybody who has an interest in education should be able to read your abstract and understand it. The same point is true for the introduction (see below) to your thesis. You also want the examiner to believe that your thesis is going to make a valuable contribution to the field, so make the introduction compelling, clear and easily understood. Take time to look at as many introduction chapters to other doctoral theses in education to see how successful candidates have written these very important chapters.

Finn (2005) provides some useful insight from an examiner's perspective:

> *Their first viewing of the thesis will be the title on the front cover, and their initial inspection of the thesis will take in the title page, the table of contents, the line spacing, font size, paragraph lengths, number of figures and tables, referencing style and, of course, the length of the thesis. (p. 118)*

Finn (2005) also points out that '… it is your responsibility to write, structure and present the written thesis in a way that convincingly demonstrates research at doctoral level' (p. 118). The following reflective questions might prove to be useful as you revise your thesis.

Reflective questions:

- Have you provided clarity: around your narrative, ideas, contributions and relationship to research questions?

- Do you justify your choices (in the literature and methodology), research journey and what has/has not worked?

- Have you checked for coherence: do all of the component parts link together to produce a clear flow from title to introduction to conclusion?

- Does the thesis contain critical interpretation and reflection?

- Does the thesis provide evidence that supports your assertions and grounds your analysis and conclusion?

- Do you provide originality and a contribution to the practice of education?

AN ABSTRACT IS NOT ABSTRACT

The abstract is usually the first thing that examiners read. It should be a distilled version of your thesis. It is short (maximum one page), usually not exceeding 500 words. It outlines the research problem, aims, research question(s) and articulates the contribution of your research to the field. It also identifies the main methods, the sample and what the most significant result is. In relation to the abstract, Brown (1994) cited in Murray (2011) offers eight questions that are useful when considering how to write a strong abstract:

> [...] questions [that] can be used at a later stage to structure the abstract, or summary [...] this approach can be used not only to reveal the central argument, but also to discover it. (Murray, 2011, pp. 217–218)

1. Who are the intended readers?

2. What did you do? (50 words)

3. Why did you do it? (50 words)

4. What happened? (50 words)

5. What do the results mean in theory? (50 words)

6. What do the results mean in practice? (50 words)

7. What is the key benefit for readers? (50 words)

8. What remains unresolved?

If you are still unsure, or uncomfortable with your abstract, use the above prompts to sum up your research and try to present it to a friend or colleague verbally in two or three minutes. Talking through your abstract with someone else can help clarify your own thoughts in relation to the nature and purpose of the study and thus sharpen your abstract.

Reflective exercise:

Read 10 or so abstracts from others' theses to get a feel for what an abstract is and what makes it different to the introduction, summary and conclusion. Try to choose the abstracts from the subject discipline of education, as this keeps them relevant, but you may also find that thesis abstracts from the wider social sciences are useful exemplars.

Most universities now have online repositories where students upload their theses; The Universities of Leeds, Sheffield and York, for example, can be found here: https://etheses.whiterose.ac.uk. The British Library is also a very useful resource and repository of theses.

THE INTRODUCTION

A well-used approach to writing an introduction to the thesis is to lay out the sequence of the chapters, providing a summarised version of each. While this is one element of an introduction, you must also be sure to include what you have done, how you have done it and why. Beginning with a grand opening paragraph that identifies the topic, the debates in which it is situated, and the contribution this thesis will make to those debates, is a good start. The introduction should not only gain the examiner's interest, but it should also demonstrate and tell them yours.

As with your abstract, get a critical friend or two to read this very important chapter. Even if your friends are not from an educational background, the introduction should be clearly understood in terms of what you are doing, how you are doing it and why you are doing it. Be clear and succinct about what the issue is, what is being said about it and how you deal with it in the thesis. Include what the research is about; what you found out; a brief summary of the theoretical/conceptual framework; what the significance of the findings are and what these findings mean; and what the implications of the research are for policy, existing research and practice within your area of education. Make sure the aims and research questions (if appropriate) and hypothesis (if appropriate) are clearly presented in this opening chapter.

Don't be Anglo-centric. The temptation for many doctoral students is to think inside your own geographical and/or cultural bubble, particularly with EdD research as these theses are often about an educational issue at a local level, for example, a school or college locally situated. The danger is that you write about your area forgetting that there is a whole world out there and one which you are contributing new knowledge to. Drawing on some of the literature and debates from the international context will not only demonstrate global educational awareness but also acknowledge that your chosen field is very likely to be an international one, even though your thesis might be looking at one local aspect of that field.

> *Reflective question:*
>
> If somebody from another country accessed and read your thesis, have you provided enough context for them to understand the issue that you are researching?

METHODOLOGY

Kate Hoskins has provided a very clear and comprehensive guide to research design and methodological approaches in Chapter 6, and we are not going to duplicate any of that here. When preparing your thesis for submission, however, there are some final checks you can make, and one is to ensure that your methodology is in harmony and has synergy with the literature review, the theoretical and conceptual framework, research questions, the findings and the conclusion.

There are many facets to this chapter including that you must explain to the examiners how you analysed the data. Remember that you can help the examiners understand your methodology by making good use of your appendices. All appendices are different; some may contain, for example, graphs, charts, interview schedules, transcript sections and questionnaires. You can make the examiner's life easier by clearly signposting this information in the chapter.

Remember too that your methodology chapter is not is an essay on methodology. Rather, it is a chapter about you, explaining to your examiners and readers, why you have constructed the methodology for your thesis in the way that you have. Examiners are not interested in you showcasing long explanations about the meanings of 'ontology' and 'epistemology'. What they are interested in is how you apply issues of ontology and epistemology correctly and how those concepts have impacted on the methodological choices you made. Ontology and epistemology should, therefore, be used sparingly as concepts within the context of your research, the journey you are making, and the choices undertaken for your educational research.

In recent years, researcher positionality within doctoral theses in education has become more important with many examiners expecting to see the extent the doctoral student is aware of the role their positionality can play in the design and outcomes of the thesis. Showing how you have reflected reflexively and critically on your positionality as a researcher will, therefore, be an important part of the final writing of the thesis. This issue of researcher positionality is increasingly one that examiners enquire about during doctoral vivas in education. For example, how might your positionality have determined what literature you have included (and excluded) in your own literature review chapter/s?

Reflective exercise:

Are your research questions consistent? Check that the wording of your research questions is identical throughout the thesis as they may change over time.

PRESENTING YOUR FINDINGS

There are various ways to present your findings, and we would always advise doctoral students to look at the different ways published doctoral theses in education present findings. You must be clear in the thesis about what it is you are doing. For example, are you going to present your findings in a discrete chapter/s and then follow this with a separate 'Discussion' chapter? Alternatively, are you going to present findings but discuss them as you go in relation to your literature review within the same chapter or chapters. These two variations are just two of a variety of ways in which findings chapters can be presented, and therefore, it is so helpful to look at similar chapters in other completed doctoral theses.

When presenting your findings, consider these points:

- Be wary of making generalisations unless they are integral to the epistemological strand of the research.

- Express your own academic authority. Do not hide behind the writings of others by using lots of quotations, this is your research, you have conducted it, no one else; you must own it and be able to argue for it. For example, if you decide to use a quote from one of your participants, ensure that you 'top and tail' this with commentary from you (rather than letting the quote 'speak for itself'.

- Your findings should relate back to the theoretical/conceptual framework deployed in the thesis.

Reflective exercise:

A very useful resource to draw on is The University of Manchester's Academic Phrasebank (http://www.phrasebank. manchester.ac.uk/referring-to-sources/) which provides a bank of introductory phrases with which to present, not only your findings but also other parts of the thesis such as reporting methods, discussing findings and writing conclusions.

In the following example, the writer chose to present the findings in a chapter called *Research findings: an interpretation of the data*. While this would be considered a discrete chapter, dedicated to laying out the findings, it also includes links to theories, the literature and the theoretical framework chapters. This is one example of the various ways to present your findings. In this extract of an EdD thesis, the writer has intertwined interpreted interview data (presented in italics) with the 'cycle of failure' theory as presented in the literature and referenced from Askham (2008, p. 92):

> *Tammi told me:* 'I felt as I said, before I felt dumb'. *For Kasim, his perceived failures were openly expressed to him:* 'I've always been called thick and stupid when it came to education. A teacher called me a spastic as well when I was at school! So, I never really thought of myself as

having any intelligence when it came to academics'. *With these perceptions of themselves in relation to education, it is no surprise that they developed into adults who felt that higher education was not the place for them, and was out of reach. Just as Baxter and Britton (1999) noted that education is a 'key site for the construction of identity' (p. 179), my participants had already constructed themselves as educational failures from their experiences of school. Askham discusses the 'cycle of failure' (2008: 92) which places limitations on learning; Askham describes the learner's state of mind: 'I had a poor experience at school, so whatever else I might have achieved in life, my self-esteem as a learner is low; so when I return to education I do not expect to perform well' (ibid). Askham's theory resonates in Kasim's words when he said,* 'I've overcome a lot of things; the only thing I never overcame was education'.

In this extract we can see the way the author has included findings with links to theories and literature. Your best approach to presenting your findings will be agreed between you and your supervisor. It might be that intertwining findings with links to theories and literature is appropriate, as above, or you may decide on laying out just the findings alone.

Reflective exercise:

Using the link https://etheses.whiterose.ac.uk, survey some theses that have presented findings as discrete chapters, and some presenting findings intertwined with links to theories and literature. This will help you to decide which is the best approach in your thesis.

CRITICAL WRITING

Many doctoral students struggle with what it means to write critically. The temptation, in early draft chapters, is to present literature, often in report form, without engaging critically with it. This tendency may occur because of a lack of confidence in writing, a fear to engage or taking a back seat and not 'getting involved' in the argument; students at doctoral level do need to step out of their comfort zone for doctoral-level writing. You may already have experience of writing critically from your previous undergraduate/ postgraduate courses. At doctoral level, this skill needs to sharply develop to include well-informed judgements, criticisms and evaluations of the literature you have presented in your thesis.

In addition to the guidance provided by Leena Helavaara Robertson in Chapter 4: writing the literature review, we have included some additional tips here that will help you to sharpen your writing. The University of Manchester's Academic Phrasebank states that:

> *As an academic writer, you are expected to be critical of the sources that you use. This essentially means questioning what you read and not necessarily agreeing with it just because the information has been published. Being critical can also mean looking for reasons why we should not just accept something as being correct or true.*

At doctoral level, everything is debatable. Wellington, Bathmaker, Hunt, McCulloch and Sikes (2009) comment on being critical as 'questioning the work and ideas of others, and students are often advised to be critical … anyone's work may be challenged and exposed to criticism' (p. 83). However, they also warn against pejorative approaches to criticism, such as being 'judgmental', 'scathing' and 'nit-picking', as this will come across as being 'hostile, rude or confrontational' (Wellington et al., 2009, p. 83), not at all advisable or acceptable in academia. The authors provide a useful interpretation of what it is to achieve criticality in your thesis:

> *being critical involves the exercise of careful, deliberate and well-informed judgement. It is important to be sure that your critique is based on what is in the literature and does not represent a misinterpretation or an ignorance of the literature. (Wellington et al., 2009, p. 84)*

To ensure that you can evidence sufficient critical engagement with the literature you will need to be very familiar with the literature and gain a deep understanding of the arguments that others are presenting. Interpret these arguments accurately. Present them with confidence, use your own voice and avoid purely descriptively writing what they have said. While it is tempting to remain impartial and avoid 'getting involved', you will not achieve the level of criticality needed for your doctorate without positioning yourself within the argument. The University of Leicester offers useful advice on critical writing. The university advise that the most characteristic features of critical writing are:

- A clear and confident refusal to accept the conclusions of other writers without evaluating the arguments and evidence that they provide.

- A balanced presentation of reasons why the conclusions of other writers may be accepted or may need to be treated with caution.

- A clear presentation of your own evidence and argument, leading to your conclusion.

- A recognition of the limitations in your own evidence, argument and conclusion.
  (https://www2.le.ac.uk/offices/ld/resources/writing/ writing-resources/critical-writing)

Reflective question:

Check your citations, can any come out without making a difference to the thesis? If so then they should not have been there in the first place.

HEADINGS AND SUBHEADINGS

Providing well-crafted headings and sub-headings can create effective signposting for the reader. These headings are an indication of the content of that section or chapter and can contribute to the visibility of that golden thread mentioned earlier. Finn (2005) provides some techniques to assist the reader, such as 'forecasting', 'summarising', 'signalling' and 'signposting'. Finn (2005) explains that 'these techniques help the reader (including the examiners) to comprehend the coherence and storyline of the thesis' (p. 125).

Let's look at each of these techniques with examples from a previously written thesis:

Forecasting

According to Finn (2005), 'forecasting involves letting the reader know in advance what will (or will not) happen in the text' (p. 125). This can take place in the first one or two sentences. Some writers call it 'setting the scene', and this may even include laying out the sequence of the section.

Here is an example of forecasting from an extract of an EdD thesis:

> *The term 'working class' is going to be used frequently within this thesis, even though the main focus of the thesis is on mature students as a non-traditional and under-represented group progressing to higher education from further education. Mature students tend also to be working class, and all of my participants define their backgrounds as working class, therefore it would be helpful to include a section where the term 'working class' can be discussed and defined.*

The writer has let the reader know what to expect by providing a forecast in this paragraph, and a justification as to why this is going to happen.

Summarising

Finn (2005) notes that 'summarising' is a related technique to forecasting (p. 126). The difference is that this usually takes place at the end of the section. Summarising is a useful technique for tapering the section to an end and also for keeping the main points fresh in the reader's mind.

Here is an example of summarising from an extract of an EdD thesis:

> *This section focuses on the theoretical perspective used within the thesis. The chosen theorist is Pierre Bourdieu (1930–2002). Bourdieu's theories of habitus and cultural capital enable us to conceptualise and understand why some people participate in higher education and some do not. Focussing on the working class as the marginalised social group in HE, Bourdieu demonstrated how*

education perpetuates inequality and lack of opportunity. I examine the theories in the context of my own research and explore my participants' experiences of HE using Bourdieu's theoretical framework.

This summary represents a theoretical section of the thesis, which was over 4,000 words, and it was used as part of the introduction to that section.

Signalling

Signalling, argues Finn (2005), 'involves the selection of words to display the various logical links in the research plan and to direct the readers' interpretation of your writing' (p. 126). Finn provides various examples of these words in his book. One particular example, and one that is useful to create a contrast between two ideas, is the word *however*. When the reader reads *however* they will know that a contradiction, comparison or contrast will follow. Here is an example from an extract of an EdD thesis in which the signal *however* is used to contradict two ideas:

I use the theoretical framework of Bourdieu's theories of habitus and cultural capital to explore the concept of class and educational success and failure, and why, according to Bourdieu, some classes succeed in education and some do not. However, my research findings do not support an uncritical application of Bourdieu's theory; rather that one's habitus can change to accommodate new practices.

Finn (2005) stresses the importance of these words as 'devices with which to convey more fully the meaning and interaction of sequences of logic in your text' (p. 126). In this example, the writer has highlighted that the research findings do not completely support the idea of an unchanging habitus.

Signposting

Lastly, signposting, according to Finn (2005), 'is similar to signalling; however, while signalling is embedded in the text, signposting usually operates at a higher level' (p. 127). Signposting can be achieved through the use of headings and subheadings and also statements such as this example from an extract of an EdD thesis: '*The concept of mass HE will be thoroughly explored further on in this chapter*'.

Although 'mass HE' had been mentioned, in order to let the reader know that it will be returned to, a signpost is provided. A footnote with a brief definition could have been provided instead but, the concept of 'mass HE' is a very significant one, and a lengthy and elaborate explanation of what it meant was needed.

Reflective questions:

Go back and look at all of your headings and subheadings. Ask yourself these questions:

- Do the headings and subheadings do what they are supposed to?

- How much text have you provided underneath each heading?

- Does the text following the heading do justice to what the heading promises?

- Check your introduction and concluding sentences of each section and/or subheading for consistency and clarity; is the story consistent?

THE CONCLUSION IS NOT JUST A SUMMARY

This chapter is your opportunity to pull your thesis together. That cohesion and synergy that is present in the title, abstract, introduction, literature review, research questions and/or hypothesis, methodology and analysed findings – is all brought together in this 'grand finale'. To achieve this cohesion and synergy, you should return to the research questions you cited in the introduction chapter and demonstrate that you have done what you set out to do providing the answers to your research questions. Although you must not introduce any new ideas in the conclusion, you should make clear what your professional, practical and theoretical contribution to knowledge is. Wellington et al. (2009) offer some useful tips about the conclusion:

> *The overall argument developed in the thesis may also be elaborated in the conclusion to make sure it is completely clear to the reader. It can be useful to explain briefly what you have learned about the research process during your doctoral project, and if there are any outstanding issues that arise from your findings you might want to point to further research that would be useful for other researchers to take up. (p. 171)*

What you must not do in the conclusion is just summarise all the main points and tell the reader all about what they have already read. This, alone, would not be an acceptable conclusion for doctoral-level writing. Although a summary can be part of the conclusion, this final chapter is more than that. Dunleavy (2003) offers some sound advice for writing this final chapter:

> *The end of the thesis needs to have a clear character. It cannot just be a 'tell em what you've told em' section that only repeats points already made. It must first of all reprise each of the same themes or theory ideas used to construct the first chapter (and any other lead-in chapter). But this time the discussion of each theme should be grounded securely in the experience of the middle chapters. The focus should be on establishing clearly what has been shown by your research, and how it is relevant to your central thesis question and the themes set out at the start. (p. 207)*

In addition to discussing, in the conclusion, what you would do if you were taking your research forward and/or had the opportunity for further research, you should also include sections on what the limitations are of the study that you have carried out, how you have developed as a professional and practitioner and how your research may have an effect on yours and others' working practices within education. It also adds something to this chapter if you can suggest how this work could be taken forward by you or other researchers reading this thesis.

> *Reflective question:*
>
> Does each chapter or section finish with a short conclusion?
>
> These short conclusions can be your best friends when writing your first draft of your final concluding chapter. Copy each of the mini conclusions from each individual chapter, copy and paste them into what will be the conclusion. Doing this can act as a really useful starting point for your first draft of that conclusion chapter. But remember – this is just the starting point of that conclusion chapter.

CASE STUDY: A PREVIOUS EdD STUDENT'S EXPERIENCE

Dr Sally Underwood, Senior Lecturer in Nursing and Midwifery (retired), completed her EdD at the University of Sheffield. Here she provides a reflection on whether familiarising yourself with the work of your examiners is important for you. Although it is not the case that students are expected to reference their examiners, it could be that your examiner was chosen because they are an expert in that field or with a particular methodology or theoretical and conceptual framework. In which case, referencing them might be appropriate. If you do decide to reference your examiner(s), make sure that your reference and interpretation are correct. You don't want to annoy the examiner(s) by having them read a misrepresentation of their work in your thesis.

> *Sally: I was involved with choosing my two external examiners for my viva. Both were well known nursing researchers who were familiar with grounded theory and both had written interesting articles which I had read as part of my research process. Someone had already advised me to read and be very familiar with their work in preparation for the viva as they were likely to focus on areas, they were especially familiar with and interested in. I had actually quoted one of the external examiners within my thesis as his research was pertinent to a particular thread of my discussion.*

As part of my preparation for submission for viva, my literature search had identified a few new pieces of interesting work, which I included. As a final check I sent the complete draft to a colleague to read. She was concerned that I hadn't included any of my examiners' work to support my discussion and strongly advised that I do so. Apparently, as a professional courtesy, external examiners' own research should be referred to within the work of anyone who is defending their thesis at viva. I am not sure whether this is true or how wide-spread across the professions this is, but I didn't want to risk it and took my colleague's advice to supplement a section of my discussion by referring to her work. This section actually formed part of the discussion at viva and the second examiner stringently questioned me on the comparisons and differences between both our findings for this particular section of my research. I was extremely glad that I had been prepared.

SUMMARY OF THIS CHAPTER

We hope that the information provided in this chapter will enable you to sharpen and polish your thesis as you think about preparing to submit the thesis for examination. We started this chapter with some insight into what the examiners will do when they receive your thesis. This is based on our own and other examiners' experiences of examining doctoral theses for vivas. First impressions of the thesis are important, but there are other details that examiners will look for, and we hope that this chapter has helped you understand what those details might be. In concluding this chapter, we have provided you with some points of reflection to help you get over that finish line.

The main points for you to take away are:

- The 'golden thread', what this is and why it is important for the examiners.

- The abstract and introduction, and why these should be clearly understood by expert and lay readers.

- The methodology and why it should be in harmony and have synergy with all thesis chapters.

- Presenting your findings, in which we discuss the different ways of achieving this.

- What it means to write critically.

- The importance of well-crafted headings and sub-headings in creating effective signposting for the reader.

- Tips on how to produce an effective conclusion.

FURTHER READING

Murray, R. (2011). *How to write a thesis*. Berkshire: Open University Press.

Although this text is not specifically about producing a thesis for a doctorate in education, it is extremely useful and relevant. This book contains lots of tips, supportive information and examples. In addition, Murray provides strategies for coping with large amounts of text and data. Useful for any student at the thesis writing stage.

Thomson, P., & Kamler, B. (2016). Detox your writing – Strategies for doctoral researchers. London: Routledge.

Both authors are widely published professors of education and have produced a variety of publications supporting doctoral students and their supervisors. This particular text offers comprehensive guidance for structuring and writing the thesis.

REFERENCES

Askham, P. (2008). Context and identity: Exploring adult learners' experiences of higher education. *Journal of Further and Higher Education*, 32(1), 85–97.

Dunleavy, P. (2003). *Authoring a PhD: How to Plan, Draft, Write and Finish a Doctoral Thesis or Dissertation*. Hampshire: Palgrave Macmillan.

Finn, J. (2005). *Getting a PhD*. London: Routledge.

Golding, C., Sharmini, S., & Lazarovitch, A. (2014). What examiners do: What thesis students should know. *Assessment & Evaluation in Higher Education*, 39(5), 563–576.

Murray, R. (2011). *How to write a thesis*. Berkshire: Open University Press.

The University of Manchester: Academic Phrasebank. Retrieved from http://www.phrasebank.manchester.ac.uk/referring-to-sources/

Thomson, P., & Walker, M. (2010). *The Routledge doctoral student's companion*. London: Routledge.

University of Leicester. Retrieved from https://www2.le.ac.uk/offices/ld/resources/writing/writing-resources/critical-writing

Wellington, J., Bathmaker, A.-M., Hunt, C., McCulloch, G., & Sikes, P. (2009). *Succeeding with your doctorate*. London: Sage.

9

THE EXAMINATION PROCESS AND YOUR VIVA

Jodi Roffey-Barentsen and Richard Malthouse

INTRODUCTION

You have completed your thesis. You now enter the next phase of your doctoral journey: the examination process. This chapter will clarify the process, which consists of three stages: the submission of the thesis, the viva and the response to the examiners' recommendations (Burgess, Sieminski, & Arthur, 2006; Tinkler & Jackson, 2004), so you will feel informed and confident about the process once you have reached this milestone. Further, it will discuss the nature of a viva, the roles of the internal and external examiners as well as those of your supervisor(s) and that of the person chairing the meeting. It will enable you to prepare for the viva and draw up a plan to pace yourself. Further, it will explain the purpose of a mock viva: the importance of knowing your work, defending your work and being able to present a clear rationale for the central argument. Nobody can predict exactly what questions will be asked in a viva, but there are common areas that are usually covered. Preparing answers for these questions can be useful practice and will help you to build confidence in your work.

Next, the viva itself and the various possible outcomes will be explained. Finally, a number of case studies, based upon the real-life experiences of former doctoral students, will be presented, highlighting the differences in the approach to preparing for the viva, making it a personal and highly individual journey.

At the end of this chapter, you will be able to:

- Explain the examination process.

- Prepare for your viva.

- Anticipate questions likely to be asked on your thesis.

- Consider the possible outcomes of the examination process.

SUBMISSION OF YOUR THESIS

The first stage of the examination process is the submission of your thesis. You must ensure you follow your institution's policies and regulations regarding the completion of the correct documents and guidance on the required format in which the thesis is to be submitted (hard copies, electronic versions). It may be helpful to familiarise yourself with the guidelines issued by the Quality Assurance Agency for Higher Education (2018) on the UK *Quality Code of Practice for Higher Education: Advice and Guidance Research Degrees*. The thesis will be forwarded to the examiners, who will then prepare a report prior to stage two of the examination process: the viva.

WHAT IS A 'VIVA'?

The 'viva voce', or 'living voice', is the oral examination of your thesis. It is often experienced as the pinnacle of the entire doctoral process. It is during this examination that you will be asked to 'defend' your thesis. In some countries, such as the United States of America and some European countries, this is a public and sometimes even quite a theatrical event, attended by colleagues, family and friends, as well as the examiners. In the United Kingdom, the viva is normally a more private occasion, which takes place in a room with just you, your examiners, a chairperson and sometimes a supervisor as observer, in attendance. So, what is the purpose of this assessment?

First, it is to establish that you are indeed the researcher and author of the thesis; in other words, it serves to authenticate the thesis. Further, it is to determine your knowledge of the field of enquiry as well as that of methodological issues and your ability to critically reflect upon decisions made, demonstrating your awareness of any weaknesses or inconsistencies within the thesis. Finally, it allows you to explain convincingly how your research and findings contribute to the 'body of knowledge' and to showcase your strengths as a researcher. In short, you need to demonstrate you can engage in an academic debate with other experts on the topic. It may seem from the above that how well you do in your viva, and therefore in your doctoral study, is dependent on your 'performance' on the day of the viva. Here, potentially, could be an issue with the validity of a viva: what is being tested? Is it the thesis or the 'defence' of it? Is there a weighting of the elements in the entire examination process. Murray (2009, p. 18) points out that

> there is some evidence that the viva is itself part of the assessment, although there is also evidence that a student's performance at the viva will not change an examiner's mind.

This would suggest that the thesis is more important than the viva. Overall, it remains unclear what the criteria are, surrounding the viva in a cloud of 'mystique' (Murray, 2009, p. 21). Some academics consider the viva as a 'rite of passage'; a hurdle, jumped by all doctors, to achieve your doctorate. Others, however, argue that in the current educational climate more transparency around the viva is required. Institutions may have their own approaches, with some offering workshops and seminars to clarify the process and procedures, so it would be helpful for you to make enquiries early on to ensure you are familiar with the expectations made of you and the support available to you.

Reflective question:

How do you feel about the thought of doing your viva? Can you list your concerns?

THE VIVA PANEL

The panel present at your viva will usually consist of three or four other people: two examiners, a chairperson and sometimes (one of) your supervisor(s). Throughout the process, they have different roles and responsibilities.

During the latter end of stage two of your Doctorate in Education (EdD), you and your supervisor(s) will start thinking about your examiners. Although each institution has its own rules and regulations, there are usually two examiners: one internal and one external examiners. Sometimes, for instance, if you are employed by the institution where you study, a second external examiner is recruited to ensure objectivity and fairness of the assessment. The internal examiner is likely to be someone from the School of Faculty and is likely to be someone you know from your studies. Do not, however, assume this person will you be your 'friend'; their role is to examine your work, and on occasion, they may come across as more challenging to demonstrate their objectivity. The external examiner is likely to be a specialist in your area of study. They will have published on the topic and may have presented at conferences. It is likely that you will have heard of the person, but you may not have met them. In a way, this can feel quite intimidating – an 'expert' will be looking at your work in detail and ask some pertinent questions on it. However, having a well-known academic being familiar with your work may be an advantage to you in terms of sharing your research. It may be helpful to check the availability of your examiners quite a way in advance, as they may have busy schedules. Once you know who your examiners will be, consider doing some homework by reading up on them and look at their profiles and publications. As they are known in your field of study it is likely you have cited their work in your thesis, however, it may also be helpful to be aware of their views and perspectives, 'where are they coming from', to prepare yourself for debate. Approximately three months before your viva, the submitted thesis will be forwarded to the examiners. They will scrutinise the work and each will write a pre-viva report. The focus of these reports will generally be on the structure and quality of the thesis, the understanding of appropriate research methods, the contribution to knowledge, evidence of originality and the awareness of the broader context. The examiners will meet before the start of the viva and will discuss their thoughts before putting their questions to you. After the viva, they will write a final report with their feedback.

It is usual for vivas to be attended by an independent chairperson. This person is likely to be someone from the institution, so you may know them, but they will have had no involvement with your supervision or research. Their role is to ensure that the viva proceeds in accordance with the institution's regulations (and they will have received training in this), is conducted in an orderly manner and is completed within the time frame set. The chairperson will introduce everybody, will ensure that the examiners' questioning is appropriate and fair and that you will be given ample opportunity to respond to this. The role of the chairperson, therefore, is not to examine you but to see that you have been fairly examined and that the examiners do not put you under undue pressure (Fulton, Kuit, Sanders, & Smith, 2013, p. 157).

Some institutions 'allow' you to invite your supervisor to attend the viva. Their role is to maybe take notes to feed back to you; however, you cannot call on them to support you during the viva. They will normally be positioned away from the main table and will not engage in any debate. Some students feel they benefit from the moral, if silent, support from the supervisor; others, however, prefer to be independent and face the challenge on their own.

Reflective question:

Can you think of someone in your area of research who you would be delighted to invite as your examiner?

PREPARING FOR THE VIVA

The culmination of your hard work will eventually result an opportunity to take your viva. Arguably your preparation will have begun a few years prior as you engaged with the various aspects of your doctoral study. However, when you have completed the chapters and tidied up the thesis, the date for your viva will be decided by the institution. You will formally submit your thesis and complete the necessary paperwork by way of receipt. This will be the time to prepare in earnest. Consider the following areas in your preparation:

Manage Your Expectations

This is the first step in preparing for the viva. You must expect the process to be adversarial in nature and you must be in a position to defend your thesis. However, that does not mean that the process need be an unpleasant experience. Tribe and Tunariu (2016, p. 15) observe that the process may be compared to that of a 'job interview'. It is formal in nature, but it is an opportunity for you to explain, describe, clarify, justify and defend your thesis. So be prepared for some challenging questions. Do not take the questions personally! The examiners are simply seeking answers to their questions. Your role is to provide the answer as concisely and accurately as possible. Remember, you knew what you meant when you wrote what you did. However, what you have written may be interpreted in a number of ways by others, or what you have written may not be as clear as you had wished. Further, you can be content in the knowledge that at this stage, you may know more about your subject than anyone else. You can take some comfort in that.

Read Through Your Thesis

It could be that some parts of your thesis were written quite a while ago. You may therefore find that you are less familiar with its content than you would wish to be. For instance, the literature review and methodology chapters could have been completed at an earlier stage. Reading through your thesis on a number of occasions will enable you to become familiar with what you have written and remind you of the concepts supporting this. The document may well be quite large, so as you read it, it may be useful for you to make notes. Reading these through during the weeks prior to the examination may support your responses in the viva.

Label the Thesis

You will be permitted to take your thesis into the examination room with you: either a hard copy or in electronic form. So, as you read through your work, it may be useful to label the various parts of the thesis. You will not be expected to memorise what you have written, but it will be very useful for you to be able to access any part of your thesis quickly. Turning page after page as you search for a sentence can be an annoying distraction. It is not uncommon for the examiners to refer to a specific page that they wish to discuss. To this end, ensure that the pagination in the copies of the examiners' thesis are the same as your own. Labelling can take many forms and the extent to which this is utilised will vary. If you are using a hard copy, then thin strips of plastic, which can be colour coded, are an excellent way to label your work. Write clearly on the labels so that you can see what you are looking for at a glance.

Identify Likely Questions

There are some questions you can anticipate, and others, however, will be a complete surprise to you. For those that can be anticipated, write them down and think about a suitable response. Avoid scripting though; this is where you practise the response to such an extent you memorise your answers. The problem with this is that it removes any spontaneity. It is far better for you to be able to think on your feet rather than draw upon rehearsed responses, which may not totally fit the question asked. A further useful strategy is for you to explain to another person the concept(s) or theories you anticipate discussing. It does not really matter if the person you are talking to fully understands what you are saying. The purpose is that you will identify in yourself if there are any gaps in your knowledge. If there are, then you will have plenty of time to fill in any gaps by reading up on the subject. The section below will identify some of the questions you may anticipate.

Undertaking a Mock Viva

It is not uncommon for students to practise their responses in the form of a mock viva. This can be very useful as it affords you to experience what it is like in the viva. For example, the pressure of trying to juggle lots of information in your head, remembering where things have been written and actively listening to the questions asked. As Tinkler and Jackson (2004, p. 130) point out: 'The purpose served by a mock viva varies depending on the form it takes'. For example, you may take the position of the candidate and be questioned. Alternatively, you may witness another person's mock viva. Sometimes, the whole of the thesis is examined, and on other occasions, only a part of it is considered. The mock viva may be conducted by your supervisory team or by a person not known to you who may have a varying perspective on the thesis. Tinkler and Jackson (2004) further observe the

> *objectives of a mock viva with the student as candidate include to: refine the aspects of the thesis; foster skills useful in the viva; provide experience of thinking deeply about focussing upon answering different types of questions about the thesis; and provide experience of managing differing types of behaviour. (p. 132)*

During the mock viva, it may be useful for you to write down the question as it is being asked. That way you can remind yourself of what you have been asked if you happen to forget or if you digress. A mock viva may also be a good way for others, studying for their doctorate, to think about their own studies.

Preparing on the Day

Ensure that your diary is free, you do not want any unnecessary distractions on the day of the viva. You may be able to arrange a visit to the examination room on a prior occasion. This can be useful for you to visualise the room as you prepare. Consider what you are going to wear. Ask what would be appropriate, what not and what is relatively comfortable. Arguably, tight fitting clothes that cut off the circulation are not going to enable you to perform at your best. Your body language will make an impression, so make sure it is the right one with your choice of attire. Ensure you have eaten sufficiently even though you may not be in the mood. A rumbling tummy can be a mild distraction. If you are nervous you may experience a dry mouth. Normally, water will be provided, but take no chances, take your own small bottle. You may not have met the external examiner prior to this viva, so think, do you shake hands, who do you greet first, what is appropriate in the circumstances and what may not be appropriate?

If you have prepared thoroughly, you will be able to walk into the examination room in the knowledge that

> *[...] you know more about your research than anyone else. Remember that you are the world expert on it, and no one else knows or understands the depth of the depth of new knowledge that you have created. (Fulton et al., 2013, p. 159)*

PREPARING FOR THE VIVA QUESTIONS

Many of the questions asked in a viva can be anticipated. As a result, these can be considered and practised by you to ensure a polished account. Although usually experienced as a professional debate, the viva can be adversarial in nature and your job is to defend your thesis. In general, likely questions can be categorised into the following areas:

1. *General questions:*
   At the beginning of the viva, it is not uncommon for the questions to be very general in nature. These are employed to introduce the questioning and to prepare the way for the more specific questions. These questions can involve the following:
   1a Summary:
   Please summarise your thesis?
   What would you say is your unique contribution to the body of knowledge?
   What are the main findings of your research?
   What would another person learn from reading your thesis?
   What did you learn from conducting this research?

1b Motivation:

What motivated you to research this topic?

Why did you select this particular topic?

What is it about this topic that you think is important?

What were the reasons for you conducting this research?

1c Position:

How did your position affect your data collection?

How did your position affect your data analysis?

What prior experience did you have in relation to this study?

How did your background affect your data collection?

How did your background affect your data analysis?

What is your professional position in relation to this field?

How did your bias affect your data collection?

How did your bias affect your data analysis?

What is your personal position in relation to these research questions?

1d Publications:

Which elements of your work do you feel are suitable for publication?

Which elements of your work do you feel are suitable for presentation at conference?

Has any of the work been published?

Do you have any plans for publication?

Has any of the work been presented at conference?

Do you have any plans for dissemination?

2. *Theories and theoretical frameworks:*

Describe in detail the main research questions in your work.

What theories have you drawn upon in your research?

From where did these questions originate?

What theoretical frameworks have you drawn upon in your research?

Explain to me about the theories this study focusses upon.

What theoretical perspectives have you drawn upon in your research?

3. *Literature review:*

What guided your literature review?

Tell me which main theories you adopted in this research.
What shaped your literature review?
Why did it cover the areas that it did?
Why did it not cover the areas that it did?
Why did you include the work of .... in your study?
Why didn't you include the work of .... in your study?

4. *Methodology:*
   Please explain why you employed the methods selected?
   What was the reason for not using others, for example ...?
   What informed your choice of methods?
   In hindsight, what would you have done differently?

5. *The sample:*
   Describe your strategy for selecting the sample.
   What factors led you to selecting this sample?
   What would you identify as being problematic with it?
   (In the case of a small-scale study) Please justify why so few participants were involved?

6. *Data analysis:*
   Describe to me the process of data analysis employed.
   Why did you analyse it in this way?
   Did themes emerge from your data (a posteriori)
   Did you 'bring them to the data' (a priori)?
   Was there anything in the data that you discovered that surprised you?
   Where there any incongruities contained within the data?
   What method was used to categorise the data?
   How did you account for unconscious bias?
   Describe to me the process of thematic analysis used.
   Could it have been done in another way?

7. *Further work:*
   Are there aspects of your work that would benefit from further development?
   Describe in detail the features of this development?
   How do you propose to achieve this?

8. *Generalisability:*

   Can you generalise from your work?

   To what extent can you generalise from this work?

   What lessons can be learnt from this study by practitioners?

   What lessons can be learnt from it by policymakers?

   What lessons can be learnt from it by other researchers?

   What are the key messages from this study?

   What are its key implications from this study?

9. *Reflection:*

   Reflecting on the thesis what would you identify are its strengths and weaknesses?

   Is there anything else you would like to say or observe that has not been covered today?

Reflective questions:

Can you prepare a response to the question in each of the above sections? Are there any gaps? What question would YOU ask if you were examining this thesis?

THE VIVA ITSELF

You will have spent a considerable amount of time and effort building up your thesis into a satisfactory whole. Parts are added to and others taken away from. Aspects are changed, modified and adapted. The elements are complementary and suitably balanced, and you may feel very happy with what you have achieved. It is complete.

However, you now face the viva, and during this time expect your thesis to be dissected, taken apart bit by bit and for that wonderful whole to be analysed very thoroughly indeed. It is when the magnifying glass focusses upon aspects of your thesis, taken them out of context, that the appearance of the thesis can change. It can no longer rely on the support of the whole but stands alone, naked and vulnerable.

The viva is not necessarily a pleasant experience, although it can be uplifting and stimulating. You will be pushed and pulled in many directions. Your purpose is to defend your thesis and demonstrate your knowledge and understanding of the research process and your contribution to the body of knowledge. Depending on your institution, a viva is likely to take between one and a half and two and a half hours, although you may request a short comfort break. So, what can you expect during the examination itself?

Introductions

When you walk into the room, you can expect to be introduced to the participants by the chairperson. As stated above, normally, there will be three/four people other than yourself: the external examiner, the examiner from your institution, the chairperson and possibly one of your supervisors as an observer. The chairperson will sit aside from the two examiners and will most likely be taking notes once the introductions are complete. If the examiners introduce themselves using their first and family name but not their titles, it would be inappropriate for you to address them using their first name only, as this would assume a level of familiarity which may be false. Therefore, always use their full title at first, unless it was suggested by the examiners to call them by their first name.

You can expect some conversation that aims to put you at ease and settle you. If you do feel nervous and most people do, then remember to breath. Two deep breaths will provide your body the oxygen it requires to function normally. If food is offered in the form of a biscuit and you accept the offer, consider an appropriate time to consume it. If you know a question is just about to be asked, then you may not want a mouth full of dry crumbs. The availability of water was discussed earlier in the chapter. At this point it would be wise to consider the relationship that will be expected between yourself and the examiners. Do not appear overly confident or arrogant. This could be seen as a challenge to some examiners who would then delight in reminding you how little you actually know.

On the contrary, you do not want to appear subservient or grovelling, however, an element of respect must be shown on your part.

The viva may be seen as a ritual, a rite of passage of the highest order and therefore must be taken seriously by all participants. Look to the external examiner to guide you on the types of behaviours to exhibit, is the process veering towards the formal or informal? In any case, you will expect to be on your best behaviour and at all times be polite regardless of the intensity or severity of the questioning.

Questioning

Then, the questioning may start in relation to your thesis. Frequently, the first questions will be very broad in nature and could relate to the selection of your chosen topic. From this point, remember that you are expected not just to answer questions but to show that you benefit from the wider knowledge of the subject being discussed.

Expect a counter argument in relation to what you have done or not done. Do not be put off your stride when the observations or questions appear to belittle what you have done. This is the time for you to justify and explain your decisions. You may feel you are being goaded and this may be the case. Try to remain calm, be rational and to compose yourself. There are always many ways to do something; however, you chose to do what you did in a certain way. Now justify this.

Being Defensive

But how do you guard against becoming too defensive? Murray (2009, p. 10) offers sage advice and suggests students should 'Define – Defend'. She points out that:

> *The doctoral examination is [...] the scene of intense debate about a piece of completed work. It should be assumed that there will be disagreement and perhaps even a conflict of views. (Murray, 2009, p. 10)*

She further observes 'For students, the temptation is to respond to challenging, probing questions with defence and justification of their work' (Murray, 2009, 106). However, she acknowledges this as being understandable and offers an alternative strategy, which is,

... to begin with the definition of the work – say what you did – and then, only then, say why you did it that way. Define first, defend second:

- *Examiner's Question.* '*Why did you not do more detailed analysis of …?*'

- *Candidate's 'defend' answer.* '*I did not do that because …*'

- *Define – defend answer.* '*What I did was …*' '*My reasons for doing it were …*' '*I could have done a more detailed analysis of … by … But I decided not to do this because …*'

(Murray, 2009, p. 106)

There will be occasions when you will be directed towards a certain page. If this is the case, it is good practice to read out what you are being questioned upon out loud, alternatively you can paraphrase the wording as you read. This gives you the opportunity to remind yourself of what you said and also it will give you time to think about what you meant at the time.

Dealing With Weaknesses

Hindsight is a wonderful thing and you may wish that you had done some things differently. You may be asked to identify any weaknesses in your thesis. Do not be worried about this as weaknesses are bound to occur to some extent or another. When dealing with these, positive affirmation is useful. You could respond in the following ways:

- 'Yes, you are quite correct, this is a weakness in the method of data collection. At the time what I was trying to achieve was …'

- 'Yes, unfortunately that is the case in this single instance. What I have learned from this is, in future to …'

- 'I agree entirely. That is the result of compromise within such research. I can see now that it would have been far better to have …'

Being Heard and Linking

It may be in the viva that you feel that the point you have tried to make has not been heard by the examiners. Thousands of words are used during the examination, and it is very easy for things to become lost or for a new subject to appear before the present subject has been properly attended to. Take control. You can legitimately ask to go back to a previous point. You can then contextualise the point you were making and either reiterate it or state it again in such a way that your point is made. Being heard also includes making appropriate links to the various aspects of the thesis. You can state that one element of your research takes a certain path and you can identify the path it took, perhaps linking between the Literature review, the data analysis and the discussion. Remember that what may be obvious to you is not necessarily obvious to the examiners. There are occasions when stating the obvious is appropriate. You know your thesis better than any other person and the onus is on you to highlight what may have been lost or not seen at all.

Ending

It will be obvious when it is the end of the process. You will be asked if there is anything which you would like to add, confirm or discuss further. You will have to decide what is best in the light of your experience within the viva. You will then be invited to leave the room and wait elsewhere (usually another small room in the vicinity).

The time waiting can be unbearable and can take up to an hour. This is because the examiners need to discuss their findings and also agree upon their report. So, do not be put off about the amount of time it takes. Eventually, you will be called back to the room. The examiners will then inform you of their decision. They will provide feedback; however, it is unlikely that you will remember anything they say. This is where a supervisor's notes may be helpful. Whatever the outcome, you will receive a written report with the decision and/or conditions and recommendations, for you to address (if required) within a certain time frame, according to the institution's regulations. For most students, it is now time to contact their family and friends with the news and start celebrating!

> *Reflective question:*
>
> How will you portray yourself in the viva; how will you
> achieve this?

OUTCOMES OF THE EXAMINATION PROCESS

As Tinkler and Jackson (2004, p. 128) observe 'The outcome of
a doctoral examination is rarely either pass or fail'. Very few students pass outright, although it can be achieved, as PR in case
study 1 below. However, do not feel disappointed if the work is
not quite finished yet. On the contrary, few students fail overall, as
their supervisors would not have put them forward for completion
if they thought the work was unsatisfactory or below the required
standard. In reality, it is likely you will achieve a preliminary pass
but with the recommendation that that you make either minor or
major amendments. 'Many theses require further work and the
extend of revision may depend on the candidate's performance in
the viva' (Tinkler & Jackson, 2004, p. 128). As stated in the introduction to this chapter, there may be a direct correlation between
how well you perform in the viva and the tasks asked of you at the
end of the examination process.

It will be helpful for you to check your institution on the outcomes
of your examination. In general, there are four possible options:

- Pass without amendments.

- Pass, subject to minor amendments. Minor amendments can
  be editorial corrections or minor deficiencies. This usually does
  not require another viva.

- Pass, subject to major amendments. Major amendments
  require you to revise the thesis and resubmit. The examiners
  may require a second viva following the resubmission.

- Fail. The student may not be awarded the degree and may not
  be permitted to be re-examined, depending on the regulations
  of the institution.

Reflective questions:

How do you think you will feel on hearing the outcome of the examination? How do you anticipate responding?

CASE STUDIES

The following case studies are accounts of former EdD students who have successfully completed their doctorate. They highlight the individual approach each has chosen, confirming that there is no one correct way to pass a viva and achieve a doctorate.

Case Study 1

PR is a lecturer at a university in the south of England and gained his EdD recently.

> *I would refer to my viva as a 'cognitive assault course', although I did thoroughly enjoy the challenge and I valued the professional and respectful dialogue of the examiners.*

> *When thinking about the preparation for the viva, I felt that I had done enough writing in the thesis that therefore decided not to do any more writing: no notes, no blogs, no summaries ….*

> *I realised that I had to focus my preparation on 'vocalising and verbalising' my research, to be able to answer any questions without significant delay or fudging and confusion.*

> *To do this, I examined his thesis closely, practising responses and had imaginary discussions with the examiners; all out loud. I found that the best way for me to focus on this was by going for long walks, talking to and debating with myself. I ignored curious looks from passers-by and kept walking and debating. I felt that my background in Performing Arts, as well as my current role as a dissertation supervisor, may have been*

helpful to me, as I was confident in being able to present and debate. A key to the strategy was therefore to 'get inside the mind of the examiners' and to anticipate the kinds of challenging questions that might arise.

I appreciate that not making any notes is somewhat unusual, however, from the rehearsal preparation I felt I 'knew' his thesis, with all its strengths, limitations and flaws, inside out. During the viva, I did not try to 'unnecessarily flatter' my examiners by referring to their work yet was fully aware of their contributions to the subject of my research and had included references to each in my work.

I must stress that each candidate has to find their own, individual way of preparing for their viva. Due to the very personal experience of the viva, I cannot recommend my approach, as a tried strategy, to all. However, it was one way that worked for me to develop my 'inner researcher voice' which was a critical factor in helping me approach the viva more confidently.

Following PR's viva, there were no amendments to be made, which is an exceptional outcome and achievement.

Case Study 2

HG is a lecturer at a London university. He was diagnosed as having dyslexia a few years earlier. He felt he no longer had the label of 'Stupid' as this was replaced with that of 'Dyslexic'. This change enabled him to go and achieve. He completed a BA (Hons) followed by an MA in Education and then found himself preparing for the EdD viva.

I needed a coping strategy. Small chunks of information were fine, I would work on the various aspects without much difficulty. The difficulty that did arise was that of remembering all the information in one go. It is suggested that most people can manage 7 chunks of information plus or minus 2. Well for me it is definitely

*7 minus two and, on some days, it feels more like 2 plus 2;
it is not constant.*

*With this in mind, I knew that potentially I was going
to struggle in the viva. The examiners could ask me anything they wished from any part of the study. Although
I knew my topic, not all of it was readily to hand in my
head. I needed strategies if I was to be able to succeed.
I experience dyslexia like doors closing on me without
me knowing. So sometimes I can spell a word and then
the next moment the door has closed, and the word
has gone. The only thing is that I am totally unaware of
this fact until I need to access the door. Then I find it is
closed and sometimes locked. Information gets locked
in also and I get locked out.*

*So, what did I do, what was my coping strategy? First
of all, I labelled the thesis. It was relatively large, about
100,000 words in length. The labels were colour-coded.
Each colour represented a chapter from the thesis (for
instance, the Methodology chapter was brown, Data
Analysis was orange, etc.) This made perfect sense to
me as I also have synaesthesia which assists and catego-
rises my thinking. The labels were placed into my copy
of the thesis like steps, so that I could see the text written upon each label. All of the relevant information,
such as key terms within the chapter, was at hand. This
served two purposes. Firstly, I was able to access the
information required following a question in the viva.
Secondly, and more importantly for me, if my brain
shut the door on a word, I would be able to find it
again as all the relevant words were listed on the labels.*

*The next thing for me to do by way of preparation was
to be involved in a couple of mock vivas. I found this
very useful as it enabled me to practise using the labels
and then to find the words on the relevant pages. In
fact, as I had all the necessary words laid out in front of
me, it made the answering of the viva questions easier
for me. No doors were able to close!'*

HG achieved his EdD with minor amendments, which he addressed within the time frame given. He describes his viva as the 'biggest and most demanding test I have ever had. There is no escaping; you cannot bluff your way through it'.

Case Study 3

GJ is a lecturer, teaching Higher Education programmes in a Further Education institution. She studied for her doctorate on a part-time basis and was very pleased and relieved to reach the 'preparing for the viva' stage.

> *I had been so focused on the submission of my thesis that I did not know how to 'prepare' for the viva. I started trying to 'learn' it by reading my work over and over again. Of course, I knew exactly what I had written, so the reading did not really help. My supervisor and some colleagues from the university where I studied, organised a mock-viva for me, which left me somewhat disappointed and angry, as one of the 'examiners', a scientist with positivist/quantitative views, completely misunderstood and belittled my research. After this disastrous meeting, the 'Chairperson' followed me out of the room, reassuring me, saying I had done very well in my defence of the work. My confidence had been severely affected though. I now set out to prepare 'properly'; this was not going to happen again. I needed instant responses, supported by the thesis. To minimise fluffing around (I remember it must be here somewhere ...), I used differently coloured post-its to label the thesis; the chapters with page numbers to start with; these were at the top of the thesis. So, if the examiner referred to a page number, I knew where I was. Then, I also needed labels for key ideas and theories; these were put on the right-hand side of the thesis. I started making notes and writing explanations and justifications on a separate note-pad but found this too cumbersome (too many bits of paper), so I wrote my notes on*

the clean, left-hand side, opposite to the relevant page (in pencil, so I could change it if necessary). Now I felt I had everything together. I knew where the limitations of my research were and prepared responses, if questioned. My thesis looked like a piece of art, with coloured labels sticking out everywhere, only useful and logical to me. It worked. The viva itself I experienced as a most enjoyable (really!) professional discussion with likeminded colleagues – I felt elated at the end as well as proud of myself. English is not my first language; I was unfamiliar with the English education system and protocols; but I had done it! There were, however, minor amendments to the thesis to consider, which I had anticipated. I decided to tackle these as quickly as I could and was in a position to demonstrate to the internal examiner how I had addressed the queries within weeks. To 'help' the examiner, I produced a table, indicating for each of the points how it had been addressed and on which page of the thesis the amendment could be found. In the thesis, I highlighted the amended section, so the examiner could easily identify the changes made.

My advice to others on this journey would be to accept all help and support offered. Do have a mock viva if possible. In my case it was an unpleasant experience, but it spurred me on. Believe in your research and be convincing in stating your contribution to the body of knowledge.

I now supervise doctoral students and have examined theses and vivas myself; I consider this to be the best part of my job.

SUMMARY OF THIS CHAPTER

This chapter has tried to clarify the examination and viva processes, so you feel informed and confident when you have reached the stage of your doctoral journey. It has:

- Explained that the examination process is a three-stage process: the submission of the thesis, the viva and the response to the examiners' feedback.

- Discussed the nature of the viva.

- Helped you in preparing for the viva, including the consideration of questions that are likely to be asked.

- Talked you through what to expect from the viva itself.

- Discussed the different outcomes to the examination process.

- Offered case studies, highlighting the individuality of chosen strategies in preparation of the viva.

FURTHER READING

- Hartley, J., & Fox, C. (2004). Assessing the mock-viva: The experiences of British doctoral students. *Studies in Higher Education, 29*(6), 727–738.
  This article explores the use of mock vivas. The study focusses on the experiences and feelings of postgraduate students (in the United Kingdom) concerning their mock vivas. The results suggest that there are considerable disparities in procedures within and across institutions, and that students are frequently asked different questions in the mock and the real viva. Nonetheless, mock vivas were judged to be helpful by most of the students concerned.

- Trafford, V., & Leshem, S. (2008). *Stepping stones to achieving your doctorate: By focusing on your viva from the start.* Maidenhead: Open University Press.
  This book is aimed at doctoral candidates, registered for a PhD or professional doctorate. It is different in that it starts with the end; how will your thesis be examined, what are the criteria that examiners use? It focusses on how you can raise your level of thinking, achieving the characteristics of 'doctorateness' that examiners are looking for. This book benefits from extracts from theses, examiner reports and cameo accounts from doctoral examiners, supervisors and candidates. It also contains some visual models that explain relationships and processes.

- Watts, J. (2012). Preparing doctoral candidates for the viva: Issues for students and supervisors. *Journal of Further and Higher Education*, 36(3), 371–381.

  This article discusses a number of issues that inform the preparation of students, focussing on the role of the internal and external examiners, the viva voce process, guidance for students and some practical suggestions for supervisors and students, particularly the value of full role-play in building students' confidence.

- Wisker, G. (2008). *The postgraduate research handbook*. Basingstoke: Palgrave MacMillan.

  Looking at postgraduate research more generally, this substantial text guides students through the various stages from starting your postgraduate research, to 'getting going' and carrying out the research, the writing up and viva, to thinking about publishing and presenting your research at conferences. The section on 'Preparing for and undertaking your viva' followed by 'Dealing with corrections and life after the viva' is informative and accessible.

REFERENCES

Burgess, H., Sieminski, S., & Arthur, L. (2006). *Achieving your doctorate in education*. London: Sage.

Fulton, J., Kuit, J., Sanders, G., & Smith, P. (2013). *The professional doctorate*. Hampshire: Palgrave McMillan.

Murray, R. (2009). *How to survive your viva* (2nd ed.). Maidenhead: Open University Press.

Quality Assurance Agency for Higher Education. (2018). *The UK quality code of practice for higher education: Advice and guidance research degrees*. Gloucester: QAA.

Tinkler, P., & Jackson, C. (2004). *The doctoral examination process. A handbook for students, examiners and supervisors*. Maidenhead: Open University Press.

Tribe, R., & Tunariu, A. D. (2016, autumn). Preparing for a doctoral viva. *The Psychology of Education Review*, 41(2), 51–58.

10

POST QUALIFICATION – NOW YOU'RE A DOCTOR, WHAT NEXT?

Jodi Roffey-Barentsen

INTRODUCTION

This final chapter looks at life after achieving your doctorate (although it may be helpful to read it beforehand). From my experience, I had anticipated that being a doctor meant I had reached the pinnacle of my educational journey, the summit of what I could achieve. Only to find that a larger mountain loomed in front of me and I was at basecamp …. The focus now was on publishing in journals, conference papers, presenting at conferences, in other words, sharing the findings of the research with a wider audience. This can be quite overwhelming; where and how do you start? How do you go about it?

This chapter offers some guidance for publishing in journals and refers to general advice for Early Career Researchers. To illustrate how each journey is different, some of our authors have contributed a synopsis of their experiences after becoming A DOCTOR!

At the end of this chapter, you will be able to:

- Consider ways of sharing your research with the wider world.

- Convert your thesis into (an) article(s) suitable for publication in a journal.

- Take steps to develop from an Early Career Researcher to a more experienced one.

If you are employed by an academic institution, such as a university, you will be aware of the importance of research and publishing, or 'output'. The Research Excellence Framework (REF) was introduced in 2014, replacing the Research Assessment Exercise, and is undertaken by the higher education (HE) funding bodies in the United Kingdom (REF, 2020). The purpose of the REF (2020) is to assess research to 'secure the continuation of a world-class, dynamic and responsive research base across the full academic spectrum within UK higher education'. It further aims to

> provide accountability for public investment in research and produce evidence of the benefits of this investment; benchmarking information and establish reputational yardsticks, for use within the HE sector and for public information …. (REF, 2020)

There may, therefore, be some pressure on you to publish your research in peer-reviewed journals of a good calibre.

Burgess, Sieminski, and Arthur (2006) recommend you do some market research before you start drafting an article. You need to establish which journal would be best suited to your research and the audience you would like to reach (Wellington, Bathmaker, Hunt, McCulloch, and Sikes, 2005). You may have already considered a number of journals, probably those that you have cited from in your thesis, as appropriate for your work. In that case, aim for the highest ranking one and draft your article to meet the characteristics of that journal. You will need to focus on only one, or maybe a few aspect(s) of your thesis, so be prepared to rewrite certain parts, converting them into a suitable article. In my case, my supervisor was most helpful, and we prepared an article together. The first hurdle is to ensure you meet the criteria set out by the journal, such as word count, style, referencing, etc. After submission of the article, the waiting begins.

It can take a long time before you get a response from the editor(s). The response is either a straight rejection (this article is not suitable for us!) or it will be forwarded to a number of reviewers. The reviewers, who are peers and respected scholars in the field, then offer feedback on the article. The majority of articles reviewed will need further amendments, either minor or major, before they are accepted for publication. Although you can argue the feedback, if there appears to be a misunderstanding or misinterpretation, my advice is to do what you're asked to do and comply with the suggestion for improvement made. Remember that some journals are published twice or three times a year, which means it may take a long time before you see your article in print. You can only submit an article to one journal at the time, which means that if it gets rejected, you have to start again, tailoring the article to fit the journal which is next on your list and so on.

Trying to get published can be quite disheartening, with peers critiquing your work and maybe even rejecting it. Do not give up; a different journal may accept your work without amendments. The defence of your work did not finish in your viva, it is a part of being an active researcher and academic; rise to the challenge!

In addition, try to publish your work onto as many media platforms as possible, not just ones such as Twitter and LinkedIn but also the academic ones like ResearchGate and Academia.edu. Not all journals and books are online or open access, so putting your thesis, publications, conference presentations, etc. onto the World Wide Web gives you high search engine optimisation, meaning that when people Google your name, or keywords you have used, like your research interests and areas of expertise, they will be able to find you quickly.

The term often used for colleagues who are new to the world of research is 'Early Career Researcher', and some institutions offer support to those colleagues. As highlighted by Czerniawski (2018) in his BERA blog,

> Laudel and Gläser (2008) argue that as an early career researcher (ECR) you are not just developing one but three careers simultaneously: your cognitive career (i.e. the development of your research trail); your community career (i.e. your contribution to your wider academic communities); and your organisational career (i.e. the performance expectations of your employer organisation).

Czerniawski (2018) offers a number of tips to help you make the transition from an early career researcher into an experienced senior colleague, which include

1. Approach senior colleagues and directors of research throughout your university. Tell them who you are and what your research is about. Many will be unaware of exactly what work we do in education or the potential linkages with their own disciplines so this could open many doors.

2. Write a blog for one of the more established blogging sites. It is an opportunity to publicise arguments, themes from research and/or published work you are engaged with. Remember, blogs are increasingly being recognised as evidence of your impact.

3. Ensure you keep your university staff webpage up to date. Don't underestimate the extent to which lobbying groups, journalists, publishers, policy-makers and others look at these.

4. Offer to review articles for journals as part of a longer-term strategy to target that publication for a future article.

5. Offer to review abstracts for academic conferences. This is a brilliant way to get to grips with the work and current thinking within your own research area.

6. Schmooze grant managers/university research funding officers in your university! Get them to know your first name. When a last-minute grant comes in, with luck, they'll immediately think of you!

7. Get accepted at a conference at least once a year and ensure that you present a whole paper (rather than just PowerPoint slides) then use the critical feedback to turn it into a journal article.

8. Aim to have one article under review while writing the next.

9. Have a trusted critical friend (not an academic!) read all your abstracts, introductions and conclusions. If they cannot understand those vital sections, then it's not their deficiency in understanding that's the issue – it's the clarity of your writing!

10. Widen your methodological expertise – it is too easy to stay within our own epistemological comfort zone – widening your expertise will open doors to the sorts of research collaborations you need to develop your careers.

11. Aim to have two mentors – one within and one outside your institution – both will offer invaluable expertise while widening your professional arena.

12. Access the dedicated support available in your own university that specifically targets ECRs – it is there – but institutions are not necessarily effective in signposting it.

13. At larger conferences, talk to the people behind the publishers' stands. They're usually the senior commissioning editors or senior publishers and are there to talk about your emerging research ideas with a view to future publication.

14. Try to write and publish with your mentor or other colleagues within your 'academic tribe' – generally speaking, more authors mean more citations!

15. Seek out and contact ECR forums in other universities. They will be keen to hear from you – and in many cases will invite you to present your work – or even put on shared events at your or their institutions.

16. With a colleague or two, put in a proposal for a special edition of a journal. It's fun and can raise your game in terms of developing professional expertise, networks and publishing craftsmanship.

17. Exploit your doctoral thesis to the maximum in publications, in terms of contributions to theory, practice, existing findings, methodology and policy.

18. Join any special interest group/network within your professional community (often related to annual conferences). BERA, for example, has over 30 such networks to choose from.

19. Answer emails at the end of the day rather than the beginning! That way you might just get to lunchtime having achieved some of the tasks on your to-do list.

20. Finally, write the sorts of publications you want to write, rather than those you feel you *ought* to write. I still enjoy writing for A level sociology students. And I get as much pleasure writing those sorts of publications as I do for the REF, TEF or any other auditing requirement that we academics, often feel pressured into writing for. All writing is good – it helps us think, create, develop, review and enhance our ideas.

The next part of this chapter offers individual journeys from colleagues who have contributed to this publication, to illustrate how each of us uses their doctorate in a different way.

JANE CREATON

I undertook a professional doctorate in education at the University of Sussex from 2005 to 2010. My thesis was titled *Policing the Boundaries: The Writing, Regulation and Representation of Criminology* and explored the role of academic staff in regulating student writing practices in interdisciplinary contexts. The final paragraph of my thesis is below:

> As I come to the end of this thesis, I have just taken up another more senior management post as Associate Dean (Academic) in the Faculty of Humanities and Social Sciences at the University of Portsmouth. This means that some of the opportunities for doing research will be reduced. However, I bring to my new post the knowledge, skills and values that I have acquired in the course of doing the doctorate; a greater understanding of the higher education policies and context; a critical approach to the underlying discourses and ideologies that underpin the curriculum; and a reflexive approach to my own professional practice.

Nearly 10 years on, I am still in my post as Associate Dean (Academic), but I was promoted to Reader in Higher Education in 2017 and have been involved in a number of interesting and rewarding research and teaching activities which connect back to my own doctorate.

My EdD thesis had concluded with a number of recommendations for developing student writing and enhancing how feedback might be given, which I took forward in my own department. A discourse analysis of staff feedback was used to initiate course-level discussions amongst staff about acceptable forms of knowledge and representation practices which enabled this tacit knowledge to be shared with students. I disseminated these findings through presentations to the Academic Skills Unit, which works directly with students to support their learning, to academic staff through university, faculty and departmental staff development events; through my teaching to professional doctorate students; and through presentations at national and international conferences. I subsequently applied the same techniques to analyse feedback on professional doctorate assignments which was published as a chapter in a collection of case studies and critical commentaries from teacher-researchers to illustrate transformative practice across a range of HE contexts.

The knowledge and experience I gained from undertaking the EdD was also invaluable in informing the development of a new Professional Doctorate in Education in my own institution, which was launched in 2017. I designed the Publication, Dissemination and Impact module to promote the communication of research findings beyond the specialist academic community, through publication in practitioner journals and engagement with social media and other platforms. This was intended to stimulate a commitment to public engagement beyond the academy, and as part of the assessment, students have given presentations at learning and teaching conferences, teacher education events and on staff development programmes. They have also prepared outputs targeted at a range of academic and professional journals, and several students have had their work subsequently accepted in these journals for publication. For the Research Proposal module, I have developed an innovative approach for the allocation of supervision teams which enabled students to have more voice and engagement in the negotiation and selection process. Students are actively involved in reviewing the outputs of potential supervisors in order to identify the appropriate mix of subject knowledge, methodological and professional expertise. The outcome has been the identification, in partnership with students, of a rich and diverse range of supervision

teams from across different departments and disciplines within
the institution. This includes appropriately qualified staff working
in professional and student support services, including planning,
information services, the library and academic skills.

Since completing my own doctorate, I have supervised five doctoral students through to completion and am currently on eight
other supervision teams. I have also delivered sessions on Writing
Abstracts and Researching Your Workplace as part of the Graduate
School Development Programme and make an active contribution
to the Graduate School training and development programme for
postgraduate research (PGR) supervisors. In 2018, I led a successful
bid for a project leading the Office for Students/Research England
Catalyst Fund Project for Supporting Mental Health and Wellbeing for Postgraduate Research Students. The project is focussed on
promoting mental health literacy and increasing social support for
PGR students. Outcomes have included the collection and analysis
of baseline data from nearly 300 PGR students about their mental
health and well-being, the development of targeted online resources to support students at important transition points, structured
action learning sets to support new students in developing healthy
working practices and personal development skills and piloting
and evaluating enhanced training to support good mental health
and well-being with supervisors. I am also monitoring the ongoing implementation of an institution-wide PGR well-being strategy
to ensure the sustainability of the project beyond the end of the
funding period. A key legacy of the project has been the establishment of a series of international conference on Postgraduate
Mental Health and Wellbeing (in partnership with the UK Council
of Graduate Education and the University of Sussex) which bring
together researchers and practitioners from across HE to discuss
and develop initiatives to support postgraduate researchers.

As a result of my work on institutional policies and procedures
and my engagement with the mental health and well-being project, I was invited by Vitae to join the Concordat Writing Group,
which was tasked with revising the current UK Concordat to
Support the Career Development of Researchers. This document
sets out a statement of the expectations and responsibilities of
research funders and institutions with respect to researchers and

is central to creating healthy and sustainable working practices for PGRs during their doctoral study and beyond. It was a valuable opportunity to participate in policymaking that would have real impact on doctoral and early career researchers. My experience of undertaking the EdD and the subsequent opportunities that it has opened up are an example of the transformative effect that the doctorate can have on the professional lives of students and of the impact that they can have on professional practice.

KATE HOSKINS

Following completion of my PhD viva in August 2010, I was fortunate enough to secure a Senior Lectureship at the University of Roehampton. I was able to gain this role because of my teaching experience; throughout my full-time doctorate, I had undertaken up to 10 hours of teaching a week at London Metropolitan University on the BA Education programme. I gained a lot of experience from leading modules exploring how identity and policy influenced practice. The modules I taught included *Women and Education; Gender, Education and Empire; and Perspectives on Curriculum and Knowledge*. An important aspect of leading on these modules was ensuring that kept up to date on reading and developments in these relevant subject areas to ensure I had up-to-date reading lists for my students, and this enabled them to become consist of key debates and developments in the field of education.

Whilst I was at London Metropolitan University, I undertook supervision for undergraduate and master's dissertation students and was able to work closely with them to develop their dissertation work. I found the experience of supervising BA and MA dissertations extremely rewarding as I was able to build a relationship with my students, and intellectually challenging, as I needed to extend my own reading to ensure I could supervise their projects on a range of education-related topics. This combination of leading modules and supervising students whilst completing my doctorate was invaluable in enabling me to secure my first academic post.

In addition to teaching and supervising students, I also worked hard to build a publications profile towards the end of my doctorate and immediately after completion. To this end, I submitted a book proposal based on my thesis, and I was awarded a contract for a book titled *Women and Success: Professors in the UK Academy*, based on this research, which was a cutting-edge analysis of how women professors experienced their 'success'. The study led to invited conference presentations at, for example, the University of Oxford and GEA, and to further publications, including *The Price of Success?* which was published in *Women's Studies International Forum*. My PhD supervisor provided significant support to help get me started on publishing, particularly in terms of understanding the standard of work required and giving me advice about how to structure books and journal articles. The mentoring and sponsorship support I received were invaluable to me as I gained understanding of how to go about building a publications profile.

To assist me with my publishing, I also presented at several international conferences including *Gender and Education* and *The British Educational Research Association* conferences. I found the experience of presenting my research at these conferences invaluable as I gained presenting experience but also critical insights from colleagues in the field that helped me develop and refine my writing and research ideas. Since my PhD studies, I began to follow the approach of undertaking research, presenting it at conference, revising the paper based on the feedback received and then submitting the work to journals for publication. This approach to getting published has served me well throughout my career and is something I still do as I benefit from getting critical insights and feedback from colleagues and reworking and refining my ideas.

SUE TAYLOR

Motivation for Undertaking EdD

Before explaining life after gaining my doctorate, it's probably worthwhile sharing with you why I chose to undertake a professional doctorate such as the EdD rather than a PhD. I have been an educationist all my adult life and have always wanted to make a difference to people's lives by empowering them through learning. I therefore wanted to further and deepen my knowledge and understanding of learning and teaching to enable me to make that difference. In addition, the structured approach of the EdD suited my busy professional and personal life.

In the event, the decision about whether to undertake a professional doctorate or a PhD was not mine to make, as I changed jobs and started working as an International Leader for the International Reading Recovery Trainer Organisation (IRRTO). Accreditation for this role was via the EdD programme so theory-practice links could readily be made and the impact of my research immediate.

Academia is becoming increasingly difficult to break into, but through the EdD, I found not only was I able to make an original contribution to knowledge but also gained a range of transferable skills that have helped me as a researcher and educator. The post-doctoral route for me has therefore not necessarily been typical.

Life After the EdD

Having completed the EdD some 13 years ago, I am now programme director of the longest running and most established EdD in the United Kingdom, and recently, also gained recognition as Principal Fellow of the Higher Education Academy. This prestigious award was the culmination of the international work I have been engaged in to support learning and teaching since starting my doctoral journey. What follows is a selection of experiences and achievements along that journey.

Engaging in Scholarly Activity

Fundamentally, the doctoral journey is about making an original contribution to knowledge but the audience is primarily our examiners. Writing for different audiences and in different genres for publication in academic peer-reviewed journals, in practitioner journals or for book chapters was something I did immediately following my successful viva. To prepare for publication, I attended several workshops on writing for publication. These workshops were extremely useful in learning about different editorial preferences. Through attending and presenting at conferences, my work became more widely known and eventually, I began to receive invitations to publish. I became a peer reviewer of several academic journals and for book proposals, and this also enhanced my own writing as I developed a more critical stance. I often reread my thesis and realised on reflection that my doctoral research was really just the beginning of the 'academic' journey.

Since completion of my EdD, I have taught (and still do teach) research methods to a range of postgraduate students which maintains my own research skills by having to respond to high-level questioning and argumentation. This is another way of sharing lessons I have learned over the years to enable others to engage with their own research.

International Recognition for Supporting Advanced Professional Development

As a direct result of conducting research into advanced professional learning for my EdD, I became programme leader for an MA linked to the accreditation of professionals to become teacher-educators of experienced teachers. The MA programme had an affinity to the EdD being based on the premise of professionalism and creating strong theory-practice links through a spiral curriculum design (Taylor, 2006) and the Connected Curriculum (Fung, 2017) where research and teaching are inextricably linked. As Executive Board member of IRRTO, I was able to support colleagues attain their accreditation as International Leaders through advanced academic professional development.

Impact through Effective and Supportive Supervision

My earlier chapter shows my keen interest in effective modes of supervision. The personal reward of gaining skills as a supervisor was matched by the tremendous pleasure I felt in the growth and success of my doctoral students, both EdD and PhD. I continue to learn from my doctoral students and am often filled with pride when observing the impact of my doctoral students' research: through contribution to both professional knowledge and academic knowledge and also to policy and practice. My doctoral students have gone on to achieve many great things themselves.

Enabling through Widening Participation

I became a key member of the Centre for Doctoral Education and developed an interest in the widening participation agenda (HEFCE, 2013). As a result, I was able to use my understanding of adult professional learning to develop an innovative accelerated alternative EdD pathway. This pathway supports those students who might otherwise have barriers (actual and/or perceived) in accessing doctoral education. Barriers might include factors such as the ones I faced: first generation at university coming from a low-socio-economic background, leading to a sense of imposter syndrome, and child-care issues. From the inception of this alternative provision of the EdD pathway in 2013, almost 50% of students have gone on to study for a doctorate.

As programme director of the EdD, and with my understanding of advanced professional adult learning, I reconfigured and restructured the EdD, building in support mechanisms to enable timely student completions. I became increasingly aware of the particular challenges that EdD students face as mature professionals with high levels of responsibility studying for a doctorate and factor that into the curriculum, pedagogy and assessment of the EdD.

International Adviser on Developing Effective Doctoral Programmes

Through my continued engagement with research into curriculum, pedagogy and assessment for professionals, I have advised EdD programmes internationally. These advisory roles demonstrate the impact that continues to be made, long after completion of the thesis.

Summary

In short, whilst having worked in HE for 18 years, my focus has been on adding to the body of knowledge in advanced professional learning. The EdD opened the doors to opportunities I would not necessarily have had access to. My only regret? ... Not doing it earlier in my career.

MIKE WATTS

Picture the scene. The evening of graduation day, the whole family (big family, a real rent-a-mob) all meeting at the restaurant of my choice. We were directed to the bar area for pre-dinner drinks, dressed up in Sunday best, me disappointed that I had actually been required to hand back my cap and gown. And then, over the general hubbub, the loud-speaker announcement: 'Would DOCTOR Watts and party please make their way to their table'. Whoops, crowing, shouting, clapping, ribald comments, carnival mayhem. But the very first public affirmation of my new official status. The speaker system was the reason I had actually chosen that restaurant in the first place. It was a matter of days only before I changed my passport, bank cards and driving licence. I would have changed my bus-pass had I owned one.

I could probably account for this mild egomania by noting that I was first in a rural working-class family to reach such academic heights; by being one of the brood to spearhead the family's growing aspirations; by being one of the siblings to consolidate my mother's pride in *her* achievements. But egomania is just that, graduation was a powerful 'me moment'. In many respects, I did not need the actual qualification, but I revelled mightily in the title that came with it. I was once told never to book airline tickets using 'Dr' in case someone's heart gave out in economy or there was danger of an imminent birth in business class, when the cabin crew would call out 'Is there a doctor on board'? Oh yes, indeed! I would have been the first down the aisle safe in the knowledge that a PhD in education equips you for anything: 'Make way, please, I'm a doctor'.

So, my tale here is about intrinsic reward. I had moved out of school teaching to work on a university project in science education and the award of that doctoral degree brought both powerful completion and approval to the work I had been doing. I went on to spend a further year in post-doc extensions of the project before then moving into university work proper. So, yes, I used the employment entry-qualification of a doctorate and have continued to do so over time, but my key comments here concern the closure it brings to a very substantial tranche of study. A doctoral award requires the recipient to have made a significant contribution to knowledge in the field, and that is no trivial matter. The broad aim for students at undergraduate level is to know (and read) some of the major books and authors in their specialist area. At M-level, students are required to *master* the field, to demonstrate mastery of (and quote from) those same texts, books and authors. At doctoral level, you are writing the book – and this is one that has never been written, read or quoted from before. You have long since left your supervisors behind in your wake and are probably one of a small august group in the world who knows exactly what you are talking about. You are adding to a body of work alongside some of the great luminaries in the field – something by which to be humble, awestruck and immensely proud.

In the writing of the thesis, we all avidly consume whatever is available and, occasionally, we come across one of those 'complete papers': the ones that are clear and lucid and really capture the issues in a nutshell. The darned thing is beautifully crisp and compact, a 'seminal' article or chapter that says the very things you would have wanted to say had you been there to say it. And the doctoral thesis does just that. It takes an idea within a cognate field, twists and turns it, plays it out like the squared-faces of a Rubik's cube to create a synaesthetic whole of the component parts. Your synaesthetic whole, you 'bring it all together'. And doing that is worth every moment of the hours of philosophical naysaying, the long grind of the data-sausage-machine, the analytical and synthetical outcomes slog and the anti-social relationship-testing keyboard bashing. I guarantee not a single soul fails to reread chunks of his or her thesis at a later stage and not marvel – did I really write all that? Oh yes, you did, and it was worth all the agony.

So, what I did just after my doctorate was gloat a little. Once the gloat wore thin, I began the construction of 'so what' – where does that get me? I was fortunate to have had a supervisor who encouraged conference papers, publication of interim ideas and preliminary data along the way, and so I was already inducted somewhat into journals and book chapters. As tradition demands, my final chapter had been full of conclusions and implications and, once I had sifted the purposive from the pious, I began to think about – and work on – the directions I had pointed out. In the following years, and free from some of the shackles of academia, I explored my populist 'write for the people' mode, then my *Guardian* readers' genre, then tried highbrow affectations. Some of this worked, some didn't; some stuck, some didn't. The process, however, did lead me to find my own writing style and my own voice – such that it now is.

I became assiduous in consolidating all those contacts I had made, the business cards I had collected. During the process of the project, I joined a small interest group discussing the issues I liked best and I now became an active member rather than a dumbstruck follower. This led to a series of shared publications and book chapters. To this day, I prefer chapters to articles – journals are necessarily tighter, sharper – fustier, even. It's not that books lack quality control, it's just that one has a greater sense of freedom to really explore those ideas, to give vent to the very ideas that drove the thesis in the first place. Move over thesis, hello book.

Intrinsic interest, intrinsic rewards: do it for the doing. Your doctoral thesis as a small personal thumbprint on the world: I was here, I did this.

GINA WISKER

My advice to newly graduated EdD and PhD students is to publish the most significant and topical parts of your work as fast as possible, get it out there in conferences and use the credentials for job applications. I only published one piece whilst writing my thesis, under my supervisor's advice (he thought it would keep me from finishing as time was tight, in the end), but it was in a widely read journal for my field at the time, a *Journal of American Studies*. I was already in a very nice job in the other HE institution in Cambridge, but I think both doing and getting the PhD gave me credibility to be thoroughly invited into the degree-level teaching world. During and after, I was able to teach the third-year undergraduates at my own HEI and tutor at Cambridge which felt more a lucky act of geography than much to do with my expertise, although working in a developing new field (twentieth- and twenty-first-century literature) was also important as at Cambridge, for instance, the literature courses seemed to stop at the end of the nineteenth century.

Doing and gaining the PhD gave me credibility and entrance into some really rewarding, enjoyable teaching and the delight of working with mature returners and junior year abroad American students and undergraduates in several systems (ex-polytechnic, Cambridge University). I taught for the Open University also which means belonging to a community in the summer schools where we new lecturers exchanged ideas and practices about how to teach our groups and swopped classes. This gave me some more insights into teaching strategies and I followed that up with an advanced diploma in teaching and course development in HE at London University full time for a year, whilst I sorted out my first child, maintained my teaching in Cambridge one day a week, and then was taken on by the Centre of Higher Education Studies to be a researcher on a major ESRC project 'Enquiry into the role of the external examiner'. They assumed that as I had a PhD (actually in contemporary English and American literature) that I knew how to research (in the Social Sciences, in HE). This was a rapid introduction to a totally different research field and in many ways process and writing style. However, it all opened more doors, all simultaneously with children and having no money and commuting to try and maintain my literature teaching one day a week back in Cambridge, at Anglia Polytechnic University. I wrote course outlines, I researched for the new lectures I was giving, I supervised master's students at the Centre for Higher Education Studies University of London, taught experienced and new academic staff from London university, supervised dissertations back at Anglia. It was overwhelming, and alongside one, then two, small children. We moved back to Cambridge and as I settled full time back into my old job with the credibility of the PhD, I second supervised my first PhD, and gradually I was able to start to write a bit more.

Before and after the London experience no one really had any local advice about publishing, in fact my Head of Department suggested I wrote in something rather quirky and obscure which wasn't at all the kind of place for what I was starting to do. In London

I wrote another piece, this time about African American women's writing, and wrote some chunks for our large HE report.

Then I started to write small pieces about teaching literature, combining across the two fields. The origins of the first book on *Black Women's Writing* (1992) for Palgrave were from running a workshop at an American Studies conference in York the day before we moved house back to Cambridge. In terms of a family activity that was one of the least popular things I ever did (costly extra travel, lots of last-minute packing) and it was a day trip – but someone with a series from Palgrave was there and later he invited me to put in a book proposal and showed me what a book manuscript looked like so I gathered up international contributions, from contacts, and together we wrote it and I edited 'my' first book.

I think I would say that the acquiring and changing jobs were all supported and enabled by doing and getting the PhD, but it was also because I was interested in a new challenge, working with a range of students, and wanted to stretch my brain beyond the PhD which had been, for 6½ years, a wonderful developmental opportunity and a lump of concrete round my neck. The ideas and values of it I have only recently, in the last six years or so, realised underpin everything I do – international social justice themes, and feminism, combining across historical realistic detail and lots of dark metaphorical, fantastic expression, which I'd now call Gothic (*Contemporary Women's Gothic Fictions*, 2016). There are now some really good ECR schemes to support new PhD's (mentoring, etc. AHRC funded – I've mentored at The University of Brighton, and worked with an AHRC 18-month scheme through the Contemporary Women's Writing Association), but I was already in a job and almost immediately coping with house moves and small kids, so I didn't need those schemes, and they were in any case not present back then. My supervisor helped me get my work out at a conference late in the PhD, and I remained in touch with some of those people and indeed some of that resulted in contributions to books.

I used the Palgrave links beyond the first book and I still write for them and am now on the board making decisions about Palgrave Gothic texts. I taught and developed my work and that dialogue (research, teaching and writing) was so important to the thinking and writing dialogue, the articles and books. I've always loved writing, so I work my ideas and arguments out through it, across literature and HE-theorised practice (e.g. *Teaching African American Women's Writing*, 2010). This all started back then, merging practice and research and writing, merging HE teaching and learning and literature and social justice themes, but it wasn't part of any scheme. Much of it was serendipitous, then built on because I enjoyed writing and teaching for the writing and putting the teaching into the writing. Has it had an impact? Twenty years since I am still friends with my three original literature PhD students from the days just after I got my own PhD. My supervisor has just died, and old colleagues contacted me – and I realised I'd written about him as an example of inspirational patience in my book, *The Good Supervisor* (2012). The international workshops and projects I've been lucky to do (Caribbean, South Africa, Africa, Scandinavia and Ireland) have grown from a continued fascination in the postcolonial and international, and decoloniality which underpinned the PhD, and I'm still working in Gothic and social justice themes and writing about writing and editing and publishing (*Getting Published*, 2015). So, doing the PhD and gaining it really fuelled my continued enjoyment with teaching, researching, supervising, writing and workshopping in the varying literature and HE-theorised teaching. It looks a lot more planned than it was.

REFERENCES:

Burgess, H., Sieminski, S., & Arthur, L. (2006). *Achieving your doctorate in education*. Milton Keynes: Open University (in association with Sage Publications).

Czerniawski, G. (2018). Early career researchers – 20 tips for career development. Retrieved from https://www.bera.ac.uk/blog/early-career-researchers-20-tips-for-career-development. Accessed on January 9, 2020.

Fung, D. (2017). *A connected curriculum for higher education*. London: UCL Press. https://doi.org/10.14324/111.9781911576358

HEFCE. (2013). *Postgraduate support scheme*. England: HEFCE.

Laudel, G., & Glaser, J. (2008). From apprentice to colleague: The metamorphosis of Early Career Researchers. *Higher Education*, *55*, 387–406.

REF. (2020). What is the REF? Retrieved from https://www.ref.ac.uk. Accessed on January 9, 2020.

Taylor, S. (2006). *An advanced professional development curriculum for developing deep learning*. Unpublished Doctoral Thesis as part of EdD, University of London.

Wellington, J., Bathmaker, A., Hunt, C., McCulloch, G., & Sikes, P. (2005). *Succeeding with your doctorate*. London: Sage Publications Ltd.

INDEX